Martin James Boon

The history of the Orange Free State

Martin James Boon

The history of the Orange Free State

ISBN/EAN: 9783337283506

Printed in Europe, USA, Canada, Australia, Japan

Cover: Foto ©ninafisch / pixelio.de

More available books at **www.hansebooks.com**

THE HISTORY
OF THE
ORANGE FREE STATE.

BY

MARTIN JAMES BOON,

AUTHOR OF

"*The Immortal History of South Africa,*" "*Home Colonisation,*"
"*Jottings by the Way in South Africa,*" "*National Paper-
Money and its Use,*"*&c., &c., &c.*

LONDON:
WILLIAM REEVES, 185 Fleet Street; MARTIN J. BOON, 170 Farringdon Road

SOUTH AFRICA:
HAY BROS., Wholesale Agents, King William's Town.

1885.

PREFACE.

> O God! for a man with a heart, head, hand
> Like some of the simple great ones gone
>   For ever and ever bye :—
>
> One still strong man in a blatent land;
>   Whatever they call him what care I?
> Aristocrat, Democrat, Autocrat—One
>   Who can rule and dare not lie.
>
>   —TENNYSON.

THESE "Jottings" on the Orange Free State are but the utterings, voicings, and articulatings of one who has honestly attempted to pourtray that State as he found it.

Many doubtless have experienced similar thoughts but lacked the energy and the heart to give them utterance.

I cannot sufficiently express my gratitude to others for their noble efforts in the past for the amelioration of man's condition, whilst contributing my humble quota on behalf of human-kind.

If I have succeeded in opening up any new train of thought that may have afforded pleasure or information to the readers, I shall be gratified; and if the pecuniary results of this little venture in the cause of human progress merely suffice to pay the printer, I shall be satisfied; but as one does not live by paying printers only, my satisfaction will of course be enhanced should the harvest be more bountiful than would be required to cover typographical disbursements.

I offer no apology for anything I have written. The questions herein mooted affect not only the Orange Free State but the whole of South Africa.

                                              THE AUTHOR.

The History of the Orange Free State.

CONTENTS.

Chapter I. Pp. 1 to 18.

A glance at the early history of the Free State—Traditions and speculations as to the Aborigines—The first definite records about the years 1816 to 1820—The Griquas under Adam Kok settle at Griqua Town, and gradually spread themselves along the Orange River, concentrating chiefly at Philippolis—The colonial Dutch farmers commence crossing the Orange River, and take up their abode in the new territory, whether they are soon followed by whole bodies of emigrants—The new comers purchase or lease lands from the Native Chiefs—The Emancipation of slaves in the Cape Colony caused large numbers to place themselves beyond British control and take up their abode on the Orange River—The settlers form a government for themselves after the model of the old Dutch Government of the Cape Colony—Matters go on quietly up till 1845—After some fracas between the Emigrant Boers and the Griquas open hostilities break out—The British Government inter, venes, and assisting the Griquas with Her Majesty's troops-the Boers are defeated at Zwart Koppies—A British Resident is established in the country, with a small force to support his authority—A treaty is concluded between the British Government and Adam Kok— The terms of the treaty cause great dissatisfaction amongst the Emigrant Boers—Their acknowledged chief Andries Pretorius, fails to obtain any amelioration of the conditions—In February, 1848, Sir Harry Smith proclaimed Her Majesty's sovereignty over the territory—Discontent now breaks out into hostilities, and in July the British Resident is driven back across the Orange River—Sir Harry Smith comes up in person with a stronger force, defeats the Boer Commando at Bloomplats and re-establishes British authority in the Orange River Sovereignty—The territory remains under the British Government represented by a Resident at Bloemfontein up to the year 1854—Continual embroilments between the burghers and the Basutos—The cost of keeping up a large military force to preserve order induces the British Government to abandon the Orange River Sovereignty—On the 23rd February, 1854, a Convention is entered into between the British Government and a body of delegates which forms the Charter of Independence of the Orange Free State—A Provincial Government formed under the presidency of Mr. Hoffman—A Volksraad, or assembly of the people elected, and a Republican Constitution drawn up and adopted—The difficulties of the young Republic—President Boshoff—War with the Basutos from March till September, 1858—The Convention of Aliwal North—President Boshoff resigned his office and is succeeded by President Pretorius—Territorial annexations—Resignation of President Pretorius and election of President Brand—Renewal of hostilities between the Orange Free State and the Basutos—A treaty of peace and a definite boundary line agreed upon—The diamond fields by the Vaal River—The British Government takes forcible possession of the disputed territory—The rascality of the Trek Boers—" Land and loot" the watchwords of the Dutch from the time they occupied the Cape—the Dutch only know one book, the Bible—From it they gather that they are the elect of God and the sons of Ham are to be their servants for ever—They start with the idea that they are of the House of the Lord and all others mere interlopers—What they call their "advanced mission" amongst the natives really means extermination—England's interposition for the protection of the natives from Dutch violence—History and facts give the lie to the pretensions of the Dutch—The Raad, the Executive, and the Sovereignty of the people—" Commandeering" or "requisitioning" neither more nor less than spoliation or repudiation—The constitution, duties, payment, and conduct of the Raad or Parliament—The elements of sound political character not to be found either in the Free State or Transvaal Republics —Hollanders and Germans thrive upon the credulity of the Dutch—The Free State governed by foreigners—Exposure of the many bad acts of omission and commission on the part of the Volksraad and the remedies for the same —Money agencies, or suckers and parasites—The Queen of Sheba and her treasures—South Sea Bubble-believers— Majuba, Sir G. P. Colley, and Sir Garnet Wolseley—The Dutch love of English sovereigns—The Free Staters very, very brave behind rocks and stones, but perfect cowards in the open—How the Basutos and the Transvaal Government were supplied with arms and ammunition—England's gold and Germany's poverty—The Moses of the *Express*— The best to command are they who know best how to obey, independently of consequences.

CHAPTER II. Pp. 19 to 31.

The *Free State Express* on the dismissal of Dr. Jorissen from his position of State Attorney—The policy and cry of the Dutch party throughout South Africa "Africa for the Africanders"—The German-Hollander—Jewish faction— A magnified Cape Town dressmaker—The President of the Transvaal after conquering the natives, Shoots the leaders, appropriates their lands, cattle, &c., and enslaves eight thousand prisoners—" All shall right come"—Monarchical and Republican Governments contrasted—The Kind of Government wanted in the Free State—The presence of barristers and lawyers in Parliament inimical to the simplification of the laws—The election of medical men and scientists desirable—" Grand old men "—Napoleon the Third, but the Little, an arch-traitor, perjurer, and bedizened villain—Sir John Brand and William the Silent of Orange

—The Capital of the Free State described—The Public offices a disgrace to the architect—The Church-home and hospital the result of charity and debt—The chronic poverty of the "Sisters"—The holy, idiotic, itinerant bishop and his wretched acolytes so many walking imposters—The Dutch Church the outcome of beef, mutton, and farming produce—Any literary man would feel ashamed to own the Public Library—The Building Society "a delusion and a snare"—Although a Dutch Capital with five thousand inhabitants not a tenth are Dutch—Its Rag Alley and Petticoat Lane—Its poverty disgusting, and its immorality and disease an eye-sore to decent people—Hot-beds of disease exposed in all their intensity and all their horrors—The prisons of South Africa including that of the Capital of the Free State—Their filthy and disgusting condition render them "living hells"—The Neapolitan dungeons of King Bomba would bear favourable comparison with them—The dishonesty and corruption of the gaolers—The cruelty of long sentences of imprisonment and the physical and mental torture endured by the victims thereof—Judge or Jury.

CHAPTER III. Pp. 32 to 44.

The extortions of lawyers and agents—Political judges a nuisance in the Free State—They talk bunkum and spout treason—The Chief Justice of the Free State goes into the Cape Colony and takes an active part in setting up a "Bestuur"—Judge Reitz preferring the Presidency of the Free State to the "Judgemisfitship" sticks at no meanness to secure it—Mr. Hofmeyer and "Kitchen Dutch"—The Dutch Artillery manned by young men too lazy to work, and not fit for much better than targets to be shot at—The attack on Colonel Anstruther not fair fighting but simply sudden murder—Free State Doctors mostly quacks—Their ignorance and extortions—Twenty-five shillings for a visit, and seven and sixpence for a box of pills—Their stock-in-trade for the most part consists of impudence and a few bottles with Latin inscriptions upon them—The officials as a rule are of German or Jewish nationality—The diamond mine swindle at Jagersfontein—A member of the Free State Raad proposes to annex the Cape Colony—Free State official puppies snarling at John Bull's big dog—The Climate—The summer heat intolerable, and the winters cold and unbearable—Whatever grass or vegetation may be grown in the summer to fatten the cattle, the frost destroys in the winter, and the wind blows away for ever—German and Jewish hunger for John Bull's money—England and the Hanoverian connection and German intermarriage combination—Downing Street a curse to all our Colonies—All mineral wealth must be public property—The Compulsory working of claims at the diamond mines.

Chapter IV. Pp. 45 to 49.

An extraordinary piece of hasty legislation—The New Wine and Spirit Ordinance—Cutting off the patients head to cure the tooth-ache—Drunkenness amongst the natives, and the stringent enactment passed to suppress it—Contributions by Plato, Pliny, Saint Chrysostom, Luther, Matthew Arnold, Maccall and Boon to the Temperance Question.

Chapter V. Pp. 50 to 58.

The Bill to punish the illegal possession of diamonds—Trap-stones sold in the dark by Kaffirs—Gross perjury and treachery resulting in cruel and unjust sentences—Free State lawyers—Their ability limited, their extortion unlimited—As a rule, like the Doctors, they are old missionaries—The "black sheep" of the legal flock—Some of

the dodges resorted to by lawyers for levying black mail—
A personal momento of the Free State lawyers way of
making Englishmen pay for being fools enough to dwell
there in opposition to Germans and Jews.—The members
of the Free State Bar on strike—Mr. Sheriff Crosby as
Taxing Master takes a very determined stand against the
extortionate practices of the legal fraternity and gains the
day—The Dutch are beginning to see that under the sneaking "ferneuking" Jew, German, and Hollander, they are
in the hands of Shylocks—President Brand and his title,
salary, and many public gifts—The Alsatia of Basutoland
—The Dutch *Thunderer* or *Express* liar paper, edited by a
Jew and owned by a German, secures by flattery and sycophancy a contract for three years' printing—The old Free
State notes and the French *assignats*—Their mode of issue,
value, and the security upon which they were based explained—Surreptitious issue into France by "the political
vagabond" Pitt of *assignats* that were produced in England—Pitt sued in the King's Bench to recover the engraver's charges for making the same—Gold owners and
hard money supporters oppose some monetary arrangements—The solution of the financial problem means the
redemption of farmers and manufacturers throughout the
world.

CHAPTER VI. Pp. 59 to 70.

The Free State still a heathen country, a land still occupied with
both white and black barbarians—The Free State Dutchman dirty, mean and cruel—Many an Englishman has
met foul play at their hands—They would feel no Compunction in being the death of all the English but for the
difficulty of burying them on the quiet—The Dutch meeting
Houses are virtually courting houses where the young men
look out for wives and the young women sigh for husbands
—The opening of the New Town Hall and Public Library
—Dutch gluttony and drunkenness at the banquet—The

English the salt of the Free State—A Presidential bereavement—One Cape Town dressmaker taken and the other left—Polygamy often practised in the Capital though not sanctioned by law and to have a plurality of wives is not considered a crime—The clergy are the public advocates of lying hypocrisy and stealing—Hollanders and Dutchmen repudiate their just debts and stink in the nostrils of the English—Debts and dishonour the constant companions of all the officials in the Free State from the President and his sons down to all his army of supporters.

CHAPTER VII. Pp. 71 to 83.

The inestimable value of Public Libraries and Homes of Painting, Sculpture and all our Fine Arts—These repositories of imperishable things will form our future churches to the shame of the preachers of all denominations—Bible criticisms—A plea for the free discussion of theological difficulties—The philosophy of secularism—Orthodoxy and Agnosticism—Revelation—Lucifer in the Confessional—"The Pirates of Penzance"—The House of Peers a house of hereditary vagabonds—The Queen only a figure-head and in no case useful.

CHAPTER VIII. Pp. 84 to 99.

The construction of public works of utility by means of national paper-money—The dangers of making acquaintances in Bloemfontein—Africa peculiarly a black man's playground and a place for no honest man—To cheat and be cheated is the system all round; honesty is positively unknown—The Religious Orders and Churches in Bloemfontein are compounded of idiotcy, poverty and commercialism. The Theological College is a disgrace in every respect—The kiss of Sisterhood and after pleasures—Carnal pleasures increase spiritual delights—All the younger ones do it when the opportunity offers, although they may afterwards rue it—Dr. Twells, the young half-blood Beck and his companions—Edwin Heron on the Confessional—"Under which Lord?"—The decline of Orthodoxy—Protestants and the Bible—The triumph of truth—The Religion of the future—What we need—Press on.

CHAPTER IX. Pp. 100 to 121.

The uncertainty of the law; unique and instructive personal experiences thereof—The Hollander and German arrangements to fleece all producers—A Maitland Street Post-cart-contractor-of-an-attorney—The faith of the Dutch Government in stamps—The advantages of the Code Napoleon—The white adult Africander population lazy, thriftless and roguish—The Cape no land for emigration, but merely a half-way place to India—Oath or affirmation—The Guelphs and the Throne of England—The "jumping" proclivities of Free State born commercial assistants—The Free State, from the President, members of the Parliament, &c., downwards, a nest of polite and impolite robbers—Boon re-christened without godfather or godmother—Bloemfontein a most unhealthy spot and the "Queen City" of Cesspools, Cow-Kaals and pigsties—Boon declared to be a Mormon in heart and a Turk in practice—Bloemfontein the home of the vilest and most contemptible of human wretches—"Trust none you know not, and trust none you know"—Morality not Christianity—Self-improvement—The morality of the future—The coming man's religion—The animalism of the Free State burghers and women and its baneful results.

Chapter X. Pp. 122 to 133.

Drunken and idiotic judges—Victims of the Blasphemy Laws—The Dutch and English could live side by side happily, but the German, the Hollander, and the Jew cause strife—The Parliaments of the Cape Colony and the Orange Free State—Their manners, customs and attire—The alleged apathy and indifference of voters in the Cape Colony—More "legal" abuses and suggestions for their removal—Boon's political economy—The enormous increase in number of lawyers in the United States, or an army of locusts forming a greater pest than the host of monks and friars that infested Europe on the Eve of the Reformation—M. J. Boon *v.* V. Van Reenen—The Press a power to harass and injure as will as to support.

Chapter XI. Pp. 134 to 146.

A woman's description of the Free State lawyers—A black-blooded Dutch Sheriff—"Paradise" a hell to Boon and the finishing stroke to his patience—A Free State lawyer's bill of Costs *in Extenso*—Boon shows that private, legal, Parliamentary, and public robberies (in that of Paradise-Hell) cost him over £1500 in the course of a few months—Boon's panacea or "perfect cure" for all legal, clerical, commercial, agricultural, legislative and Presidential rascality in the Orange Free State.

Chapter XII. Pp. 147 to 153.

The President of the Free State as the fountain of *dishonour* meets the old Dutch-£2-per-day-men and Town Council—Boon proposes and describes an installation of the order of Knighthood with very suggestive titles—Bully swart Dutchmen, or half blacks with Dutch names—their insolence to the English due to the folly of a Colley and the weakness of a

Gladstone—A modern Daniel—Idolatry—The policy of the Gladstone Administration and its results in South Africa.

CHAPTER XIII. Pp. 154 to 167.

Sepinare the Free State made Chief of the Barolongs not the rightful heir—The rivalry between Sepinare and Samuel Moroka—Sepinare giving farms to lawyers, missionaries, and the Bishop of Bloemfontein to ensure their support—The extortions practised upon the Barolongs to pay the Resident and the white forces under Commandant Raaff—The defeat and death of Sepinare by the followers of Samuel—The *Friend* of the Free State on the Barolong disturbances—The annexation of the Barolong Territory—Diplomatic Relations—The beginning of the end—Aiders and Abettors—Is it Peace?—Proclamation by President Brand—A Treaty of amity *and Treachery*.

CHAPTER XIV. Pp. 168 to 188.

The financial position of the Free State in 1884—The failure to negotiate a loan in England and the causes thereof—Extraordinary Session of the Volksraad—"The way it should be done"—Patent Law—National paper-money and its use—A perfect buck animal or human monster—*Express* views on the Free State legal profession—The Free State Balance Sheet—Mr. Higgo and his day of prayer—Hard Times—More Swindling—Jewish Fire Kings and Fire Dragons defrauding their creditors and the insurance offices—The descendants of the Impenitent Thieves of the Roman Era deserve the hatred of mankind.

CHAPTER XV. Pp. 189. to 203.

A lively and amusing "Skit" on the Bloemfontein Town Council by Blikoor—The Sanitary surroundings of Bloemfontein

—Paying the piper—The water supply of Bloemfontein—How to construct public municipal water works by means of national paper-money—" Utopia is a pleasant place, but how shall I get there ? "

CHAPTER XVI.   Pp. 204 to 217.

Preparations for a May day 'Festival'—Meeting of the Volksraad The Treasurer-General's balance Sheet—A Serious debit balance of £39,722 4s. 3½d—Trade influencing Revenue—Bad Times—Measures for peace in Basutoland—What a New Ministry means—The *Natal Witness* on Railways and the Rebate Customs—But for its connection with England the Free State would be an uninhabited wilderness—German and Hollander human asvogals—Boon has a holiday and goes sight-seeing—The Town Council votes £10 for a National day of rejoicing—The swearing-in of His Honour J. H. Brand as President—The procession amusements, and illuminations.

CHAPTER XVII.   Pp. 218 to 222.

Banking power a monopoly—" Blue-backs " issued on the public and their securities stolen, consequently their market value diminished—Interested parties oppose the issue of paper-money—Boon's opinion of a few of the " big ones "—A magistrate not knowing his duties—Commercial trickery.

CHAPTER XVIII.   Pp. 223 to 228.

Settling with a Landlord—Roman-Dutch Law and Equity—Cause of hatred to a squint-eyed man—Information is vouchsafed that it is not *legal* to rob—The Africander Bond says that lawyers are to be extirpated—Hostile feeling to the legal profession, why and wherefore—The remedy for reformation lies with the profession itself—The scarcity of " free men " in Bloemfontein, the remainder of business houses expecting by, every mail to receive their *congé*—A cry to John Bull.

CHAPTER XIX. Pp. 229 to 246.

Personal remarks on an unfortunate wretch—Threatened action for £500 for loss of character—" Fortune favours the brave"—Sharpers in Bloemfontein—The Reformer—System of Thieving Practised by the Medical profession—A good salary and an enormous fee for two days' visits—The Volksraad takes the medical faculty in hand—Sharp practise, buying a farm of a dying man for a small sum— Medical Scandals—The memorial (translated into English) got up by the faculty to be presented to the Volksraad to reduce the tariff Ordinance—How to put down Quackery— District Surgeoncies—On putting up his shutters for the last time Boon is asked to deliver a parting lecture—The selected subject somewhat astonishes the Town Clerk—The Town Hall hired—A Hard-God, alarmed, summoned a full meeting of the Town Council—A Mayor believes in *free speech* but not in a *speech of freedom*—Good English sovereigns and the Town Hall refused ; consequently a "set to" prevented—A solemn warning to the Prussian thieves—"A crew to fly from "—St. Edmond-of-the-Council assures Boon that the refusal of the Hall was the saving of his (Boon's) life—Programme of entertainment and the laconic letter of refusal—The last Sunday in Bloemfontein—No longer light and sunshine, a total eclipse expected—" Away, away with him, he knows too much to leave us alone."

VALEDICTORY.　Pp. 247 and 248.

Boon does not wait for the day of judgement and of doom but mounts the Post-cart for his last ride in and out of the Orange Free State—The way to be an ever-living boon, not for the Free State only but to all States and for all time—Sad thoughts broke in upon and indignation aroused at the sight of the dry bed of the Modder-river—Boon begs to subscribe.

THE
ORANGE FREE STATE:

A GLANCE AT ITS EARLY HISTORY.

Chapter I.

THE earliest traditionary accounts concerning the territory now known as the Orange Free State convey the idea that it was not inhabited by any particular race, but rather that marauding bands from various tribes, either Kaffirs, Bushmen, or Corannas, from time to time infested it with a view to secure pasture for their flocks, or to escape destruction at the hands of some stronger and inimical races; and it is only about the years from 1816 to 1820 that the records become definite as determining the fact that a body of Griquas under Adam Kok settled at Griqua Town, and afterwards gradually spread themselves along the Orange River, concentrating their greatest number at what is now called Philippolis.

About this time many colonial-Dutch farmers commenced crossing the Orange River with their flocks in search of pasturage during times of drought in the Colony, and took up their abode in the new territory, more especially in the vicinity of Riet River. These pioneers were afterwards followed up by whole bodies of emigrants, one of which settled in the district of Boshof, on lands purchased by them from the Coranna chiefs Dantzer and Bloem, while another located itself in what was afterwards termed Vaal River district, on lands bought from the chief Mataquan, and many more either leased or bought lands in the territory of the Griquas, between the Riet and Orange Rivers. The numbers of the emigrants were also greatly increased by the influx of those colonists who felt themselves aggrieved by the emancipation of slaves, and left the Colony in 1836 in large numbers in order to place themselves beyond British control.

These settlers formed a government for themselves after the model of the old Dutch Government of the Cape Colony, and matters went on quietly up till 1845, when, in consequence of some fracas between the emigrant Boers and the Griquas which resulted in hostilities, the British Government intervened and, assisting the Griquas with Her Majesty's troops, defeated the Boers at Zwart Koppies. To prevent a like occurence, a British Resident was established in the country, with a small force to support his authority. But a treaty had been entered into between the British Government and Adam Kok in 1845, in which certain terms affecting the Boer tenure of property in Griqualand were comprehended, which gave great dissatisfaction to the emigrants; and their acknowledged chief Andries Pretorious used every endeavour to procure an amelioration of these terms, but without success. Accordingly, after the proclamation of Her Majesty's sovereignty over the territory by Sir Harry Smith, in February, 1848, discontent broke out into hostilities, and the British Resident was driven back across the Orange River in July, 1848, until a stronger force could be brought up by Sir Harry Smith in person, which force met the Boer Commando at Boomplaats, and after a short but sharp encounter, defeated it, whereby British authority became re-established in the Orange River Sovereignty.

This territory now remained under the Government, represented in the person of a British Resident at Bloemfontein, where a fort had been erected mounting three guns, and the Seat of Residency had been established up to the year 1854. During this period many Europeans and colonists of European descent also took up their abode in the Sovereignty. Owing, however, to the continued embroilments of the burghers with the Basutos, under Moshesh and Moletsaine, not in their own quarrels, but in those of allies of the British Government, and the cost thereby occasioned of keeping up a considerable millitary force, the abandonment of the Orange River Sovereignty was recommended to the Home Government and carried out under the special commissionership of Sir George Clerk, who, notwithstanding the opposition of many of the inhabitants, especially of Bloemfontein, made over the government of the Orange River Sovereignty to a body of delegates representing the various districts, in terms of a convention entered into on the 23rd February 1854,—which convention is the Charter of Independence of the Orange Free State.

Two articles of this convention are as follows :—" The British Government has no alliance whatever with any native chief or tribes to the northward of the Orange River, with the exception of the Griqua Chief, Kaptyn Adam Kok ; and Her Majesty's Government has no wish or intention to enter hereafter into any treaties that may be injurious or prejudicial to the interests of the Orange River Government ; and the Orange River Government shall have freedom to purchase their supplies of ammunition in any British colony or possession in South Africa, subject to the laws provided for the regulation of the sale and transit of ammunition in any such British colonies and possessions." And these articles were approved and confirmed by Her Majesty's Government.

A Provisional Government was at once formed by the delegates, under the presidency of Mr. Hoffmann, and afterwards a Republican Constitution was drawn up and adopted by the Volksraad—the assembly of the people—the members of which had in the meantime been duly elected.

For some time after its erection into a separate state, the Government of the Orange Free State was principally engaged in meeting the difficulties arising out of the many boundary questions with petty native chiefs in and bordering on the Free State, the principal settlement arrived at being the definition of the Vetberg line between Adam Kok and Cornelis Kok and Waterboer, in 1855. And it was only during the able presidency of Mr. Boshoff, commencing in August, 1855, that attention could first be given to the internal affairs of the country, and some order established by salutary local ordinances, which are in force at the present day, regulating, amongst other matters, the establishment of law courts, tariffs, sale of gunpowder, the liquor law, &c. But this dawn of order was soon to be clouded by territorial disputes with the Basutos, which assumed greater importance, and eventually, in March, 1858, culminated in war between the burghers of the new

Republic and their thievish neighbours. The hostilities lasted with varied fortune, and were finally brought to a close by the convention of Aliwal North, on the 29th September, 1858. The following year, 1859, saw the Orange Free State deprived of the further services of President Boshoff by the resignation of his office, and although there are those who may have differed with him, still the almost universal voice was one of regret at the loss of the man who not only did so much for the internal regulation of the country, but also so ably conducted the State through its early difficulties with Witzie, the South African Republic, Scheel Cobus, and the Basutos.

A successor to President Boshoff was elected in the person of President Pretorius, the son of the well-known Commandant-General Andries Pretorius, of Boomplaats celebrity, who assumed the reins of office in 1860. The two principal events during his term of office were—first, the annexation to the Orange Free State of the Bethulie lands by special treaty with the chief, Tephin; and secondly, the purchase from the Griqua chief, Adam Kok, on his migration to the territory of Nomansland in 1861, of all his lands, and those he inherited from Cornelis Kok, of Campbell whereby the Vetberg line became part of the boundary of the Orange Free State, and the Government of that State obtained right and title to the Campbell lands, situated to the north of Vaal River.

On the resignation of President Pretorius in 1863, a new election was held, and President Brand, one of the leading barristers of the Supreme Court in the Cape Colony, assumed office as the chosen of the people in February, 1864. The peace secured by the treaty of Aliwal proved a hollow one, and as the Basutos not only repudiated their treaty engagements, but continued their depredations and committed various outrages on the burghers inhabiting their frontier, President Brand's first endeavours were directed to the attainment of a satisfactory settlement of the boundary line, and he succeeded in getting this defined by the arbitration of Sir Philip Wodehouse, Governor of the Cape of Good Hope, in October, 1864, whose award was entirely in favour of the Orange Free State. Notwithstanding this peaceful solution of the question, the attitude of the Basutos grew daily more and more threatening, and the Orange Free State saw itself forced to arms, and took the field in May, 1865. The struggle lasted eleven months, and then hostilities ceased, a treaty of peace, on very advantageous terms for the Orange Free State, being signed at Thaba Bosigo, Moshesh's stronghold on the 3rd April, 1866, by which, among other conditions, a large tract of country was ceded to this State.

The new territory was inspected by commissioners, and divided into farms which were granted and sold on conditions of military tenure, and as Basuto squatters had here and there re-occupied portions of this tract, it became necessary to clear the country of them by a commando called out for that purpose on the 12th March, 1867. But this measure had not the desired effect, for in the months of June and July following, parties of Basutos re-entered the territory, and murdered two subjects of the Orange Free State named Bushe and Krynauw, and defiance was flung at its Government when it demanded the delivery to justice of the murderers. Consequently, in the month of August, 1867, the Commando of the Orange Free State burghers took the field afresh, and soon victory crowned the Free State cause, as stronghold after stronghold was taken from the enemy, and there remained now only to Moshesh his own fortress of Thaba Bosigo, when hostilities were brought to a close by the intervention of the British Government, according to proclamation of His Excellency Sir Philip Wodehouse, dated 12th March, 1868, whereby Moshesh and his subjects were declared to be British subjects.

An armistice was agreed upon, during which this contravention of Article 2 of the Convention of the 23rd February, 1854, formed the topic of a lengthy correspondence, and it was only after a deputation from the Orange Free State was sent to England that a satisfactory settlement of the question was arrived at, as defined in the Convention of Aliwal North, dated 12th March, 1869, whereby the terms of peace and a definite boundary line to the new territory were finally fixed, as agreed upon between Her Majesty's High Commissioner and the Orange Free State Government.

Immediately after this settlement had been arrived at, negotiations were carried on with the Transvaal Republic which resulted in a Deed of Submission by which the definition of the boundary line between the two Republics was confided to the arbitration of

Lieutenant-Governor Keate, of the Colony of Natal, and his decision was communicated to the respective Governments in February, 1870; and the award, although virtually at variance with the object for which the arbitration was agreed on, was nevertheless, in the interests of peace and a good understanding with its sister Republic adopted by the Orange Free State.

But another boundary question which had from time to time engaged the attention of the Volksraad—viz.: that between the Orange Free State and Nicolas Waterboer—now assumed prominence owing to the discovery of diamonds on the Vaal River, near Pniel, a mission station of the Berlin Mission Society in the district of Jacobsdal. A Deed of Submission had been agreed upon between the Orange Free State Government and Captain Nicolas Waterboer, whereby the then Governor of the Cape Colony, Sir Philip Wodehouse, was appointed to arbitrate as to the claims set up on behalf of Waterboer to the Campbell Lands to the north of the Vaal River, which had been purchased from Captain Adam Kok by the Free State Government; but the deed was rendered nugatory by the removal of Sir Philip Wodehouse to the Governorship of Bombay in British India.

Under these circumstances every endeavour was made to bring the matter to a satisfactory solution, without further loss of time, but without avail; and at last the Orange Free State Government, after a meeting with Waterboer and his Council at Nooitgedacht, on the Vaal River, on the 18th August, 1870, from which meeting the latter unceremoniously withdrew, saw itself constrained to proclaim the territorial boundaries of the Campbell Lands to the north of Vaal River purchased by it from Adam Kok, as heir to Cornelis Kok, in 1861.

Meanwhile, a large influx of people from all parts of the Cape and Natal colonies and from foreign countries, to the Diamond-fields on the banks of the Vaal River, took place, and gradually spread itself to the dry diggings at Du Toit's Pan, Bultfontein, and Vooruitzigt, in the districts of Pniel, which had been newly created out of the districts of Jacobsdal and Boshof, in order to provide for the establishment of a more efficient control and special regulations for the moral and sanitary condition of the mining population; and while the Orange Free State Government was engaged in the consideration of the required measures to meet the altered circumstances of this portion of its territory, Waterboer, urged on by his agent, presented a petition to the British Government representing that a great portion of the territory had been encroached upon by the Orange Free State Government, and requesting its acceptance of himself and his people as subjects, and its intervention on his behalf.

Lieutenant Governor Hay, then Acting High Commissioner of the British Government, thereupon identifying himself with Waterboer's representations, and without awaiting an answer to his official inquiries as to the right and title of the Orange Free State Government to the lands claimed by Waterboer, forthwith, in violation of the second and other articles of the Convention of 23rd February, 1854, appointed commissioners and empowered them with authority over the diggers, which authority was at first only exercised on the north side of the Vaal.

On the arrival of Governor Barkly at the Cape in 1871, a proclamation was issued on the 27th October, 1871, declaring Waterboer and his people British subjects, and claiming as his territory not only the Campbell Lands, to the north of the Vaal, but also all the territory on the south side of that river up to a straight line from Platberg to David's Graf, at the junction of the Riet and Modder Rivers, and thence in a straight line to Ramah and the Orange River. This proclamation was followed up by forcible possession being taken of the lands in question, in a time of profound peace; and in order to avoid a collision and the dire effects which a war with a consanguineous race in the Colony would inevitably entail, the Government of the Orange Free State withdrew its authority and officials from that portion of its territory by proclamation of President Brand, dated 8th November, 1871, under solemn protest against this invasion of its rights. It has since endeavoured to obtain justice for the violation of its territory in arbitration, and deeds of submission thereto, on the merits of this question, are still under discussion and correspondence between the Government of Her Majesty and that of the Orange Free State.

Many events have occurred in connection with this question, each in its turn threatening to disturb the peaceful relations between the parties concerned in it; but sufficient proof has been given that the terms of the Convention of 1854 have not received that due regard which a weaker power may with the more justice expect from the stronger, and that the endeavours of the Government of the Orange Free State to secure the definition of the boundary line made over to them, with all its attendant difficulties, by that Convention, have but too often been thwarted by those from whom it had a right to expect every possible co-operation.

Such, then, are the principal events which have occupied the Orange Free State Government to such a degree that the internal affairs of the State have not received that attention which many important branches urgently demand; and to this it is owing that the judicial, administrative, and educational departments still call forth the earnest study of every well-meaning citizen with a view to their establishment on the best possible footing.

Being a Republican, I necessarily took a deep interest in the Orange Free State and Transvaal Republics. A system may be good in theory but very defective in practice, or in consequence of the imperfect way in which the system is carried out.

The Trek Boers who had left the Colony in haste, as they said through fear of the English, in reality did so because they were no longer allowed to do as they liked in stealing, first the cattle, then the land, and finally the persons of the natives to make them slaves under the guise of indentured servants, whom they agreed to pay wages either in money or in kind. It invariably happened however that the Boers, lacking common honesty, dismissed their victims without paying them; and thus they goaded the unfortunate natives to help themselves, which resulted in their being called a band of thieves; whereas, to speak truthfully, the Boers were the thieves in the first instance. I know there are some who will, upon reading this statement, indignantly challenge its truth; to them I say, "reserve your judgment until you have followed me to the end of this chapter and book."

"Land and loot" have been the watchwords of the Dutch from the time they occupied the Cape; and Mr. Merriman, of the Cape Government, said as much in the House of Assembly in the Session of July, 1883, after the Dutch Emigrants had trekked into Tembuland, and were backed up by the Dutch Members of Parliament, who advised them to resist lawful authority and defy the Government.

This was only on a par with the movement in Stellaland where a number of families moved " to fields afresh and pastures new," and without any definite idea of government, banded themselves into a sort of community, and for general practical purposes elected a Head ; and according as they prospered or otherwise, this man was remunerated or discarded—a mode of procedure that after all was but a repetition of the method in vogue in old times.

I don't deny that many of the old leaders were brave men, who with full confidence in the rifles and powder supplied them by England, boldly went into the forests, risked their lives among the native tribes, and in many cases, as in Weenen in Natal, became the victims of treachery ; but still with marvellous pluck they continued to face their enemies, whom they relentlessly mowed down with their rifles and elephant guns until they ultimately attained their ends.

There was nothing at all wonderful in this ; the Dutch only know one book—the Bible—from which they gather, and don't want to learn anything beyond what is to them the all-important fact, that they are the Elect of God, and that the sons of Ham are to be their servants for ever. In this they are in no way different from many who make use of that unfortunate book solely for the purpose of upholding their own special views and interests ; and who, without so much as having heard of Tamerlane or Suarrow of Catherine's time, would in imitation of them even " make a desert " of either of their so-called Republics if they thought it necessary to do so in order to put down opposition and remove all obstacles from their path. Now, starting with the idea that they are of the House of the Lord and all others are but interlopers, they take possession of the land for their daily sustenance ; then all they ask is to be left alone to carry out their " advanced mission " or—as it really means—extermination in their own way.

In the very Free State where I penned these words, the Dutch had to be restrained by the English, who refused to abandon that sterile mountain-top part of Africa until they had obtained from the Dutch a promise of protection for the natives. Notwithstanding their solemnly reiterated pledges, such were the encroachments of the Dutch upon the natives at Philippolis and in Griqualand West, that the English had again to step in and protect the natives once more from what would eventually have been extermination. That they are trying to repeat the process is to be seen by those who read in this year 1883—4, in Mackarani country on the other side of Kimberley, where they have attempted to set up a miniature Republic to the detriment of the natives and also of the white population. I know that the Dutch will swagger and maintain that they are the victims of England's greed ; but nothing of the kind. I, living on the spot, had good, full opportunities of finding out—and I took the trouble to ascertain—the truth ; and I fearlessly assert that history and all the facts of the case give the lie to the pretensions of the Dutch.

The Free State, as a Republic, possessed the basis of the best possible form of government ; but all its real advantages were entirely ignored, both by the Raad and the Executive. The principle of the sovereignty of the people was tacitly understood, and by the people cherished in good faith. Within the last few years they had no standing army, every burgher being at all times liable to be called upon for service. What is known there as "commandeering"—a system somewhat similar to the "requisitioning" practised by the Germans in the war with France in 1880-81—was carried on in the Free State; and in most cases was neither more nor less than spoliation or repudiation, unless the victims were prepared, by way of compensation, to occupy lands conquered, or to receive cattle that had been looted, with a certain quantity of "black ivory" thrown in as future slaves. The equality of man is at no time recognised, and to such a pitch of frenzy have they arrived, that they are now disposed to shout Africa for Africanders of European descent, totally ignoring the Africanders of the soil. As it is possible that the natives may determine to resist these raids upon their lands and cattle, the Republic now maintains a standing artillery force, and keeps on hand a supply of dynamite wherewith to attack the natives in their hills and strongholds if they object to give up their lands and cattle, or pay taxes as tributaries.

The Raad, or Parliament, is constituted mainly of farmers, and they meet annually. Dignity and honour are to them words without meaning. In order to give no cause for complaint, they assemble in the winter months, when pastoral and agricultural operations generally cannot be undertaken, receiving for their services the sum of £2 per day; and I fearlessly assert that but for this public bribe, not a tenth part of their number would leave their homes. I am a supporter of the principle of payment of Members of Parliament, but then I expect they will give an honourable return for their remuneration. The bulk of these men never understand the questions brought before them unless they relate to cattle or pounds, but are entirely guided by their Predikant and the few leaders, so that in reality they might as well vote by proxy; and they would do so were it not that they must be present in order to secure the £2 per day. Such is their joy at getting the same to take back to their wives and children, and their greed to increase the amount, that they unnecessarily prolong every Session, and even have extraordinary Sessions so as to make it more; whilst their travelling expenses are allowed them at all times. In almost all cases these men free the farming interest from taxation, and lay it heavily upon the commercial portion of the community, who generally are not of Dutch extraction, and they feel the burden most acutely.

Once in every five years, the Raad or Parliament nominate one of their body for election as their President, and he is finally chosen by the general population; but such is the supineness of the rural inhabitants that they never question what is provided for them, thus opening the way for any unprincipled adventurer who may be proposed as their President to assist in the nefarious designs of the Assembly.

The Republican is the highest form of Government by virtue of the fact that it requires the highest form of intellect to understand and follow it up to its final conclusions. This truth should commend itself to the whole world; a properly constituted Government can only exist where the people are thoughtful and honest, and where they manifest fidelity to the principles of honour and the service of public utility; and I fearlessly say that these elements of sound political character are not to be found either in the Free State or Transvaal Republics. Attached to both Republics are a number of Hollanders and Germans, who thrive upon the credulity of the Dutch, so that you may say in reality of the Free State that it is governed by foreigners, who maintain their position by traducing the English and levying all the taxes upon imported goods; and thus it will continue until they eat up the native-born Dutch, who must continue to suffer unless they again ask and obtain protection from England.

The Late Session of Volksraad.

The various Acts of Legislation recently passed through the Volksraad are so entirely at variance with the best interests of the community at large, and so obviously caused by the utter ignorance of, or indifference to, the real condition under which alone a young Colonial State can prosper, that we cannot refrain from trying to point out where, in our opinion, the root of the evil lies, with a view of eliciting an exhaustive discussion of the whole matter; which may eventually lead to the improvements in our general position—the imperative necessity of which everybody will admit. Amongst the many bad acts of commission and omission lately passed of which we have great reason to complain, are :—

1. The refusal of admission to foreign Banks, excepting the Bank of Africa.
2. The refusal of the veto right to the President.
3. The bad principle of favouritism by giving out, contrary to law, important Government contracts without calling for tenders; which bad example is bound to act as a very bad pattern and precedent.
3A. The neglect of suitable Postal arrangements.
4. The new liquor-law which aims at destroying the liberty of the subject, and inaugurates the antiquated and ridiculous attempt of improving morals by an act of law.
5. The highly important decision of the hon. Volksraad in the matter of compulsory working of claims in the Free State diamond mines, the consequence of which will be to destroy all faith in the validity of our titles or tenure of property under Free State laws.

Our hon. Volksraad being chiefly composed of farmers without any experience of business, or any wide range of knowledge beyond that of the immediate requirements of their own class, it cannot be wondered at that their deliberations on these important measures are so wide of the mark, as these matters would tax to the utmost the best powers of men who are endowed with the highest intellect, and alive to the interests of a progressive new country. At present the farming interest is the only one which can be said to receive any special attention at the hands of our Legislative Assembly. Whenever questions concerning any other class of burghers, be they business men or diggers, are to be regulated by law, experience has shown the majority of members of the Volksraad to be altogether ignorant of the simplest questions involved, and their interference has naturally had the effect of making a mess of these matters to the detriment of the best interests of the whole State.

Now it is our opinion that this deplorable state of affairs is principally due to the great indifference shown to the political institutions by the more enlightened inhabitants of the State and to their political duties and rights. Up to within the last few years legislation in this country was carried on in a rather noiseless way, without interfering much with the rights of those classes of the community who were not farmers ; but the result of the war in the Transvaal has entirely altered the aspect of affairs, and the formation of the Africander Bond has tended to bring to bear a very decided and strong influence on legislation, with the object of ruling all classes of the community, regardless of their legislative needs, according to the ill-considered views of the more unenlightened class of farmers. To put the case briefly, an intelligent minority and their interests—which are likewise very important interests, common to all burghers of the State—are at present not represented in the Volksraad at all ; and it is of the highest importance that they should exert whatever influence they may have to mend this great grievance. There is not, in our opinion, any complaint of malice or ill-will against the majority of the present legislators ; it is principally their want of knowledge of the real bearings of the cases not immediately connected with farming interests which leads so often to those bungles in law-making, and a remedy can only be effected by strenuous efforts which, however, may be easily made successful.

It is suggested that the classes most interested, all over the State, should forthwith be communicated with to send delegates to Bloemfontein with a view of discussing the above matters, and either of forming a separate association, for the protection of the injured vested interests by the aid of supporting a good newspaper and an agitation for the purpose of returning more suitable members for the Volksraad at all future elections; or of joining the Africander Bond in a body for the purpose of guiding its influence in the proper direction for the development of the best interests of all classes of the community. The necessary agitation to be decided upon by a Central Committee, the members of which to be resident at or near Bloemfontein, and immediate measures to be taken in order to bring the worst grievances before the impending extra Session of the Volksraad.

While I write, these flattering foreigners, finding that the prospect is not so bright, have conceived a new idea; and in conjunction with the Dutchmen of the Colony hold it over the heads of the colonists *in terrorem*. Having no money of their own, depending upon an English currency, not possessing too much natural wealth, and not knowing yet how to make or construct their own railways and other public works without bonds, loans or mortgages, as I have in my other works explained, they have conceived (more especially since the Majuba affair in the Transvaal, which I will discuss hereafter) the idea that the colonists ought to pay black-mail, on what they are pleased to call a rebate on Custom dues, which if they were such fools as to do, they say would enable them to pay interest for the money to build their railways; and led on by the foreigners, I have named, cry out like spoilt children for English gold, irrespective of justice, or without giving any sound reason for the same. They ignore the fact, or rather choose to forget that it is the colonists that have incurred debts—over twelve millions—to make harbours and breakwaters, railroads, and main roads, to facilitate transit up and down, and that in reality it is but an insurance fund to guard the outside of the Colony, positively making it possible for the Dutchman to live on his farm, and these political impostors to fatten on the credulity of the farmers.

Of course as might be expected, there is to be found all sorts of money agencies at work, to get enriched at the expense of the community; and it may virtually be said that there is not one farmer out of ten who is not under some monetary obligation to these agencies, and simply because the foreign governors ask to share the plunder with their friends at home. It is not too much to say that these suckers and parasites are beginning to think that the Free State is played out, and I must admit they are not far wrong. The English market at Kimberley and the late wars have enriched all, but as these circumstances are not likely to last or occur again for some time to come, they are packing up their trunks and making their way to the Transvaal, to bamboozle and persuade the rotten Government there to pass away in the form of Conventions, valuable tracts of land which they say are the exact spots where the Queen of Sheba got all her treasures. What wonderful faith some people have in these days. If I was disposed to give an opinion, I should say that in her wisdom Her Sheban Majesty took all away from that spot long long ago, but such is the simplicity of some people in haste to get rich, that they will give away, like the dog over the brook, the substance for the shadow ; and will only realise that they are dupes when they, like the South Sea Bubble-believers, find themselves deficient of all their means.

The present leaders of the Transvaal are but the accidental outcome of the mistake made at Majuba by that unfortunate impulsive man, Sir G. P. Colley, and afterwards overlooked and condoned by the weak and vacillating policy of a false, peace-at-any-price, paltry, party Government ; and which has had the result not only of making the very name of Englishmen a bye-word in both Republics, but has brought about the positive ruin of thousands through putting faith in the words of Sir Garnet Wolseley, that " as long as the sun shone, no alteration could take place or cause the removal of the British Flag ;" and yet in the face of all these promises, a most unjustifiable peace was proclaimed. One could have tolerated much, if the Transvaal leaders had started with honour and dignity, and if, having been saved from bankruptcy and native devastation, they had offered to re-coup the outlay of the British Government. Such a course would have been decent and becoming, but to attempt to repudiate all the advantages given, was the act of blackguards and blacklegs ; and the sudden attack on the troops, while playing a parade tune, was an act of infamy that no future apology can wipe out. It was simply a wild-animal blood-seeking attack, which no Government ought to have overlooked, much less the English Government. The whole campaign including the conclusion of peace by telegraph was so disgraceful, that in very shame Englishmen try to forget the bitter humiliation they were subjected to, and such a wretched makeshift for right will yet necessitate the alteration of the whole of the conditions, if Englishmen are to be respected.

This peace gave birth to a wretched compound called an Africander Bond, ostensibly got up by the Germans in order to stir up the Dutchman to get rid of the English—and to make way for an offshoot of the German Empire. At the Congress at Richmond, a resolution was moved to encourage patriotism as a preparation for a United Flag of Africa.

The States of Africa can never be independent while their natives increase and multiply as they do, any more than India could be governed by its white population. In India the experiment was tried and it failed, so that at last the whole had to be ruled as a conquered province. It is true that the Whig, to save expense desires the Colonies to take care of themselves; but Africa is not like our other Colonies where the native population decreases, making it possible for white occupation. On the contrary, the Kaffir increases, notwithstanding the various epidemics and the many wars that have taken place time after time.

It would be a sad day for all the Dutch, if ever the English Flag was lowered, for even now the Boers are regretting that the English are gone, and many would be glad if they would but return. The fact is only now and then let out, so don't tell it in Gath, or make it known in Ascalon—they do love the English golden sovereigns. But for the last few years Africa has stank in the nostrils of Great Britain. The English people have spent millions to assist in putting down native disturbances in the Colony, Zululand and the Transvaal, principally for the benefit of steam companies, controllers, tariffs, contractors, and officers; and for all this outlay, they should have had peace and good-will among all the people. It is also my firm conviction notwithstanding all the past loss and mismanagement, England would spend millions more, if it was needed, to prevent the overwhelming of the white population by the black; but if she does, it will be in her own way, and for the benefit of the whole, not a part.

The wretched attempt of a Sprigg to control the Basutos by unjustifiable means, cost the Colony over three millions, and then such was the stand made by the Basutos, for what even the colonists (not Spriggites) considered they were not entitled to, that the party of land and loot had at last to ask the English Government to take over a land that they could not control and govern. The acceptance of this duty by England is the one gleam of light through many a long day of gloom. Once let the English flag fly as representative of England's might, and all will be well from the Drakensberg to the Zambesi. This prospect has called forth a howl of fright, and even the gallant so-called reliant Free State, that prided itself upon beating what they are pleased to call a nation of thieves—after having robbed the Basutos of the land as well as the geese and cattle that were sustained upon it—shout out for mighty England to protect, not only the Colonial Border, but even their's, for fear it might cost them too much to do so themselves. Bah! the Free Staters are like their Transvaal brethren, very, very brave behind rocks and stones—but perfect cowards in the open. This assumption of Basutoland may eventually lead to the amalgamation of the Transkei, Nomansland, Natal and Zululand, as a whole Province to the advantage of all, if wisely carried out—after the style of the old Romans. Once let England plant her flag there should be no retreat, let the consequences or expense be what it might. For England there is no retreat, but after death; let who may say to the contrary. This is a view by no means impossible, and even the Free State is alarmed, and in addition to asserting that they have paramount claims to be considered, they have the impudence to say it was Colonial mismanagement that brought the Free State into jeopardy, and that the taking over of the Basutos was a breaking of the Aliwal Treaty. The despatches, on the taking-over question prove nothing of the kind. They simply reminded the Orange Free State of certain conditions contained in the Convention which they would have to fulfil; and one of these conditions was, that they should not invade Basutoland, or wink at its principals —German, Pinch-Us, Boo-Man, Green and traders in its Capital and elsewhere, supplying the Basutos with arms and ammunition, as the President had done for a long time, as well as allowing his own sons—who rented or owned farms in the conquered territory—to do the same for many years with impunity. Methinks, I see an attempt to deny all this; but having lived in the Free State, when the Colonial Government stopped their ammunition supply, I can hurl the lie in their teeth. I boldly assert, and

B

could prove that it was mainly due to the large supply of ammunition and the very best arms by the Free Staters, that the war was so prolonged, and which caused the Colonists to depart from Basutoland in disgrace. The Free State Government lent and sold ammunition to the Transvaal Government, to compel the Mapochs to surrender, and what with the help of the English volunteers and others—whom they had compelled to enter their ranks—notwithstanding that the Convention specified that British subjects should be exempt, they did at last make the poor wretches after many, many months of besieging, deliver themselves up—some to be shot, others to be transferred as servants among the farmers, to be articled, they say, for a number of years, to sow again dissention and revolt among the native tribes. Although it may be a fact, that the natives will settle down where there is water and grass, still they remember the land of their birth and the mountain stad of their chief. The close proximity of the British flag seems to many to forebode the beginning of the end of Dutch rule in South Africa, with the top of the wedge at Masaru and Cape Town as the future New York of South Africa, with its railway right up to Kimberley—supplying from the Western Provinces the whole of the interior trade, with the prospect of the Bechuanas, placing themselves under British protection, and afterwards the line of railway round on the Colonial side of the Transvaal to the Garden of Rustenburg, and finally on to Pretoria, will keep the Free State out in the cold, and without her railways, engirdle her still more with British influence and might.

The Natal and Zululand and Delogoa Bay or St. Lucia's Bay Railway on the Eastern side will also encircle the whole; and thus at last it will drop imperceptibly as it were into the hands of the Englishman. A gleam of this strikes the Dutch already, and they are even suspecting the Germans of being two-faced, watching which pays the best, to take advantage of England's gold or Germany's poverty. To such a length has their fear gone that, a Moses—the leader of the *Express*—feels somewhat astonished at such treatment. The best to command are they who know best how to obey, independent of consequences.

Chapter II.

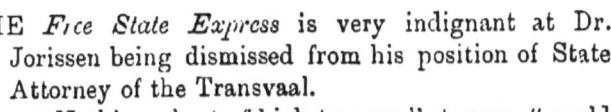

THE *Free State Express* is very indignant at Dr. Jorissen being dismissed from his position of State Attorney of the Transvaal.

"Nothing short of high treason," it says, " could surely justify such treatment of a man who has so eminently served the Transvaal. Dr. Jorissen was the guiding mind in the war of liberty. It is all but impossible to believe that—in return for his zeal, devotion, and patriotism—he should have been treated so outrageously. In either case, it shows anything but a healthy state of political life, and it is most painful for a staunch friend of the Transvaal and its people to have to say this."

But the Transvaalers are only true to the policy of the Dutch party throughout South Africa. The cry of the party is "Africa for the Africanders." The leaders declare that the people born of the soil are quite able to govern themselves, and they ask all other people to leave alone. Dr. Jorissen, is a foreigner ; he is a Doctor of Theology, brought to the Transvaal by President Burghers to be Superintendent of Education. The Volksraad do not want him, they feel strong in themselves ; and hence give him, as they gave other foreigners, notice to quit. There are a few demented men who think differently ; as did the Boer on the Pretoria Market, who when failing to get a bid for his produce, exclaimed,—" Where are the English people ?" He was but a Boer, with a lamentable weakness for sterling money, and may be passed; but to find the Bloemfontein *Express* holding up its hands in token of horror, is astonishing. The Editor called it "base ingratitude," but in so doing forgets his party, like the Boer farmer, perhaps because of personal interest. There may be base ingratitude ; there may be treason ; but the dismissal of Dr. Jorissen is only carrying out the policy of the self-styled Africander-party ; which is to get rid of everyone whose family is not of Dutch extraction with several generations buried in colonial soil. The indignation of the *Express* is amusing; apparently it has not before understood the doctrines it has diligently proclaimed. When they are understood by others, a similar effect will be produced, and Free State farmers may give notice to a German Borckenhager to clear out immediately.

The Transvaal have lost faith in Foreign Hollanders, and under the cover of needing a *legal* Attorney-General, have got rid of one of their ablest men, who acted so shamelessly against the English at the time of hostilities.

All this indignation is truly laughable, coming as it does from the German-Holland Jewish faction, who doubtless see in this removal, notice to quit likewise, and perhaps they will feel some day like the engineer "hoist with his own petard."

The President of the Free State has made his arrangements for future office, and longs for a trip to Old England to recruit his health and air his new Sir-Ship in company with her who is now not only his wife but his "lady" also, and once a Cape Town dressmaker; who after fluttering in England during their brief holiday will return once more to disgust the stout dames of South Africa, and when the services of her husband are no longer required, they can retire upon a pension to some more congenial clime.

The President of the Transvaal having thanked God for victory over the black sons of Ham, shot the leaders, and taken possession of the land, cattle, &c., of the conquered, put their eight thousand prisoners all out to a life-long service. Then, being in need of a holiday, the President instead of going to Holland to be congratulated, or Germany to be tabooed, goes to England in the vain hope that he will there receive some honour and secure an alteration of the terms of the Convention. Whilst there he laid in a stock of bell-toppers, white ties, and black suits to strut about in during the remaining brief period of his authority in the Transvaal Presidency; for, according to Mr. Hofmeyr, the Republican President and members of Parliament are most particular about being dressed in English court-costume when performing their Senatorial duties. Truly this portion of the world, like many other parts is governed by precedent but with very little wisdom, and without going to the root of things.

These men—to keep up an appearance of decency, and to satisfy the cant and humbug of those who in lawn-sleeves, with upturned eyes, bless flags and arms—go to their places of worship and call upon the God of battles to help them to crush out their enemies. Acting in this contemptible spirit, Joubert, the Commander of the Transvaal, went to a spot where no white man had ever stood, and in full consciousness that the God of battles was on their side a volley was fired, and then in a stentorian voice he gave out the first verse of the Psalm No. 134, after singing which they retired thinking they had done a noble work. The President of the Transvaal was but a successful farmer, and an accidental leader—the outcome of Boer savagery, in the war as they call it, of independence against the English. This war was undertaken to enable them to repudiate the *debts* they had contracted, and to take possession of English spoil in the Free State in the shape of buildings and the portable wealth and the gold, the result of fancy and impartial prices, and which they secured during the English occupation, after the English had destroyed ecocone and paid off all their liabilities.

It is said in private life, if you want to make a man your enemy —place him under a money obligation. This was their exact position—without means or credit—prior to the English going to the Transvaal. Directly the Boers waxed fat, through such occupation, they began to kick ; such is the usual way of men, especially where there is no sense of honour or dignity.

The President of the Free State is a well-meaning gentleman, originally a practitioner in the Colonial courts, but not a prominent or successful one. He was requested to accept the Presidency, in the hope that his knowledge of English good-nature would enable him to secure from them English means, as John Bull was known, when in a good humour, to be rather soft and liberal. The President is a decent country gentleman, with ordinary lawyer-official-like ability, but possessed of no genius and without any special aptitude for governing. His special advantage over more intelligent men, is the silent unconcerned manner in which he takes all matters, and his undoubted faith in the pure simplicity of John Bull. The one grand speech of his life, which ought to be placed on his tomb when translated into English, was, " all shall right come ;" and I must admit his unbounded faith in his own words, for judging by the little improvements that have taken place, during the last twenty years, no one will credit him with aiding in any way to produce two blades of grass, where one only grew before. To live, and be merry, and to secure the good things of this life for himself and family, is a paramount desire on his part and as I shall have later on to show, in this, he has been exceptionally successful; but even all this would have been impossible, if it had not been for the close proximity of the diamond-fields, enabling the Dutch to sell at very high prices, but alas! for which they are not even thankful or grateful.

"A President" is not a necessary feature of Republicanism, but rather, an offshoot of Monarchical power reproduced in an elective form. In my opinion, a Republic would be better without a President. As Goldwin Smith remarks; 'A single head of the State is a fancied necessity.' The Swiss Constitution, which instead of a single man, has a Council with a President whose function is only to preside, presents great advantages in this respect, and is the safest model for adoption. A single head is certainly not a universal necessity, since Switzerland does without one. An office such as the elective Presidency is at once the grand prize and the most powerful stimulant of faction; it keeps selfish ambition and intrigue constantly at work; it breeds and advances to influence a crowd of men skilled in bad electioneering arts. Every four or five years it brings burning questions to a dangerous head. . . . . The periodical revolution which it involves is fatal to anything like stability of policy or forecast on the part of the Government. Why should we not all do as Switzerland does, with an Executive Council elected by the national Legislature? Harmony between the Executive and the Legislative might be preserved, and steadiness of policy secured at the same time, by having the Council elected—not all at once, but by periodical instalments. The first of these two essential objects would, perhaps, be better secured by such a system than it is by the present."

In recording thus of the political situation of Republics in the United States, it must not be supposed that any depreciation of Republicanism is intended. I regard Republican institutions, if wisely used and morally and intellectually enforced, as the model of all true government. But the ideal Republic should be the outcome of the mental vigour and unfettered freedom of the people whose genius and honour should protect its purity and maintain its strictest integrity. That such a Republic will ultimately obtain recognition I firmly believe. All nations have the proper foundation, and are not deficient in the materials with which to construct a solid and harmonious edifice. All nations are but comparatively young. Increasing in age, they will also accumulate experience ; and disassociating themselves from Monarchical influences inherited from their mother countries, they will flourish upon their own merits and be sustained upon their native resources, the catholicity of their institutions, the breadth of their political rights, and the discrimination, loyalty and intelligence of their liberty-loving people.

The Kind of Government Wanted in the Free State.

" Sir,—I have been wondering whether a few thoughts from an absent Englishman on the best kind of Government for any country generally, and England particularly, to have would be acceptable to you and your readers, and whether it would help to solve the problem before you as a country at no distant future. I presume, and take for granted, that the people are in favour of a free government. They believe that a free government means a government by the people for the people. I take it to be doubtful whether such a government in its purity can exist where there is any *one man power*, let the government be called a ' Republic.' ' Limited Monarchy,' or by any other name whatever.

" A single ruler, although elective by the people, is actually a monarch *pro tem.*, and he is apt to become more or less a despot according to the measure of ambition and cupidity that reigns in his heart.

" The people should be represented in the Executive branch as well as in the Legislative, and the best representation to meet such an end would be by an Executive Council of three, five, seven or nine.

" This would liberalise the government effectively, make it truly representative, and do away with ' rings,' ' cabals,' and ' backstairs influences ' behind the throne, and greater than the throne itself.

"The members of the Executive Council should be equal in authority and power, and decide all questions by vote, of which a public record should be kept.

"The argument of the Monarchist is that one man must govern *ex necessitate*. Two or more would differ, quarrel, and never agree about anything : therefore the world must ever be governed by the one-man power. If this were true, then the Legislative branch, and also the judicial branch should be governed by one man. The principle is the same in either case. If a difference of opinion can be settled by a vote of the majority in the one branch, it can be equally so in either of the others. Parliament has its differences, but readily settles all questions by a vote. The judges have their differences, but come to a decision with amity, dignity and decorum. And to say an Executive Council could not do the same would be absurd and wrong. The history of the world is against the argument of monarchists. All the Republics of the ancient world had plural executives.

"Some had ten archons, and Rome had two Consuls to administer the executive power ; and Switzerland—the model Republic —has a chief Executive Council of seven, which has successfully administered their executive power for over five hundred and seventy years.

"The Executive power in Great Britain has been in reality administered, and most efficiently, by the Cabinet composed of twelve members of the Ministry.

"The change could easily be made by substituting an Executive Council for the Crown, and making the Council elective by the people or Parliament.

"With the present system of government a great many reforms are impracticable, and the whole fabric will sooner or later topple over of its own weight of errors.

"England, and all countries will have soon to consider the question seriously."

With reference to the election of barristers or lawyers I am distinctly of opinion that their presence in the House is inimical to the simplification of the laws and I believe my views on this question are held by many of our leading politicians, their judgment being founded on past experience of the conduct of legal members of the Legislature. Nevertheless, I can admit that a lawyer's genuine opinion may in some cases be of value, but the difficulty lies in the fact that one is so seldom sure of this genuineness. The people would do far better if they returned scientists and medical men. Questions of health, hygiene, the sexual relationships, and other cognate subjects, can only be perfectly understood by these gentlemen. There are few questions comparatively, which do not involve considerations of health, life, disease and death. In all these matters, the voice of the doctor must be above every other; and the judgment of a lawyer, as such, would be of no more use or value than that of a bricklayer.

A German Republican cannot swear allegiance to a King or Queen, and their heirs for ever; and, if this is needed, he cannot sit among the Commons so-called. It is the duty of a Republican to serve to the best of his ability his constituency and country, and if he can sit among those who are elected to serve their country, all is well; but if he cannot sit without giving or taking oaths, to some one on a throne, then let him like the "grand old men" in and out of France, who being elected to serve in the French Assembly, declined to sit, rather than swear allegiance to that arch-traitor, perjurer and bedizened villain, Napoleon the Third, but the Little.

It must never be supposed that John Brand, now Sir John Brand, can in any sense be likened to William the Silent of Orange of the Old Dutch Republic. This giant's words were indeed silvern and his silence golden—just the thing at that time when a mighty work had to be done, and for anyone to criticise and make speech thereon was only to bring about their own discomfiture.

I don't allow these men to misunderstand or judge me; to allow them to do so, would but admit that Lilliputians had the right to judge giants. What I have written is after due care and consideration, and for any to dispute the same would be the outcome of fear or ignorance.

The Capital of this Republic has not too much to boast of. The Public Offices are a lasting monument of disgrace to the architect, and being built in the "West End" of the town, among the aristocratic houses, their appearance is anything but dignified. The church-home and hospital, close to the public buildings, were the result of charity and debt. The "sisters" admitted that they were always in a chronic state of poverty, so much so, that even clothes,—sent out by the charitable from England for the poor blacks—were sold at a public church bazaar to assist in paying the interest on their accumulated liabilities, which, if not stealing, is certainly raising cash under false pretences. Getting into debt with the tradesmen and not paying twenty shillings in the pound if possible to avoid doing so is carried on here upon the principle of robbing mammon, and making friends with the children of this world. But even this now has its limit, and the children of this world begin to look upon its holy, idiotic, itinerant bishop and his wretched acolytes, that officiate in white and black surplices, as so many walking impostors—youthful shams. Its cathedral is the outcome of the success of its Bishop and of the old ladies of England, and it would starve if it had to depend upon the contributions of its members. The church members amuse themselves, as elsewhere, in looking after each other's bonnets and making up general scandal of their neighbours, who don't go to church or subscribe to their follies. I myself came under the lash of their small talk, because I exposed their littleness and would not bow down to their little men nor attend their insane meetings. The Dutch-church, an imposing two-tower building, is the outcome of beef, mutton, and farming produce, begged out of the Dutchmen by their Pastors. The Dutchman does like to get hold of English gold, but he does not like to part with it, so he satisfies his conscience by giving a few heads of cattle and sheep, sending them on as his paying passport to Heaven, and the Pastor sells them on the public market, time after time, as he stands in need. The Pastors bless and curse in accordance with their needs or satisfaction.

The city boasts, after twenty years of prosperity, of a Public Library, that any literary man would feel ashamed to own, and which is the result of weekly entertainments. The public Post and Telegraph Office has yet to be built. Its Building Society is a delusion and a snare, a rich investment for those who never buy out of the society, but for those who build, the old adage is well proved that "fools build houses, and wise men occupy and own them" for certainly, almost all—after miserable efforts to keep up subscription and house-payments and fines—have at last to sell out for the benefit of the money classes. But the time must come for the public building of houses, as I have drawn attention to in my later chapters on house building. Strange to say, that although a Dutch Capital, out of five thousand inhabitants, not a tenth are Dutch, the remainder are all of different nationalities. It boasts of its Rag Alley—its Petticoat Lane; its poverty, disgusting, and its immorality and disease are simply an eyesore to decent people. Dr. Stollreither drew attention to it in its most glaring forms; its sluits are hotbeds of all kinds of diseases, until its young victims in diptheria, scarlet fever and opthalmia reveal it in all its intensity and in all its horrors.

I may say, about the same of all towns in the Free State and the Transvaal, with very few differences, let who may say to the contrary. I have written this true history without malice or prejudice, although I know some will say to the contrary: but all past historians have desired to flatter. I write as I found, and defy anyone truthfully to dispute all and everyone of my well-authenticated facts.

Of course, where there are so many churches there must be a gaol; but such was the condition of this building, that the most desperate characters made a boast, that directly they so desired, they could take off their irons and bolt, once more to prey upon Society. This was specially so with horse-stealers; till, at last, those who had a steed—either for pleasure or every day work— never were certain of finding the same in their stable. And such was the care of the Government, that one well-known horse-stealer got his liberty because the gaoler could not produce the warrant authorising the detention of his person, revolver or clothes; and such was the order in the Records of the Courts in this much belauded Republic, with the "all right shall come" man at its head, that even the officers could not produce the committal documents, so that there was no power to hold one of the most unprincipled men of his day—according to his own confession published, after he was set at liberty, in the *Daily News* of 1883. The bulk of the officers at the gaol are lazy brags and, in some cases, understood thieves.

The following will so well illustrate the condition of the gaols in South Africa, that I feel it incumbent to print the same, as it shows the illogical position taken up by the Judge—one of the attorneys pitchforked into a judgeship.

"The prisons are filthy in the extreme. At night, for eleven hours, a tub is placed in the cell for all common purposes, where perhaps ten men are stowed in a space of about eight feet by sixteen.

"A water tub in the centre of the yard, into which all filth can pour, and out of this tub the prisoners drink their water and wash their persons and clothes. Talk of the gaols of Bomba, in Naples; in comparison they were superior. At no time did the Gospel preachers think it their duty to call, unless some poor wretch had to be hung up, so that the prisoners had no opportunity to complain or get redress. The food was at times disgusting to look at, much less eat ; but this was not to be wondered at, when gaolers so manipulated it that they fed their families out of the cost of the prisoners' rations, and then, like the gaoler of Fauresmith, retired upon the plunder. Doctors, with no bowels of compassion, gave no help or redress ; they were like so many hogs on a visit, when they had to call at the prison to entitle them to their fees. No division of prisoners ; so that murderers, thieves, perjurers, and unfortunate, accidental, or innocently suffering prisoners were all crowded together—the latter being in simple torture, and passed their time as if in a living hell."

If Judges were capable of feeling, they would indeed hesitate in their sentences. What a year in prison, even to the guilty, must be, is horrible to contemplate ; but in the case of an innocent man, nothing can repay him for the constant physical and mental torture and insults heaped upon him.

Could juries and judges think what a year in prison means, —the isolation from a man's family, that cuts out a year from a man's life, a year from a man's work, a year from a man's tongue, —is a penalty so terrible, that if madness or suicide ensues no one need wonder. When will it be understood, that half, if not more, of our man-made laws are man-made crimes, that only indicate the savage nature of one portion of society to the other. May the time arrive, when Nature's laws being recognised and carried out, there will be no need for Judges or prisons; and then, no future Howard will find the work of visiting prisons needful.

Judge or Jury.

Mr. Justice Shippard has during the present Circuit started or re-started the question of Judge or Jury, by finding it to be his duty in more than one town to dissent from some verdicts returned by Juries. At Colesberg, Peter Albertus Hanekamp was charged with "assault with intent to commit grievous bodily harm." The evidence was conflicting, and the *Advertiser* reports :

"At about 1.30 the Court adjourned for luncheon, and the jury were locked up and luncheon provided for them. On the Court resuming at 3 p.m. the jury had not agreed, and saw no prospect of agreeing on a verdict. His Lordship in discharging them, remarked somewhat severely on what he considered a failure of justice, owing to no verdict having been returned, and said this added another to a list of cases in which he considered that the ends of justice had been defeated owing to the defective working of the system of trial by jury in this colony."

A good many persons who do not think, are too ready to proclaim that the learned Judge would have done better ; but even so able a jurist as Mr. Justice Shippard is not beyond the liability to give a contradictory, and hence, unsatisfactory verdict. As some persons are aware, a Judge on Circuit visits the public prisons, and, on the 7th of March last, Judge Shippard visited the Fort Beaufort gaol, and gave the following document (which we find printed in the *Journal*) to the gaoler :—

[Copy.]

"I have this day visited the Fort Beaufort gaol, and find everything remarkably clean. The prisoners have no complaints to make, and the general state of the prison does very great credit to the gaoler.

"I would suggest that the ceilings and roofs be looked to, especially with a view to destroy the bugs that infest the ceilings, and drop on the prisoners at night.

"(Signed)

"S. G. A. SHIPPARD,
"Judge on Circuit.

"Fort Beaufort, March 7, 1884.

"Certified a true copy."

"B. W. HOLLAND, Resident Magistrate."

Everything in the gaol was found "remarkably clean," but "bugs infest the ceilings and drop on the prisoners at night." No more contradictory verdict, no verdict more against the evidence, has ever been given by a colonial or any other jury; and we fail to understand how the learned Judge could have written such a report, indeed we would not now believe that it was written from his pen, had we not the certificate of the Resident Magistrate; for how can a place infested by bugs be clean—remarkably clean?

And in truth, a Judge's verdict is not of necessity better than the verdict of a jury. We believe that some Judges now on the Bench would try criminal cases impartially; but enough is known of Judges to prove that there are among them men who could not be less impartial in some cases than juries are. While we say this, we repeat what was written lately, that jurors should be more carefully selected, and also be paid for their work. There is no reason in the world for making some thirty men attend court, and there do the most important work of the court, without any remuneration, when every one else is handsomely paid for what he does.

It is quite a mistake to suppose that always, and everywhere, jurors are against the natives. At Uitenhage, last week, a labourer named Andries Booke was arranged and charged with stealing two head of cattle from Daniel Foxcroft, a farmer, but the jury gave the man an acquittal; and James Magoba, a native doctor, who gave a native woman a dose of medicine which killed her, was also found "not guilty" of culpable homicide. There are many such verdicts given in this Colony. Whether they are, or are not, such as should be given is an open question, and when the Judge happens to endorse, or when he disapproves of a verdict, there are some, who having heard the case, disagree with the Judge; and facts so much depend upon the way they are looked at, and upon their surroundings that courts of law will not hear an appeal, if it means reconsidering anything but points of law.

One reason for some verdicts may be found in the practice of the Courts. When nine men are called upon—some for the first time in their lives—to hear a case, they are confused by the addresses for the crown, and for the defence, and the directions of the

Judge, and forget the evidence upon which alone their verdict ought to be based. Then there is, we fear, a growing habit with Judges to tell juries a great deal too much. They announce so many times what the finding should be, or they so often tell jurors to give prisoners the benefit of the doubt, that an independent jury put up their backs ; or a weak jury lets the prisoner go, to find then that there was no doubt to which the prisoner was entitled. Occasionally, too, a Judge is so obscure in his address as to make it impossible for any jury to understand what he is really driving at.

Another fact must also be remembered. The general public —from whom the jurors are drawn—believe that the prison which may appear remarkably clean, has been whitewashed specially for the Judge, and that it is not a fit place for any decent European to be kept in. It is also notorious that no classification is made at Convict Stations, which may also be " remarkably clean " with " bugs that infest the ceilings and drop on the prisoners at night;" and jurors who know a European prisoner, or who see that he is respectable in appearance, decline to have him punished, when it is known or assumed that the sentence will be imprisonment with hard labour. The time has now fully come for appointing visitors to every gaol, who shall have access at any hour of the day or night, and be compelled to report on every part of the prison once a month ; and the time has more than come for separating black and white convicts. Until this is done, jurors will decline to find every white man guilty who has committed crime ; but better this sometimes, than doing away with trial by jury, and leaving prisoners to a Judge Menzies or a Justice Bell.

Chapter III.

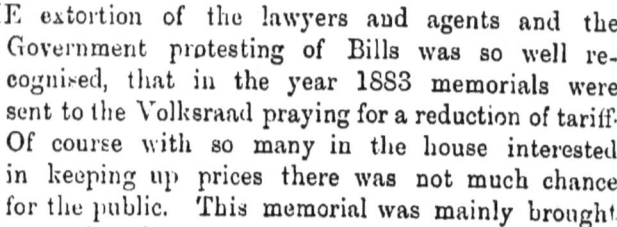HE extortion of the lawyers and agents and the Government protesting of Bills was so well recognised, that in the year 1883 memorials were sent to the Volksraad praying for a reduction of tariff. Of course with so many in the house interested in keeping up prices there was not much chance for the public. This memorial was mainly brought about by the excessive charges in mine promoting and diamond stealing defending, and it would be simply disgusting to give the particulars of the extortion practised. In one case of Company-defending, charges amounting to over twelve hundred pounds were incurred, and a governmental reduction of five hundred pounds occurred in the case of two Kaffirs wherein a lawyer's charge of eight hundred pounds was made, and a set-off of five hundred pounds allowed. Can anyone wonder after this that lawyers and doctors, procureurs and agents build fine houses, enclose lands, and become sheep-farmers, fare sumptuously every day, and wear fine linen, and boast that they have my Lord Beaconsfield's carriage and other vehicles belonging to the aristocracy of England to ride in?

Political judges were another nuisance in the Free State; talking their insolent bunkum in person under the Cape Colony flag, and spouting treason in a criterion, public hotels, with a Cape political mountebank and Dutch enthusiast as a companion. This companion, for the purpose of tickling his Dutch and German audience, lied about his neighbours of the Colony, and his compeers in the Cape House of Assembly.

Political judges have in times passed disgraced their countries in England as elsewhere, and I protest against the Chief Justice of the Free State going into the Cape Colony and taking an active part in setting up a "*Bestuur*"—which means setting up some other form of Government, although it was only attributable to his want of wisdom. As a genial dinner-eating individual no one can find fault with him, but it is time to speak when he sets up as a general leader, the coming light of the South African world and the future President of the Free State. One is perhaps expecting too much in comparing him with the enlightened men of the Western world, but it is truly lamentable what a few years of easy official authority will do for a man of small parts. Conceit in some men has been likened to an egg full of meat, and it is no less true of this Judge Reitz, the foreigner, who being fully persuaded that the Presidency of the Free State was a better position than its Chief Judgemisfitship, stuck at no meanness to secure so good a future income as £3,000 for doing so little, and the prospect of so many other fat things.

Mr. Hofmeyer says that his compatriots cannot read English, which certainly does not speak very highly for the Dutch colonists, and one can only feel for and pity the unfortunates who have not learnt to speak the commercial language of the world; but how any man can ask that the Dutch *patois* should be continued, would almost puzzle a native of Tasmania, for a more wretched mode of expressing one's desires, feelings, and thoughts, is not continued in any other part of the globe. This upholder of Dutch conversation, commonly known as *kitchen-Dutch*, publicly lied when he stated that better manners and order were to be found in the Free State Parliament than in that of the Cape Town House of Assembly. Also when he assured his hearers it was a treat to see its members all dressed in black coats, white ties, and tall hats. Well, if being dressed like waiters in a French restaurant is delightful, then they are welcome to look upon themselves as things to be admired, as "a thing of beauty is a joy for ever." But I, who have also looked upon these unfortunates when dressed-up, as it was called, was convinced that they must have felt as uncomfortable as the old soldier did in his stiff cravat and tall busby in the days gone by, and that for these honourable gentlemen and other public officials, to ape the worst style of our officials in England, did not in any way add to their Senatorial dignity, but rather to their discredit.

Another item is worth noticing. This speaker intimated that the burghers were a fine body of men; but the artillery was made in England, and manned by young Dutchmen too lazy to work on their farms, who were specimens of humanity by no means to be envied. The artillerymen were certainly not fit for much better than targets to be shot at, and so far as the burghers were concerned, certainly, if turning out when they spied plunder was to be considered manly and national, and to be admired, well and good; and when the opportunity occurred for shooting down Kaffirs, women and children, and securing cattle and land, I must admit they are willing to show up, but always with the understanding that substitutes and Englishmen, as in the late Transvaal War with Mapoch, go to the front, do all the fighting, and get killed, leaving all the plunder for the Dutchmen afterwards. Such plunder consisted of their lands, cattle, men, women and children, who, being prisoners, virtually became their slaves on their own farms, notwithstanding all they may say to the contrary. I know that many will assert that the Dutchman is better than the English soldier in buck-shooting. This is true, but he could never compete at the target; that he held Majuba Hill is also true, but this was one of the accidental victories due the folly of a commander, who paid for his folly with his life, but alas, his conduct gave the opportunity to a Governor to degrade the English name in the face of all, and to forget the slaughtering of Englishmen on their way to Pretoria, and thus, by their unsatisfactory settlement of the Transvaal country, leaving for the future another crop of slaughterings to come, and all the ills of bad government, for the sudden attack on Colonel Anstruther, was simply sudden murder,—don't forget, not fair fighting. I repeat it, sudden murder, which ought never to be forgotten.

To verify my remarks on the Free State doctors, I record the fact that the chief municipal officer was but a travelling quack, who, by dint of flattery and funniness, got a document from the State President authorising him to physic and kill without enquiry; and who, to keep up his character of the successful quack, while in his capacity of Mayor, by building a huge barn, dignified by the name of Town-House, involved the town in debt, almost to the verge of bankruptcy, in fear and trembling left in haste, but not by the way of the Colony, his old ground of quackery and failure, but by way of Natal on his road to England, in the hope that by some fluke he might be dubbed M.D., and thus be made respectable ever after. By leaving just before the time of opening the New Town Hall he escaped being greeted with the curses of those he had helped to impoverish. But then this man was in no way different from most of his fellow-practitioners, whose stock-in-trade for the most part consists of impudence and a few bottles with Latin inscriptions upon them, to awe the ignorant if necessary. One could give the history of the Free State's wealthiest doctor, so-called, one who had learnt the art of calling twice a day upon all his patients to swell his account, and who could with Free State impudence charge twenty-five shillings for a single visit, and seven and sixpence for a box of pills. If he prescribed a dose that deprived a man of life and a family of their breadwinner; thus creating a condition of life-long sorrow for this family—of course, it was only a case of "death by misadventure." This man in his early career, when just emerging out of his missionary chrysalis state, was the principal cause—of course in ignorance of the nature of the deadly poisons, and the means of detecting the same—of helping the Dutch, out of spite to the English, to get an Englishman sent to glory in a few days after trial by means of a rope round his throat. As a rule, all these officials are of the German and Jewish nationality, who having liberty to enter and live in English colonies, take advantage of English protection, and afterwards traduce the country that sheltered them; and when found out they go their way and commence the same practice elsewhere.

One of the most important outcomes of public feeling, was the exposure of certain doings in connection with a mine which I have said I thought had been salted. I allude to Jagersfontein, and the occurrence took place in June, 1883, in that so-called rising township. The whole position of this town and neighbourhood shows the want of wisdom of the President and its insolvent inspector. The President ought never to have appointed this man, who has since been removed from his position; and who, though knowing the law, yet for some selfish end did not note and acquaint the President with its evasion. The mining Ordinance specified that all claims must be worked or forfeited in a given time. Now the evading of this, simply threw the land into the hands of speculative men, who ignoring the original conditions, held and passed on until the bubble burst and exposed the trickery.

It was held to be the redeeming feature of this mine, that there was a chance for the working men, but the men who salted it with diamonds got from the illicit trade in Kimberley, principally Jews, as is now proved by the numbers of these roving tribes at the breakwater at Cape Town. The *scricp* successors now maintain that the mine will never be a poor man's working ground, and that therefore this clause is useless. Of course, some men are sanguine if allowed to work there, and had the Government notice of April, 1879, signed by the Inspector, been enforced regarding compulsion of work in one claim, in a block of ten, that protest and meeting need never have been made or held. One Beddy, a successful speculator, contended that capitalists would not invest their money in the mine, unless it was *bona fide* property. He further said that no Company had proved the mine payable. Mr. Quinlan said did they think, after the experience capitalists had had of the Jagersfontein mine that they would make further investments? Before that day arrived his hair would be white. James Armstrong intimated that as labour was wealth, and that by labour the soil became productive—the profits of such labour should be to the workman's advantage. If the mine was thrown open to workers, they would have a class of men there who had made Australia, California, and New Zealand; and as the companies had failed, it was but fair that the working men should have the opportunity of trying; that they should try and not allow, as at present, so much ground to be idle. Labour meant success, and a future prospect for the Free State mines.

Now all this might have been accomplished if the President had but seen the claim law enforced; but this is on a par with most things in this delightful very, very Free State. It would have been a delightful free pastoral country, but for the natives, Germans and Jews; but supposing the Government to know that this place was in reality diamondiferous they should work it out as a national speculation, either with convict or free labour, and then picture the future.

The Unworked Claims of Jagersfontein.

The question as to the enforcement of the clause relating to unworked claims is now mooted, and it is hoped to prevent this place being turned into a mere speculator's playground. "You will drive away capitalists," is the cry of those who are opposed to the measure. If so, so much the worse for the capitalists, is my reply. The interests of a moneyed few should not be studied to the detriment of the hard-handed toiling many. What capitalists call "the mine of the future" is now lying idle and unworked, while hundreds of men with small means, willing to work, are eating their hearts out in sickening despair, at want of any outlet for their energies. From Pretoria and Kimberley, to Durban and Cape Town comes the cry: "What can we do? Where can we go to better ourselves?" The Free State has always had an unenviable name as a mere grazing run, a Boer's paradise; now is the chance to show otherwise. Throw open the doors to any and every man willing to work the precious soil, which waits only to be wooed to enrich the wooer. Look to the future, and imagine what a successful Jagersfontein means. A splendid revenue, a large and prosperous township enriching the neighbouring farmers and encouraging them in the paths of industry. Avoiding the mistakes of Kimberley, profiting by its errors, and building on its experience—what a glorious career is open! A busy Anglo-Saxon town, bustling streets, the clang of workshops, the hum and roar of industry, the firm establishment of English ideas in the very heart of Boerdom—a continual stream of native industry and the enormous increase in the value of property for miles around! What blessings are to be gained! The surrounding farms would be thoroughly prospected by adventurous spirits seeking for wealth. The rich mineral wealth concealed by our jealous mother earth would be brought to light, new mines would certainly be worked. Every kopje and kloof would be ransacked by the class of men who in a few years converted Australia from an unknown, dark, savage continent to a glorious, rich, proud and enlightened group of colonies, superior in magnificence to many an ancient European kingdom. The railway would be a necessary adjunct to a town of such importance, and the increased revenue and value of property would enable the Government to extend the iron-road from length and breadth of this country—a country which is a "railway engineer's paradise," so few are the natural obstacles (alas, that the dull, heavy, prejudiced minds of many of its inhabitants are indeed natural obstacles). This large country now lies a vast sullen, monotonous, and barren flat. But let Anglo-Saxon energy and indomitableness have fair play, and in a few years how this scene will change. The restless Transvaal, the childish Natal and Exeter Hall ridden Cape Colony will look with envy on this compact and wealthy Free State.

If the mine is as rich as made out, let the Government take over and work it, and give the benefit to the Republic at large, and thus save taxes ; it will then pay better, and give more satisfaction all round.

During the sitting of this ever-to-be-remembered Session of 1883, while discussing the frontier and the Basuto question, one of the uninformed well-dressed black shining hat members of the Raad, who certainly showed a tendency to become an occupant of one of the rooms of the new lunatic asylum that the Free State had constructed, desired that an amendment be put at once to the effect that if certain things were not done, the Free State Government would annex the Cape Colony. The President facetiously reminded the member that all strong men were merciful, and objected to such remarks for fear that it might be thought they represented the feeling of the Raad. Truly, in his latter days the President desires to make jokes. One thing he well knows, that but for the strong Englishman being merciful to the Dutch inhabitants of the Free State, the English would have been seen over the plains and mountains long before this. Some people say that the Free State farmer, since the abandonment, has bred his own horses, shorn his own sheep, raised his corn, planted his orchards, lived prosperously and undisturbed, while wars have raged all around him, with the exception of his little war with the Basutos in 1868. This is not strictly true. During this time the farmer himself has done but little. As a matter of fact, a lazier man does not exist; he grows but little, and depends upon the foreigner for agriculture, and other countries for food supply ; but owing to the diamond-fields and Cape wars, he has been able to sell his miserable sheep and cattle for fancy prices, and John Bull, in the Colony, like a fool, allowed him to have unlimited supplies of ammunition, which he sold at fabulous prices to the Basutos and Transvaalers, making the fortunes of the Bloemfontein Ladybrand and Ficksburg German and Jewish merchants, and of which the border farmers had their share. But since this, as all failed, general bankruptcy has followed. The summer heat is intolerable, the winters are cold and unbearable to any man that can possibly spare the means to travel to the Cape sea-board or remove out of the Cape Colony. Whatever grass or vegetation may be grown in the summer to fatten the cattle, the frost destroys in the winter, and the wind blows away for ever; and yet the conceit of these unfortunate men, who cannot leave for elsewhere, enables them, like puppies, to snarl at John Bull's dog. Truly, this big dog is merciful to the weak, but as usual, the little dogs cannot understand such mercy. I know this will make the little dogs squeak and howl at being found out, but while they continue to do such dirty deeds and credit my countrymen with them, I will never spare the lash. One had the insolence to move as a resolution, " that owing to the inherent weakness of the Colony, they, the Free State, had better annex the Cape." I refrain from giving this madman's name. There is no fear of this while its legislators take their £2 per day and live in a small room upon a loaf, sardine, and a bottle of Cape brandy daily. Their want of good treatment made known their little weaknesses.

The telegram announcing that Gladstone contemplated taking over the Basutos, created an excitement among the German and Jewish fraternity that was quite repelling to any decent Englishman contemplating the possibility of John Bull starting once more upon a Quixotic campaign, and spending in South Africa, the taxes so easily raised in England at the point of the bayonet or the staff of the policeman. It is something disgusting to notice with what eagerness the Germans and Jews openly tell you they hope that those who control the nation of shopkeepers will spend lavishly John Bull's money, and who so insolently remind an Englishman that they have no love for him, but that is the English money that they hunger after. Upon my objecting to this low estimate of my countrymen, and reminding them of obligations that the Continental nations were under to the English during the Peninsular wars, one of my hearers intimated that the soft and good-natured Englishman had been taken in, to which I replied, " True, on the principle that honest, simple men were often fleeced by swindlers and blacklegs, and that the Hanoverian connection and German intermarriage combination with our people was not a connection that reflected any credit on us, but that the time was coming when we would either send them back to eat their sour-krout, or ship them all off in company with the Norman aristocracy to some island, where they might prove themselves useful in their lifetime, a new order of things for them, and highly advantageous to other people."

It was quite a pleasant relief to read the utterances of Mr. Abram Barend de Villiers, a son of one of the Hugenot families, that, after being compelled to leave France on account of their advanced views on the Government arrangements, settled in the Cape at the time the Dutch held possession, and whose rule they found almost as intolerant as that of their native country, even if it was not worse. This descendant of a Frenchman, and a large winemaker, after he had grown the grape on one of his large estates, having time at his disposal for studying the improvement of his country, advocated among his schemes for the advancement of the Colony, the right of the colonists to settle all "native" disputes as they might deem best, seeing that they had to pay the expenses and suffer the loss of life from among their burghers; a proposition that was but fair from the South African point of view.

There can be no doubt that Downing Street is a curse to all our colonies. The frequent transfer of office from Tory to Whig and *vice-versa*, brings in its train all kinds of change and new situations to the detriment of the colonies.

The most important change that Mr. De Villiers asked for was, the issue of ten millions of Cape notes on the security of real property, for the construction of Municipal and Governmental works, in order that they might free themselves from the everlasting extortion of the foreign banks. The notes to be legal tender for all purposes.

The education of this gentleman had undoubtedly made him acquainted with the money system of France during her revolutionary epochs, as well as at the present time, and he could well testify to the advantages of the same in freeing the agriculturist, the manufacturer, and the merchant from the imposition of banks in general.

Of course, like all good things, this was pooh-poohed by the combined forces of the bank interest; but it was indeed a pleasure to read the utterances of an Abram, crying in the wilderness to carry out the right, and if ever one regain faith in South Africa, it will be when men of all parties send to their House of Assembly advocates who will fearlessly tell the Colony that they are being shorn, year, after year, by the foreign money owner, and that for the sake of the present and all future generations, this public robbery by Act of Parliament must cease to continue.

It is truly painful to read time after time of concessions and gifts of public domains on this African continent, to be held by speculators and sheep farmers in the Cape Colony, and especially in the Transvaal at the present time, when they need the legal tender to carry on their government, and assist the country to emerge from its late troubles.

The last concession of mining rights in the Transvaal has drawn from the *Volkstem* the following protest :—" The most significant comment on, and at the same time the most cutting condemnation of this most unfortunate practice of indiscriminately granting concessions on mining rights, is an observation of a gentleman who is himself part holder of a concession on other property, and which has been reported to us. When the Volksraad's resolution was passed, this gentleman is said to have made the following remarks :—' Well, I am glad I have got my concession ; but I must say I am surprised to see a people selling its birthright so cheaply.' We said above that we would not add much to what has been said the Volksraad Hall upon the matter, and we abide by this resolution. We shall, therefore, ask only two questions of the Government and the majority of the Volksraad members, who are all of them so eager to grant away immense tracts of public property to any and every applicant. The first question we wish to put to them is this :—Have they ever considered the cost of either protecting the numerous gold concessionaires in, or compensating them for their reserved and guaranteed rights should the conceded areas be rushed by a large population of diggers ? And the second question is this :—Have they ever considered whence the capital has been derived for all the concessions, without distinction, granted hitherto, and have they forgotten what British capital has done for Egypt barely two years ago ? The Egyptian illustration may not be of much account, but it is certain that the Transvaal Volksraad are squandering valuable assets, and it is to be feared that amongst those who promote this extravagance motives are at work in some instances of a not altogether disinterested character."

For the sake of all interests, these continual practices of parting with public wealth must be discontinued. They have produced untold misery, an awful increase of immorality in the Colony, and station after station of convicts. The convicted have in some way inwardly decided that dame Nature never recognised the giving away of her wealth under such conventual arrangements to one in preference to another. The taking away of what is known as the outcome of men's brain and labour, is understood to be robbery, and no one sympathises with a thief; but the accidental picking up of Nature's diamonds or gold, when the picked-up is not within the circle of conventual arrangements, is not to be acknowledged or countenanced as a theft, much less as a crime. The fact is, we must break down, by education, the notion that the wealth of the world must be in the hands of monopolists. All mineral wealth in England and elsewhere must be public property, worked for the benefit of the nation at large for the advantage of all, and not to the enriching of a few, who in securing the same become the taskmasters of their fellow-man, and destroy the liberty and independence of their fellow countrymen.

Compulsory Working of Claims.

The question whether the Government shall allow claims to lie fallow, or compel owners to work them has been discussed in some circles a good deal of late. Jagersfontein has not been a success—at any rate, it has not been profitably worked. Legislation has been invoked several times to its aid. The I. D. B. traffic was supposed to be the cankerworm, which was eating the very vitals of the diamond-mine industry, so laws were passed to suppress it. Now, it is discovered that no company pays expenses. Indeed, as far as we can gather, every joint-stock company in the mine is in liquidation. Formerly it was asserted that private digging would not pay because very few men commanded sufficient capital to work on a large scale. Those who advocated joint-stock companies, rather more than two years ago, said a company which could wash ten times as much as a private individual, might, with the improved machinery and working a large block of ground, make it pay where small men would starve. Now, it is maintained that companies are too cumbrous and too expensive for Jagersfontein, and only private diggers (like the Kerr Brothers and a few others) can make working pay in the mine. It is difficult to say whom we are to believe. It appears to us, however, that the men required for Jagersfontein, are people possessing the number of claims and the money of the companies, with the thrift and the knowledge of private diggers like those mentioned above. Reckless extravagance, and ignorance of practical mining have been the main causes of the failure of diamond-digging by joint-stock companies.

Now the question arises how to benefit the few people who are nearly destitute at Jagersfontein. As companies do not pay, many wish to have a law making it compulsory on all claim-holders to work their claims. If this law were passed by the Volksraad, it would soon be discovered whether the mine would be payable or not. It is thought by many, however, that the tenure of the claims will not allow of the Raad declaring them "jumpable," for not working them. By Ordinance No. 19,—1881, provision was made for registering the transfer and hypothecation of claims by the Registrar of Deeds. Some hold that as this law has been passed, it would be absurd to allow claims to be forfeited simply because they were not worked; what use would it be to have a bond on a property which could be "jumped" at a moment's notice? They naturally ask where is the security? No doubt the Raad will have to be exceedingly careful of what they are about before they interfere with vested rights and interests, for owners of claims will not lightly give up property which has cost them thousands of pounds. We take it, the question at issue can be decided by referring to the original Ordinance on diamond-mining, under which Jagersfontein and the other mines were thrown open to the public, viz., Ord. 3,—1871. Ordinance No. 19,—1881, only provides for the transfer of claims and the registration of the bonds on them, but it cannot in any way affect the original tenure. This being the case, the Raad will have to be guided by the former Ordinance. If the Ordinance of 1871 made it lawful that claims should be either worked or be forfeited, then there is no necessity to pass any more Ordinances on the subject; but if, on the other hand, every claim-holder has a freehold, or copyhold right in the ground, we do not see how the Volksraad can force the working of claims under penalty of forfeiture. It seems neither law nor common sense to do so. The lawyers will, however, most likely be called upon to decide this knotty question, and to make their profit out of the swindle.

Chapter IV.

NE of the most extraordinary pieces of hasty legislation was passed by the Raad in June, 1883, at the suggestion of many of its country inhabitants. It is often said that the gods make mad those whom they wish to destroy, and it would almost appear as if the Dutch were rushing on to their own destruction, as they have never been known to accomplish any sensible things except when sitting side by side with Englishmen. So many unwise arrangements have been made by them that Englishmen, in a short time, will leave them to experience once more the meaning of ruin and want in their midst. The following taken from the *Friend* explains all :

The New Wine and Spirit Ordinance.

"The Raad is not doing anything by halves this Session. The Ordinance which passed its second reading yesterday, with only nine dissentients, will be almost as stringent in its operation as the famous Maine Liquor Law. So many complaints have been made to the Executive and the Raad by the Dutch Church Synod, and by the Wesleyan district meeting, of the great harm done to the people of this country, and especially to the natives, by the reckless manner in which ardent spirits have been sold in the country canteens, that the Raad had to take cognisance of the evil, especially as the Good Templars are very active in getting up memorials on the subject. Our landfathers do not care to place drinking shops under *surveillance*, any more than they wish to guard the frontiers of the State, so they proceed on the principle of the man who cured the tooth-ache by cutting off the patient's head! They have accordingly made most stringent laws against the sale of strong drink. In future, no person can procure a licence for the sale of strong drink by retail or wholesale except in towns and acknowledged villages. No shopkeeper in any town or village will be entitled to obtain a licence for the sale of liquor, either by retail or wholesale ; neither must he allow spirituous liquors, with or without any money consideration, to be given away or consumed on the erf or premises where the business is carried on, under a penalty of £25, or in default imprisonment not to exceed three months. No native is to be allowed to buy "drink," whether he is provided with an *order* from his master or not. No doubt this latter provision is a good one, for many of our canteen-keepers made a multitude of natives drunk under the colour of one such order. We have frequently written against the way in which the old law is hourly broken by the canteen-keepers, who apparently do the principal part of their business with the coloured population. If the new law is carried out, we fancy the occupation of the canteen-keeper will be, like Othello's, gone."

I am not the man to complain of all and any fair attempts to enable people to be temperate, but in the name of common honesty it is advisable at all times that legislators should be considerate—not hasty—and honest towards their fellow-countrymen and others. Men who have invested means and time in their wayside properties, in the belief that they and their houses are wanted to accommodate the public, and in the legitimate expectation of a fair return for their investment, ought not to be exposed to ruin by any sudden act of Legislation. Now, it happens that most of these legislators are of the pastoral, coffee and biltong-eating class ; men who from their birth, have no love but rather a hatred towards the trading class, and would destroy what they conceive to be the interests of the small wayside hotel-keepers and traders, at whose establishments their young men in a social manner meet to chat about the topics of the day over the genial glass of friendship. True, it will always be the case that some men will waste their time and means in constant tippling ; but this is no reason why the public are not to be accommodated on public roads.

I know of one case in which a lease was taken for ten years and an outlay of over £300 in stone buildings, besides other liabilities incurred in the very natural hope of reaping the usual advantages from such an outlay. By hasty legislation, however, as described in the beginning of this chapter, all these hopes were destroyed in a week by an Act passed in a passion, and the unfortunate investor a loser of £600 or £1000 ; and yet these men expect to be honoured, when by a public Act they rob and plunder without even as much as suggesting compensation. Drunkenness and debauchery is one thing, the glass of good-fellowship another ; and the following words of Maccall explain the whole position so well, that I cannot refrain from printing them, in the hope that they will guide men to be temperate at all times, and liberal-hearted likewise :—

Temperance.

"We take over, for the benefit of fanatical Good Templars, the following well-written and sensible letter, addressed to the editor of an English journal :—

"Sir,—Plato, a great Greek philosopher, saith, ' Wine fills our souls with courage.'

" Pliny, a great Roman naturalist, saith, ' By wine the blood and the hearts of men are nourished.'

" Saint Chrysostom, a great Christian orator, saith, ' Wine is the gift of God : drunkenness is the work of the devil.'

" Luther, a great Protestant reformer, saith, 'Who loves not woman, wine and song, remains a fool his whole life long.'

" The Eddo, that great treasurer of Norse poetical traditions, saith, ' Wine is the joy of man.'

" I take these sayings as texts for a brief discourse on a subject not much understood.

Temperance is either the wise and moderate use of things allowable and desirable, or the balance and harmony of a man's whole faculties. The one kind of temperance implies the other. A man who has the sweet and melodious equilibrium of nature can never be led to excessive indulgence in anything ; and a man who in all things shuns excess spontaneously and habitually harmonises his own character.

In regard to wine and alcoholic drinks it is manifest that the temperate man is he, not who abstains from them, but he who uses them commensurately with the health and the harmony of his entire being. Who can in reference hereto be another man's judge ? The German poet, Goethe, who was as famous for his

Olympian calm as for his brilliant genius, was in the habit of drinking every day after dinner four or five bottles of Rhenish wine. His brain, nevertheless, remained clear to the last, and he was in his eighty-third year when he died. On the other hand, a very small quantity of drink confused and vanquished Charles Lamb. If Goethe could drink immensely and be all the brighter and better for it; and if Lamb could not put drink to his lips without being intoxicated, it was obviously Lamb and not Goethe who was the drunkard. Thomas Carlyle, who died in his eighty-sixth year, drank very moderately, but smoked ten or twelve pipes daily. He disliked drinkers as much as Goethe disliked smokers, but each of them took the enjoyment which suited best his taste and constitution.

Drinks, however, and drinking have reference not to the individual alone; they play a grand, and, on the whole, a beneficent part in social existence. At this aspect of the matter fanatical teetotallers refuse to look. Public feasts have enormous sympathetic influences. Working men enter taverns not because they are fond of drink, but because they rejoice in each other's company. When they meet and take a glass together, they are induced to feel an interest in each other, and to be mutually helpful. Working men are more hospitable, especially to relatives and friends, than any other class. The moment they turn teetotallers they cease to be hospitable; and cold, covetous, and canting, they shut themselves up in the gloomy circle of sordid cares.

A community of total abstainers would be the dreariest, the most monotonous of all communities, because everything would be sacrificed to prudence and calculation. When the generous instincts are annihilated, holiness, heroism, the divinest virtues, the sweetest charities perish.

The Blue Ribbon and other noisy, silly, pretentious pharisaical movements, give under the guise of temperance, birth and nourishment to the worst forms of intemperance; to bigotry, to slander, to monstrous spiritual presumption.

I am not aware that teetotallers abstain from beef because some men are gluttons, or from marriage because some men are debauchees or systematic seducers. But if consistent they ought to do so. Perhaps a time is near when Local Option is to determine a man's right to eat a mutton chop or to marry. Woe to the butchers and the pretty girls when that season comes.

Yours obediently,

A MINORITE BROTHER."

Mr. Matthew Arnold says he drinks wine not because he finds it indispensable, but because it seems to him to add to the agreeableness of life. Society generally has discovered that moderation in its cups adds also to the agreeableness of life; in other words, that there is more pleasure to be got out of existence by refraining from excess, than indulging in it. Gradually the lower class are learning the same lesson, and are beginning to understand that habitual sobriety pays and conduces to the constant agreeableness of all life. The young official men who either as past or present Landdrost clerks, and who gradually get reduced and become stamp-sellers, because they lost their heads when otherwise acting in public life, must be put out of consideration, although one could fill sheet after sheet with their silly, mouthy remarks. They are simply so many walking, touting, smoking, tailor-made men who certainly will never shine as lights of the world, no never, nor even as decent citizens of Bloemfontein.

The general ignorance of the members of the Raad is so dense, and their stolid obstinacy so great, that even the President with all his general knowledge, is often unable to move them from a position once taken up by them. The general success—due to England's purchasing power—has at last converted many to the belief that they are miniature God-Almighties, and since the defeat of the English at Majuba Hill, some of these antediluvian blackcoat, tall-hat, rough, Boer-farmers, have several times burned to declare war against England, feeling sure that they could beat, and then—O what a prospect! come into her possessions! The free-livers and reformed drunkards in the persons of several lawyers and other officials do their best to increase this conceit in them for their own selfish purposes.

Chapter V.

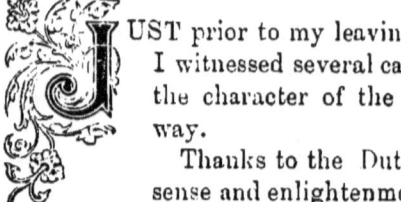

JUST prior to my leaving Bloemfontein for the Colony, I witnessed several cases of injustice that reflect upon the character of the State in a very unsatisfactory way.

Thanks to the Dutch Legislators having no more sense and enlightenment than the world's law-manufacturers generally, in an evil moment, and in the short space of a week, without previous discussion on the part of the people, the Government passed a Bill giving power to proceed summarily against those who might be found in possession of diamonds. Although there was no clause in the Bill giving the right to entrap—trapping being in opposition to old Free State ideas—after the Act in question came into operation, it became a common thing for men, priding themselves upon being considered gentlemen, to assist in trapping their fellow-men by means of trap-stones sold in the dark by Kaffirs. It was said and sworn that they gave the stones for the purpose referred to, and although in several cases no such stones could be found in the possession of the accused, three ordinary men, acting as judges, sentenced these luckless victims of perjury and treachery to ten years hard labour and fifty lashes.

This was done by men who looked upon Englishmen as fools; and not a single word of protest against the injustice and cruelty was ever uttered by any member of the Legislature or by the Officials, including the President himself.

Again, to enable a magistrate to ingratiate himself with the Dutch population, and to share with an informer to add to the Government chest, a trap is set to help him, or them, to get into their possession a sum of ten pounds. This magistrate—the chief one of the Free State—accepts the evidence of a white German, a man who swears that while buying goods for the road, to go to

Pretoria, he also bought a bottle of brandy. This is denied by the respectable store-keeper, who stated that, in kindness, he gave him the bottle of brandy as a present, he being an old customer. Here we find an individual, who is but an indifferent inhabitant of a large town, allowed to swear against a responsible, respectable man, whose word is not permitted to weigh against that of a common informer ; and the occupier of the seat of justice with such evidence before him, fines the defendant—thus placing him in a false position with his neighbours. He was desirous of procuring the annual licence, but owing to Dutch and German jealousy, and the vote of a boy acting as clerk to this Landdrost at the time— his application for the same trade liberty as others failed. Justice is rarely administered in the Orange Free State to an Englishman, and since Gladstone's Ministry trailed the English flag in the dust to be scoffed and laughed at in the Transvaal, Englishmen put up with losses rather than appeal to the Courts of Justice, so called, in which men sit who are hardly fit for clerkships, and who if tested for competency in any other country would be sent back to school again. Very little can be said in favour of the judges for ability ; they are simply good-natured, simple-minded gentlemen, good for a feast where neither wit nor flow of good language is needed.

So far as the Free State lawyers and attorneys are concerned, the less said the better. Their ability is limited, but their extortion is positively unlimited ; as a rule, like the doctors, they are old missionaries, who have found it pay better to *doctor* and *advise* than to remain followers of the gentle Jesus. They know this so well, and the fact is so patent, that they chaff each other on their antecedents. An instance occurred in which one lawyer accused another of always making his account equal to the receipts, when he had clients soft enough to get him to collect their over-due accounts. He was known as the " black sheep," and kept himself handy to do the dirty work of the other lawyers in town and about the Courts. One lawyer held a bill of sale over this " black sheep " to keep out his creditors, while he was doing their dirty work, to save their reputation. Several lawyers never thought it wise or worth their while to pay any debts, in the hope that their creditors would need some legal adviser, or assistance, and thus enable them to levy their " black-mail."

I can quite endorse all this from personal experience. I was more than black-mailed in pocket, I was black-mailed in my feelings: for under a kind of friendship, I gave an account to collect and to sue for. I keep that account as a warning, and intend framing the same as a memento of the Free State lawyers' way of making Englishmen pay, if they happen to be fools enough to dwell there in opposition to Germans and Jews. My own case was not an isolated one, for well do I remember a friend, who to recover £40, was eventually let in for the whole of his opponent's expenses as well as his own, which amounted to nearly £200.

While dealing with legal subjects, I may mention that a precedent was established in the Supreme Court one Saturday morning which has considerably exercised the gentlemen of the long robe. Ever since the appointment of Sheriff Crosby as Taxing-master, war has been waged between him and the advocates on the question of costs, and although several appeals have been made against his decisions, the Bench has almost invariably supported him. A practice has lately sprung up of dragging in a junior counsel to assist in cases of the most unimportant character, thereby greatly swelling the bill of costs and giving the juniors a job—and sadly they need one, as any one can testify who spends any time in Court. Against this, and other extortionate attempts, Mr. Crosby has taken a determined stand, and the thanks of the public are due to him for the bold front he has presented. On the Saturday morning referred to, Mr. Attorney Leonard presented himself and informed the Court that not one of the advocates would take up his brief—in fact, had struck work. Anticipating that there would be a hitch, the advocates to a man were in their seats, prepared to enjoy the discomfiture of the attorneys, and, through the attorneys, Mr. Crosby. Judge of the surprise of the advocates when the Chief Justice blandly told Mr. Leonard to step forward and conduct his own case; which he did, and succeeded in defeating Mr. Upington, Q.C., ex-Attorney-General, and his able coadjutor, Mr. Innes. Further, the Court awarded Mr. Leonard five guineas for arguing the case, and ordered that the briefs should be paid for, as the attorneys were not to know that the Counsel would refuse to act. A meeting of the Bar was held afterwards, but with closed doors, so that I am unable to give the result; but the sympathies of the public are entirely with the other side, and the discomfiture of the Bar has been the cause of great merriment and jubilation.

But there, what can one expect in a State that possesses a man at its head who for twenty years sat as its President, had received several farms as a public gift, and had always had a good income from the Dutch legislators (for as a matter of fact the Dutch population never troubled themselves about governing), and who in the fourth epoch of his presidency had £3000 a year, a house found him, and travelling expenses paid at all times—yet had the meanness when proposed for the fifth time at a salary of £3000 and all found, to ask like a pauper for a gift, and make it a condition of his accepting the office to have £2500 given him when sworn in on the fifth occasion. Such is the influence of the example of our Crowned Heads and Presidents of the Old and New Worlds, that even the little men of these small pastoral States have the impudence and audacity to ask alms in so barefaced and public a manner as to convey the impression that they are needed. Personally this man is no worse than hundreds of others in the Free State. As a rule all the members of their Volksraad accept the honour of sitting, for the sake of the £2 a day and travelling expenses allowed, for about sixty or eighty days.

These men were so ignorant of the common wants of civilised people, that they opposed telegraphs, railways and road-making for years, and whose remarks were so absurd that for the dignity of the House, I refrain from giving them ; but one can quite believe that, but for the sake of the £2 per day, they would put themselves to no inconvenience to assist in misgoverning and living upon bread, sardines and brandy when sitting in the Raad.

It is often said that, but for President Brand, the State could not have weathered the storms that assailed it. Possibly so ; but it is at least a question whether this so called safe man has been quite of the advantage that some people suppose. Like the late Bishop of London, he has the reputation of being a good man, simply because he is a quiet, safe man, whom no active change would allow to lose his position, and some maintain that but for his timely aid the State would have been ruined. One thing is certain, that if he had persisted in his unrighteous demand for the diamond fields, the men of action on that spot would have annexed the Free State, and thus he knew that his calling would have gone. The whole of the Free State is prosperous, owing to its connection with the English colonies and nation; and although they protest against the influence of the English, they hunger after English sovereigns. Ah! well it is but a question of time for the Dutch even to ask for the protecting arm of Englishmen, if it is only to save them from Hollanders, Germans, and the worse class of Jews who trade upon their credulity. Even now, they are beginning to see that, under the sneaking "ferneuking" Jew. German and Hollander, they are in the hands of Shylocks, and that in having their pound of flesh, they lose their farms, and that the Hebrews are their masters, while the English would be generous and give new life to their country by their speculative feeling and the prospect of obtaining money and credit from England, which would be far preferable to the treatment they get from their German false friends. It is astonishing, and can only be due to the general simplicity of the rural mind, that they have been so blind to the fact, that while the Jews and Germans have been speaking falsely of the English, those *pimps* of society have gradually absorbed the land, and that in future it will be well to free themselves from these Eastern strangers, who while being protected by the might of the English, have shamelessly traduced them, and who, to use the language of the poet Heron, will, after they have served the inhabitants, as he describes, leave them to fall before the natives, as they have ever done from the time of borrowing from the Egyptians, and never honestly repaying:—

> "These Jew men owe no duty to the land they drain,
> They see no home where they collect their gain,
> They're keen, because they've nothing else to do;
> They're shrewd, since nothing else distracts their view."

The argument advanced that it was for the good of the whole country that the President should have been so often nominated and elected, on the assumption that it was for the benefit of the Republic at large, is open to doubt. The country at large had no opportunity of showing whether this sum of £2,500, voted by the Volksraad, was a spontaneous gift or substantial expression of gratitude and affectionate regard, or a sign of the helplessness of the Republic and scarcity of men fit to take the helm of State, rather than a proof of statesmanship appreciated.

To prove their utter reliance upon this man they—after passing a vote that he should not accept a title offered him by the English Government for assisting them in their dirty, dishonourable work in degrading the English nation in the Transvaal—at his earnest request, re-opened the subject so that he might accept the cheap, muddy glory from a bastard Government, ate their leek and huge humble pie by giving him the option of accepting or refusing.

Picture, if possible, the head of an independent State asking and begging to be allowed to accept a title to rank no higher than a successful butterman of an English city might attain. When the Free State produces men of ability, it will no longer need such men, who are practically but simple executive officers. As a proof of want of good generalship, up to 1882, the post office was officered by boys, and public robbery was a constant practice ; the telegraphs were constructed in the State by the Colonial Government ; the money collected for road-making used for other purposes, and road-repairing rarely undertaken; yet this man—for being well paid, sanctioning the large pay to the forty odd members of the Raad, and at all times flattering his subordinates so that in turn he could command their votes, and the money of the State—is to be lauded as a little god, and all are to fall down and find no fault, but worship him. Truly, with what little wisdom is the world governed !

The material prosperity of the State is due to the diamond fields of the English, as will afterwards be seen. The farmers give no special care to their breeding of anything, and their agriculture is simply of the rudest and most meagre kind. The very territory that they took in violence from the Basutos, which they hungered after,—like David did for the vineyard of Naboth —was taken simply because it was the garden of the Basutos' territory, although they justified the seizure on the ground that the Basutos were a nation of thieves, ignoring the fact that they themselves had not only stolen the cattle on a thousand hills, but like our Norman conquerors, had also robbed the inhabitants of the land on which the cattle grazed ; and when the rightful owners asked for restitution they were designated rebels, thieves, and vagabonds. The "garden" stolen from the Basutos by this much vaunted Free State, was considered the Alsatia of Basutoland, full of land, cattle and merchandise thieves and swindlers, and with all the opportunities it presented for men who would work for an honest living, it was in one state of crime and insolvency. When the Government refused to help them to continue the robbery, like the Israelites of old, they borrowed right and left from their English neighbours, started with their ill-gotten wealth over the Border, and jumped the lands of Mankoroane, and to give their deed a high recognition, called it Stellaland. They thus again proved how Dutchmen or Bastards,—who while called after their fathers' name, and never knew or liked to tell who were their mothers,—could go into a land where neither magistrates were nor policemen needed, and in the name of brute force, secured by past robberies, set up a form of Government. They elected for their Landdrost, or chief magistrate—a man who deliberately took out a load of goods from an English firm, in Bloemfontein to trade with, and who started in life there as a capitalist with the proceeds of this robbery. For these facts and particulars, I refer my readers to the public papers of the years 1880 to 1883. These things occurred with the full knowledge of the Dutch *Thunderer*, or properly speaking the *Express* liar paper, edited by a Jew and owned by a German,—who secured by flattery and sycophancy a contract for three years printing. So well were these facts known, that even the Judges complained of the difficulty of obtaining convictions against some Dutch horse-thieves and traders, who were afterwards requested by their Dutch brethren of the jury to clear out for fear that they (the brethren aforesaid) should have to bow to public opinion and convict, and thus get Dutchmen on the roads for hard-labour.

To give a further illustration of the abilities of the members of the Volksraad. They were memorialised to assist the Burghers with a sum of money to help them out of their monetary difficulties brought about by the mine fiends who had offered such tempting baits as to induce many to open their leather sacks and invest, and who in so doing impoverished themselves and enriched the German and Jewish fraternity. These men asked for a loan in Free State paper-money, giving as security to the State the deeds of their lands and other property, only stipulating that as the money would be Free State made, only a small interest or rent should be charged for the same. This reasonable request was pooh-poohed, and even the proposed notes were classed as "blue-backs" that never had the same kind of security, and for want of sense, the members could not comprehend the difference between such notes and their security, and the old paper-money of the State. Let it never be forgotten that the old Free State notes were issued in good faith upon farms and the public domain, which were afterwards sold by a dishonest Government, making these notes occupy the same position as the *assignats* did in France after the first revolution, when the political vagabond Pitt issued surreptitiously into France *assignats* that were produced in England, and thus created panics in France in opposition to the genuine *assignats* that represented the public domain. For proof of all this, see Doubleday's history, which so fully describes the particulars of Pitt being sued in the King's Bench to recover the engraver's charges for making the same. No wonder that Pitt and the officials of his time got rich, when for engraved paper they secured the wealth of France to the loss of Frenchmen. No depreciation could finally be effected by the issue of a State's paper-money, if secured at all times upon positive property, and redeemable year after year out of the income of the farmers.

Their Bank, called national, owes its existence to money given by England in a fit of generosity at the expense of the Colony—which by a system of double rates and extortion, secures them a considerable annual income.

The financial problem solved, means the redemption of the farmers and manufacturers, not only in the Free State, but in the wide, wide world. It is to the interest of gold owners and hard money supporters to oppose sound monetary arrangements. As gold monopolists they get rich, and nowhere so readily as in the Free State, where the normal condition is ten per cent., which means that any bank or individual bringing in £1,000,000, can in ten years take out in production the £1,000,000, and still have in their hands for future financial gold plunder their original £1,000,000. No wonder that bankers retire with colossal fortunes and build palatial residences; but don't let it be forgotten, all at the expense of the labourers of all climes, and let it also be further remembered, that no alteration will take place until the workers understand the dodge, that while they are working and sleeping, the gold owners,—who neither toil nor spin, but simply look on,—are getting richer and richer, while they are getting poorer and poorer, and work harder and harder than ever and fare worse. But once let them comprehend that money should be representative, that it should be created as fast as worked-up productions demand the medium of exchange, thus making it as easy to sell for money *tokens* based on wealth, as it is now to buy with the money in existence—and labour becomes emancipated from all unrighteous demands. To prove their ignorance, at the very time that the discussion occurred in the House, the Report of the National Bank was before them, and was afterwards printed in the papers of the town on June 24th, 1883.

Therein is the distinct item of £55,000 as Notes which they have a Government right to use, and through which they exact from the borrowers a large interest when they lend. Now what are these but "blue-backs?" They are not representing gold, but simply are issued as a credit capital upon which they secure an interest, that pays all their officials, and leaves an interest of eight per cent. on the original capital given them by the Colony at the dictation of England, the interest of which again pays the salaries of the Executive servants; so that in reality the people in direct taxation pay nothing for the Government; it is really secured out of England's gift and their issue of "blue-backs." If this is not public robbery with a vengeance, we must invent a new name for it. Good heavens! when will the eyes of the public be opened to such infamy? Many, Sunday after Sunday, utter the words: "Thou shalt not steal," and implore the Lord to enable their hearts to keep this law, but never ask that their hearts should be kept from public money stealing. With such facts as these before us, can anyone wonder, that we write so strongly? Don't let it be supposed that the Free State is the only place where such deeds are done; in England and in all our Colonies the same system of robbery is going on, as I have and am showing in my past and present works on political, social and other kindred topics.

CHAPTER V.

HE first week in July, 1883, was a red-letter week in the history of the inhabitants of Bloemfontein. After many efforts on the part of the foreigners, backed up at last by the English—who constituted the go-ahead portion of the community, and assisted by the high prices realised by the sale of Erven for building purposes in the town, the Town Council were enabled to build a very fine Hall out of the proceeds of the money so raised.

To give an idea of the anomalous position of this much vaunted Free State, it is a remarkable fact, that the capital of this Dutch State is principally peopled by English, Germans, and foreigners; nine out of every ten are aliens. The town councillors are not Dutch, and in no way do the Dutch control the internal or external condition of the town. As a matter of fact it would have remained a dirty "dorp" had not the English had the *go* in them to give the Capital some dignity in its public and private buildings; for deny it who may, there is no onward tendency in the Dutch community.

Even with an allowance of £2 a day, their Legislators will buy a tin of sardines and a sixpenny loaf, carry the same under their arms to some out-room attached to some friend's house, for which they pay no rent, and there regale themselves with the same in common with some other Legislators provided with some similar refreshment, supplemented perhaps with a bottle of two-shilling common Cape smoke. When these articles are purchased by them with English money, change must be secured with plenty of three-penny pieces amongst it for the religious service on the following Sunday. One could admire these men for their economy if they gave their services for their country free of charge.

No doubt many will howl with rage when they read this statement, and inwardly wish the writer was in their hands, but the Free State is still a heathen country—a land still occupied with both white and black barbarians, and although some may call me an Anglo-maniac for uttering these things, the truth shall be spoken and made known.

It is a common thing to speak kindly of the Free State Dutchman; but this is the courtesy of men at a distance, who would rather speak well of all than ill of any; but for one who has ridden with them, travelled through their land, eaten and talked with them, these kindly sentiments must be dispensed with. They only appear to be possessed of any sense of justice when they are near neighbours of the English, and cannot get outside their influence or do without their assistance. Many an Englishman has met foul play at their hands, and at this they rather rejoice than otherwise; and they would feel no compunction in being the death of all the English but for the difficulty of burying them on the quiet, which is all that troubles them. They would not consider it any crime to free their land from the "intruders," as they describe and profess to conceive them, but they dread being found out.

This may seem too horrible for belief, but I speak without fear or favour, and tell the truth honestly. The Free State Dutchman is dirty, mean, and cruel; he isolates himself as much as possible, rarely goes now to "Nachtmaal," and when he does, he thinks he does his part if he buys a tickey-worth of sweets to eat while at the Kirk, and a tickey for the plate on retiring from the place of conventual meeting, or house where young men may look out for wives and the young women sigh for husbands—i. is virtually a courting-house.

The modern Dutchman stands in no fear of his "Predikant" until on his death-bed, and then his only trouble is, who will get his land, flocks and herds after his decease.

With the usual courtesy of the English, the President and the members of the Raad, the judges and other public officials were invited to take part in the opening ceremonies. The opening was a small matter, but O my! the prospect of an after-meal of the most sumptuous kind, washed down at the expense of the rate-payers, principally English, with all kinds of delicate wines and champagne was a glorious opportunity, causing even the stolid Dutchmen to indulge in a hearty laugh at the folly and generosity of the councilmen, which they availed themselves of to the utmost to drink all they possibly could, even at the risk of a headache next morning, if the conduct of some of them at the evening concert, and their appearance on the following morning, afforded any indication as to their condition. Their gluttony and headache were compensated by the knowledge that these two festive days, at the expense of the public were in addition to the £2 per day they received out of the coffers of the State funds.

Such was the well-known obstinacy and meanness of these members of the Raad, that an Act that can only be known as one of legislative public swindling, was allowed to pass without any public expression of indignation, or even protest, lest in their hatred, and passion they should pass a more stringent set of laws against the English trading classes. This small body of farmer-legislators, were under the impression that God had in some way or other fitted them to be the regulators of the children of Ham as their bondmen for all time. For proof of this assertion see their strong, earnest effort to annex the Barolongs, (since accomplished) an independent tribe at Thaba 'Nchu, whose independence was arranged for, when the English gave it over to these Dutchmen. Although this land is in winter one howling wilderness, it is coveted by the land-hungering Boer, who, if he dared, would smite hip and thigh the, to him, English Philistines, who oppose this tribal robbery—in the high veld near the Capital of the Free State.

I have met many traders and merchants in the Colony, and I was commercially connected with a German who also was a Jew; but owing to his talking, walking, eating, and living among civilised English people he was a gentleman. The Free State from the beginning was the Alsatia of the Colony and Natal, and was *free indeed* to all the rascals of the neighbouring Colonies, who there had space to melt in their own fat, and thus in time cease to be an abomination to other people.

The procession on the occasion of the opening of the Hall was headed by a band, the inhabitants all marching round the Market Square and finally mounting the steps leading into the Hall, the band, which was composed of the younger portion of the Grand

Army of the Free State, with no musical taste whatever in them, meanwhile playing the Free State *God Save the President*. Thus, it can be fully imagined by those who have heard the German Bands that howl in every street in London that there was a general wish that the whole of them had been transported out of the Free State at their Country's expense, long ere the conclusion of their brass-mouthed discords. The President made an earnest appeal to Dutchmen, and a still stronger one to the English and foreign portion of the burghers, to amalgamate their interests and feelings, and create a nation of *Dutchmen*. This no doubt was highly flattering to the Dutchmen; but what an invitation to the English to lower themselves by conforming to this "rest and be thankful" policy. The feeling on the part of the English go a-head burghers was " not if they know it : " rather than sink into the narrow-minded Dutch element, they would abandon all they valued and betake themselves to some of the other Colonies of Greater Britain. As it is, they are as the salt of the Free State ; but only let them leave it in disgust, and the Boers will find themselves socially, commercially, and politically ruined.

After sundry appeals to the egotism of the listeners, and the impatience of those who had free tickets to eat at the expense of the rate-payers,—and who had purposely refrained from several preceding meals in order that they might enjoy free gifts the better,—the President moved towards the tables groaning with the good things of life. Once more the band blew its brass-windy discord to the torture of all, and then with all haste the consumption of eatables took place, followed by the usual toasts.

If, on a certain memorable occasion, the ghost of Banquo gave trouble at the festive board, no less did the spirit of Bloemfontein's late Mayor, Dr. Exton, give torture to the councilmen over this prandial feast. The vast expenditure had been sanctioned, because this man had pledged his *honour* that the money borrowed would be sufficient for all purposes ; but his honour was like his promises, of very little account, as was afterwards painfully experienced by the soft confiding burgesses. " May his shadow never be seen again," was the earnest prayer of many of the Councilmen, who had no funds even to pay for the feast, and who, in a perfect perspiration, contemplated the pay-day to come.

The proposer of the toast of "The health of the President," had the ignorance and presumption to say that it was due to him (the President), that the Free State had prospered, and attained its high position; his benign and wise rule had done it all. What a false and anti-historical statement! The diamond fields alone had been the source of its prosperity; and as for wisdom, if speech is silvern and silence golden, and it is desirable to observe such rules as the RULES "do nothing that you can get another to do for you, or put off to-day what can be done to-morrow," then indeed praise him for his wisdom, &c. Nothing was expected of the President, owing to his late bereavement. Fancy, what bunkum; as it is as certain we have all to die, as that we are born. Wisdom teaches us to look forward to expect this of all our friends, and our own future passing away.

An elderly sister-in-law had died a few days before, and if there was anything to distress him upon this bereavement, it must have been the regretful thought that whilst he had chosen, out of many others, one dress-maker of Cape Town, all mankind had passed this other by, and in consequence thereof she had not had the opportunity of fulfilling legitimately woman's mission of adding to the world's numbers. It might have been different, in many parts of the Free State. To have a plurality of natural wives is not considered a crime, and although polygamy is not sanctioned by law in the Capital, it is often practised. The one thing that the President might feel bitterly and often grieved about, was the uselessness of his sons, who as farmers, traders and citizens caused him constant anxiety and expense; compelling him to go hat in hand, after having had over £30,000, to his Parliament for a gift to pay their debts. It is truly disgusting, this apeing older countries in their follies and practices, and deserves—and so far as I am concerned shall have—denunciation at all times.

The toast to the Judges was a capital joke, and must have been given ironically. To be told that the Bench possessed a number of men of unsullied integrity, and that the Bar was composed of men of erudition and honesty, was to most people a surprise; and if some of the more important cases of late years are considered, the statement was of somewhat more than doubtful accuracy.

Judge Reitz—the chief Justice, as a private gentleman, is not to be reproached; but as a judge and a candidate of the future for

Presidential honours, he has no special qualifications. His past work seemed principally to be to flatter the Dutch population, that they were the coming race, and like most insignificant politicians, he used the class prejudices of the Dutchman. His ideas and knowledge were so limited, as to lead him to advocate the Africander Bond, and say, that he believed it possible to create out of the mongrel white population of South Africa, a nation of men, who could defy the outer world and hold their own without external assistance. No such population could exist, for even if they killed all the natives off, and made the land a perfect desolation and wilderness, the whites could not toil in an African sun for many generations to come. All this public bunkum proves the need to "tell the truth and shame the devil." This successful son of a Swede is a fortunate mechanical sitter on the Bench, but a man of no genius.

The seconder of the toast, was the son of a quack-doctor, who for many years ate the bread of idleness and pleasure in London to give him dignity at our Inns of Court, and who on his return to his father's land of adoption—the native land of the black, to whom his father was sent out as a missionary, but who found it paid better to practice in physic than divinity—through his father's influence, was allowed to practise in the Free State, and act as its Solicitor-General, and with all the base insolence of his German fathers, he talks and *utters* nothing but *common-place remarks*.

> " This is the crew I fly from—shall I see
> Hybrids like these take precedence of me?
> Shall these adventurers strive, and take our place ?
> These men of guttural names and dubious race,
> Who a few years since made a noise—
> Went round the world with Hambro' Sherry, hemp and toys ;
> Is it no matter that such English stock as ours,
> That have been the source of all this country's power,
> Have laid the broad foundation of many a State,
> Built up our nation, and made England great :
> That now, like vultures scenting out a prey,
> These supple tradesmen hustle us away,
> Give them their way, in every English place
> The rarest sight will be an English face.—
> Give them their way, and the oceans o'er—
> Self-banished—the Englshman will seek another shore ·
> Where for some time, until there's cream to skim.
> These keen-eyed cormorants will not follow him."

Such is the class of men who hope to rule and control the Free State when they gammon Dutchmen to give them full power, and thus make way for the Hollander and German to be their future task-masters and regulators in all social, theological and political conditions.

The toast to the clergy was replied to by the Revs. Messrs. Morgan and Croghan. The proposer of the toast, Councillor Cheap Jack's-son, stated that the clergy of South Africa had always been a fighting clergy and remained so to-day; a fine character of the followers of the lowly Jesus. Certainly brother is against brother, and a sword seems to be in the hands of those who differ in matters theological, and ignore the human brotherhood of man. But the insolence and lying of those who replied to this toast was most bare-faced. Surely they could never have supposed that they would be reported, or their exuberance of verbosity would have been drowned in the champagne cup. These men maintained that the Church of Christ had always been aiding in the spread of civilisation, the arts and sciences, and social order.

So utterly untrue is this, if history is to be relied upon—as in Mosheim's *Ecclesiastical History* fully shown, also in Buckle's *History of Civilisation*, and Leeky's *General Information for the People*. It is high time that any clergyman, so-called, of any denomination speaking in the name of the past or present, should cease lying; but it seems as though they could not help it and that the father of lies,—the devil—is their great god in this world; they are eaten up with the Mammon of unrighteousness—they are the public advocates of lying, hypocrisy and stealing. The time was, when "thou shalt not steal," or "bear false witness against thy neighbour," and "love your neighbour as yourself" was considered the duty of men; but since the teachers of Christianity as they teach it, and call it, strive after the good things and the portions of this world, they have converted themselves into liars and receivers of stolen property. To those who can see with their eyes, and hear with their ears, these things are not unknown; and these reverend old fossils of the past hope I shall go, and if they had the power they would send me, where the bad niggers go. They must teach this doctrine of eternal torture if they want to keep up their position, and continue to trade upon

E

the credulity of their worshippers; but I have no fear of their thunderings, and am fully determined to expose them in all their deceit, seeing that they are becoming as leeches and consumers of the people. Truly they are the blind of this world; but instead of making a happy despatch of themselves, before they lead other blind people into the ditches, they guard and truly make themselves friends of the children of this world, condone their faults, enter into their houses, feast themselves to the full, and, in reality, let the more simple folk fall and obliterate themselves.

My contention cannot be more forcibly illustrated than in the following lines:—

> If, as you brood upon the ills you see,
> The grip of greed, the wrath of misery:
> If, as you count the force on either side,
> The rage which frets against the hand of pride,
> And as you watch the mischief, it may seem
> Your Church can heal it, scout the idle dream.
> Time was, when they who preached could rouse the soul,
> And make the tide of misery backward roll;
> Time was, when men were dough, and words were leaven,
> And the voice seemed to issue forth from heaven—
> When his strange message the bold preacher brought,
> And staked his life upon the truth he taught;
> When, meditating on his sacred page,
> He woke the slumbering spirit of his age;
> When, seeking anxious hearts and greedy ears,
> He stirred their anger or dispelled their fears;
> Telling his moving tale to every sense—
> The tale of sorrow, wrong, and recompense—
> Of how God's arm was bared to ease their grief,
> Of how His Spirit aided their relief,
> Of how the enemy must turn and fly
> Before the strong right hand and kindling eye;
> Of how men fought for God in ancient days,
> And having won their battle, sang His praise;
> Or, if their sorrows found no mortal friend,
> God's self would give them vengeance in the end.
> Preachers like these have, in their darkest hour,
> Given men new hopes and made their Church a power.
>
> *   *   *   *
>
> What is the union of your Church and State?
> Your priests are merely lackeys of the great.
> Your bishop is a prince—a lord, a peer,—
> A man of several thousand pounds a year,

Whom kindly Providence permits to hive
A copious family, and make it thrive.
Chosen to fill his see on no pretence
Of courage, foresight, learning, or eloquence ;
A schoolmaster, an ignorant cadet,
A priest with kinsfolk near the cabinet,
A pompous don, of kindly, stupid face.
These, Paul and Peter ! occupy your place.
There, though we miss the groaning voice of Trench,
One Irish howl still issues from the bench.

  * * * *

To the dry bones of dogma can they give
The prophet's power, be clothed with flesh and live ?
Can they perform the work which has been done,
Revive the nation's faith and make it one ?
Can they do that which Knox and Melville did,
And make the people follow as they bid ;
Lay down a policy, exact its laws,
And win all hearts to struggle for the cause ?
Of course not ; and they know it. Not a word
For Justice, Right, and Truth is ever heard
From that Right Reverend Bench, on whose soft perch
Roosts the fine linen of the English Church.
They know it ; grateful Ellicott displays
The saintly gifts for which the nation pays,
When, raising up his apostolic hand.
He spoke in scorn of those who own no land.
Blessed the good food, consigned the poor to God,
And mindful of the child, spared not the rod ;
Bade the bluff farmers try the good old rule
And duck their critics in the nearest pool ;
Those evil men, who seek to cut the knot
Which ties the peasant to his wretched lot.
Such speeches, if that peasant ever sees,
How must he bless that prelate on his knees,
And thank the destiny which lets him live
Where farmers hear the advice which bishops give.
       —EDWIN HERON.

The other toasts were too commonplace to notice, and, as the wine got in, there was no possibility of any display of wit or flow of soul from any of the revellers. Not a member of the Raad uttered a word of wisdom, and at last the body being satisfied, and there being no food supplied for the mind, the party adjourned for the foot-ball match, and the coming concert in the evening. The balls, and other matters connected with this week's rejoicing, were all of the usual kind, and need no telling, as they had no special feature in any case.

The opening the day after of the new Public Library so-called was another effort on the part of the English and foreign portion of the inhabitants. To give it an appearance of magnitude, the President, his officials, and members of the Raad were invited to take part in the ceremony. The President and a few of the officials assisted; perhaps all would, but for the fact that, like many others, the members of the Raad had not recovered from the effects of their indulgence the day before. They would have made a supreme effort to be there, if the opportunity had been given them to indulge in unlimited eating and drinking again at the expense of the ratepayers: for, deny it who may, the tradesman knows as a fact that the Dutchman dearly loves to eat, drink, and get into debt, but never makes much effort to get out of liability. "Opschrijven" is his motto and practice all the days of his life; and when he has well-nigh overwhelmed himself in debt, and had the hint given him by his friend, a Dutch sheriff, that the indignant trader is about coming down upon him, he gathers together under cover of an ante-nuptial contract, with his wife, all his cattle and sheep, and places his household goods in his waggons, that are not paid for, and passes on to some lands that his less fortunate brethren have previously taken from the natives, squats himself, and builds a "Hartebeest" house, near good grass and water, and, with this stolen property, lives in a new Stellaland.

As time passes on, and population increases, his wealth gives him a position that, to those who knew not of his previous movements, magnifies him into a wealthy man, and the original process is repeated, either by himself or his grown-up sons, who have, on the faith of their father's supposed wealth, got other credulous men to "opschrijve," or give credit. Hard work and the Dutchman fell out at the very beginning of his Cape career. If kind Nature in her grasses and water favours him, all may be well; if not, a state of chronic starvation ensues, and contracting debts and repudiating the same is his constant practice. No one can deny that there are many rich Boer farmers; but they are so more from good luck than good management, some of them by living near old markets, or where the English have created new ones, or being near the seat of war could not fail to amass wealth.

As a fact, such now is the well-known meanness, trickery, and bad settlements to be expected from the Dutch customers, that all honest traders try to get into a centre of natives, who, until they are impregnated with the practices of the Dutchman, are always ready to pay punctually in cash, cattle, grain, or some other commodity. Their natural in-born sense does not allow them to stink in the nostrils of the white merchant, and, for fear that my readers might misunderstand me, this characteristic is not confined to the Boer farmer, but applies equally to the white trash to be found in all the up-country divisions; to suppose otherwise would be to know only half the facts.

In the capital of their Free State the lucky men of land and houses and official position, if not worse, were as bad. I myself inspected school and other accounts that had been running for years, and which no amount of dunning had any effect in securing, and not even raising a blush of shame when repeatedly requested to pay up. One can pity and sympathise with men who have struggled for many years and cannot possibly pay, but only bitter contempt can be felt for those who will not, but who, if they would only cease from personal indulgence, could pay up honestly. One fool, with one-half of black blood in his veins, nearly related to the public sheriff-hangman, and who certainly would be more in his place as positive hangman, if such work was needed, month after month imposes upon the school authorities by taking unlimited credit, with the intention of finally repudiating the same. When requested to pay a private account of three years standing, and for a small amount, this worthy lied repeatedly in saying that it had been paid, whereas it remains unpaid to this day. But what must we say of a man who, holding a near position to the Solicitor-General, owed over three hundred pounds for school fees and was deeply in debt all over the town, although in receipt of seven hundred a year, in addition to having the right of private practice and an income from house property? This was the way with many officials in receipt of good positive pay in English sovereigns—men with large fixed incomes, and who, owing to the depreciation of all goods, could live for one-half less than in more prosperous times, and yet were unwilling to pay up; thus it is that Hollanders and Dutchmen stink in the nostrils of the English.

It may be said truthfully that this represents the exact position of hundreds of officials in the Free State. Debt and dishonour are constant companions to them all, from the President and his sons down to all his army of supporters; these are the officials who believe in putting off till to-morrow what they ought to do to-day, and never doing anything themselves that they could get another to do for them. How like the officials of other climes, and how catching in old and young communities is this man-made disease! It but proves to what a low level these men have sunk, when they allow their flesh and blood, in the form of their own likenesses, to be in such a false position in these public schools, in one sense almost eating the bread of charity!

I know that many of these fathers and mothers, if allowed to give vent to their cruel tendencies, would willingly rend me limb from limb; but they say there are devils to shame by speaking the truth. I dare do so, but with no hope that these well-dressed paupers will alter their ways, or cease to treat unkindly their neighbour, who acts honestly, though not so showily, at the expense of baker, butcher, bootmaker, dressmaker, tailor, linendraper, greengrocer, etc.

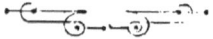

Chapter VII.

THE speeches at the opening of the library were common and untruthful on the part of the officials. The honesty of the Dutch borrowers was once more to be tested, but, as this was suggested by one of themselves, we will pardon his mistake. The well-known trait of "jumping" in the Dutch settlement, dignified by the name of "kleptomania" in other parts of the world, is so well known that it is well understood that it is the common, every-day practice for storemen to watch their customers, and to charge them considerably over the original price, to make up for what they do not detect. The morality of the Dutch people in Africa is so low, that it is now understood to be the fashion to rob and steal from counters, and then laugh at the trader boldly in the face; and this accounts for so many Public Library books being found on the market stalls, bought by Dutch and other travellers, when passing through the towns from whence the books have been purloined, and afterwards sold for the benefit of the "jumpers."

Nothing too earnest can be said in support of Public Libraries; they are the future homes of all classes, who will be able to read the thoughts and emulate the actions of the Great Dead of the past—to follow whom would indeed be an honour. It should be the ambition of all towns and villages to have their sanctuary of books, where on all days, Sunday included, the old and young of both sexes could study the teachings of the illustrious dead, made imperishable by the printer's art, and, when means permitted, a home of painting, sculpture, and all our fine arts. These public repositories of imperishable things, and our museums will form our future churches, where all really divine things can be seen, marked, and inwardly digested, to the future shame of the preachers of all denominations.

The President congratulated the Town Council on their liberality in giving the old Town Hall for the use of its Public Library, and he drew their attention to the gift of that noble Englishman, Sir George Grey, who, with exemplary liberality, gave books of great value to Cape Town—a gift unequalled, and which no Dutchman has ever imitated, and, unless they graft or get grafted on some English stock, they never will. In the good old times, men considered it the greatest act of their lives to give the greater portion of their individual wealth for public purposes, to be handed down for the benefit of future generations; but it is not so now. In these degenerate days it is only in some fit of weakness or on a dying-bed that men whose fears are moved by some witless clergyman to leave to their particular sects some means to erect a home, not to the honour of the true living God of creation, but to the gratifying of their votaries, in perfumes and costumes and their own glorification. Good heavens! When shall we have more living for others, and the continuity of humanity? Are we everlastingly to see such shams officiate in our public offices and protest not? If it was necessary in the first century for a Christ to turn money-changers out of a building that was devoted to the Highest, as they then conceived it, the time has now come, if words will not do it, when a little compound out of an illicit chemist's shop might be used to advantage in the removal of houses dedicated to error and folly.

The Chief Justice drew their attention to a gift, namely a Bible, that had been used in the Dutch Church for many years, and said it was the best book of all, which was another proof of his incapacity and deficiency of good faith. No intelligent man in this age would, in the face of our scientific works, put the superlative to the Bible, a record of tyrannical and filthy acts committed by that unfortunate race, the barbarous Jews. Then again its "science" and its "history" are totally unreliable. No one can consider it was an ordinary book, written in an age of manly effort to find out some of Nature's secrets, with merely a peculiar mode of explaining things in general, whilst for truth, morality, or any high form of thought, no parent would place it in the hands of his boys, much less of his daughters, with any degree of confidence, without first pasting together its objectionable pages, containing its false cosmogony, history, science, so called, its account of many public prostitutions, its harlotry, its seductive but lascivious poetry, and its erroneous false teaching in general. I of course allude to that old Jewish compound, known as the Old Testament. I would it were unknown, and yet to know it is all that is really wanted now for it to be discarded. My space and time do not allow me to discuss this matter fully; but my earnest desire is, if this book must be read at all, that all should read it carefully, and see if I have not truthfully depicted its salient features.

In these remarks I do not include the New Testament. The supposed Founder of Christianity, who taught the Fatherhood of God to us all, and desired the human brotherhood of man, has my profound reverence; but, through not being understood, He is worshipped like a fetish, by those who live upon a Church called Christian, but which, in reality, is Paulian, with this difference, that Paul lived by his hands, and made it his boast while teaching, as he conceived, a higher ideal of life. His successors live without work, upon public gifts, and robberies of the past; and by the aid of bayonet and staff, they are the recipients of public plunder, in face of their Sunday utterances, "Thou shalt not steal," &c. I cannot allow this opportunity to pass without protesting against the black-robed gentlemen, who officiate in the various places of public worship, and do their best to repudiate the giants of science, of history, and of travel—men who have even fallen martyrs to their endeavours to find out Nature's laws and ways; while these pigmies are incapable of so much as giving a lecture on astronomy, geology, history, or any other subject calculated to raise man's hopes, or give their Church a power. Why, even their best, the son of a nobleman—a *little-town*—can only give, as an evening's entertainment, for the elderly ladies of the gushing sisterhood, some of his college experiences, but only that portion thereof that gratifies his vanity by enabling him to indulge in self-praise. Away, away with such things; they constitute but our human lumber. Are such as these to be the teachers of our children, and our fellow-citizens' children? *Not if I know or can prevent it*, and in support of my views, I submit the subjoined testimony of recognised theological disputants:—

A Plea for the Free Discussion of Theological Difficulties.

At the beginning of the English Reformation, when Protestant doctrine was struggling for reception, and the old belief was merging in the new, the country was deliberately held in formal suspense. Protestants and Catholics were set to preach on alternate Sundays in the same pulpit; subjects were discussed freely in the ears of the people; and, at last, when all had been said on both sides, Convocation and Parliament embodied the result in formulas. Councils will no longer answer the purpose; the clergy have no longer a superiority of intellect or cultivation; and a conference of prelates from all parts of Christendom, or even from all departments of the English Church, would not present an edifying spectacle. Parliament may no longer meddle with opinions unless it be to untie the chains which it forged three centuries ago. But better than councils, better than sermons, better than Parliament, is that free discussion through a free Press, which is the fittest instrument for the discovery of truth, and the most effectual means for preserving it.—*Froude, in " Short Studies on Great Subjects.*

The Philosophy of Secularism.

Real life—that is, an original relation to man and to the universe, worship of one's own ideal, consecration by one's own love—has for ages been postponed by despairing hearts to another world, and thither where their hearts were their treasures followed. But that waking dream grows dim. The future is all unsure. Lost opportunities are lost for ever. He who throws away his life upon dogmas or dreams is as one who throws life away in dissipation. Let every heart arise and claim its full measure of existence! The weakest will is strong enough to select its right elements and organise its fair life, if it be only free—free to concentrate itself each instant upon the nearest need of life—the essential condition of every farther step. It is the single, simple will, intent each moment on its truest and best, which finds those moments ever weaving the general life into beauty, and virtue into joy.—*Moncure D. Conway.*

Orthodoxy and Agnosticism.

" On my side," said the Rev. Mr. Lascelles, " I affirm a personal

God, the inspiration of the Bible, and the truth of revealed religion ; the separate and distinct acts of creation ; the miracle of the sacrifice and the atonement ; an immortal soul, to be judged at the last day according to the deeds done in the body ; and a future life of bliss or woe." " On my part," responded Mr. Richard Fullerton, " I deny all these articles but one, and that I neither deny or affirm. It belongs to the domain of the unknowable ; and neither you nor I know what comes after the death of the body—if anything, or nothing but the disintegration of the forces which made what we call life. Scientific analogy is against you, universal belief is with you ; but in this, as in many other things, the confession of ignorance is the greater wisdom and the truer modesty.—*Mrs. Linton, in " Under which Lord ? "*

Revelation.

Men admit that all knowledge of " philosophy, politics, medicine and the like," has been slowly gained by the experience of man and his own toilsome efforts, unaided by any supernatural power ; but they say religion has been revealed to man direct from a perfect omniscient God. We find, however, that men are no more agreed about religion, which has been revealed, than about science —which has not been revealed. Of what advantage, then, is revelation ? And is it not derogatory to God to suppose he could reveal what men cannot understand ? The fact that men differ about religion, philosophy, politics, and medicine, proves that God has never given direct, positive instruction on these subjects. It seems, to my mind, that religion rests on just the same authority as science—namely, human experience and research ; and God has never spoken about religion in any way, that he may not be said to have talked politics or given medical lectures. " The Lord spake unto " Solon and Galen as truly as unto Moses. When men recognise the truth that religious ideas have no higher authority than medical ideas possess, they will become as charitable about theological differences as they now are about varying medical theories. Will it not be a social improvement ? *R. C. Adams, in the " Index."*

I know that for writing all this, that they (the pigmies) will try and find out my vulnerable part, maintain that I must have murdered my grandmother, robbed a bank, or committed some other horrible deed. which will yet bring me to condign punishment. Try again; come on ye manikins, and tax your little brains to injure me ; but it will all be of no use.

The minister of the Wesleyans never did, and never will, " set the Thames on fire " or *hurt* anything or anyone ; there is but one thing he fully understands, and that is the universal law of "increase and multiply"—and understanding it thoroughly, like a big man, he practised it diligently ; and though in poverty, he lived in hope. As the President said, " All shall right come "— and for which, as an anti-Malthusian, he has my best respects ; but he would have had my esteem if he had followed some useful profession, enabling him to provide for his children, and preached —as he and others called it—for the love of the cause. It is no use hauling in the sentence that "the labourer is worthy of his hire."

In these modern days, Paternoster Row supplies the world with any quantity of ready-made sermons for all seasons and conditions. A full portmanteau of these, when starting with a constant monthly supply, will always fill up an hour's reading without any effort ; if not to the edification of the listeners, to the passing away of the allotted time. There are no Oracles of Delphi to consult in these days. Paternoster Row is a never-failing well to all the talking cripples that go out to South Africa and our other Colonies, which supply out-door relief and a refuge for the incapables of England ; to the relief of the heads of missionary societies in England, on the same principle that Governors not wanted, are sent to some parts of India or the West Coast of Africa to be got rid of, so that they should not trouble their theological and political friends any more. .

This much I must say, that of all religious and scholastic bodies in the Capital, the only party out of debt, and that pays its way, is the so-called Roman Catholic —in practice not catholic. They are too poor to be dishonest, as no one trusts or even fears them in these days. They have a full conviction that there is a veritable hot place called Hell, and that it is in the exact middle of this earth, where the Devil is constantly tormenting and worrying the unfortunates that they say are there. In the case of the man who did not want to go to the wedding-feast, but when forced in, upon being found without a "wedding-garment" that he could or would not buy, and that others did not, was turned into outer darkness, as some say to dwell with devils—we are furnished with a proof of the justice of a man having no free will. The outcome of these unfortunates damned below (if all is true they say), to be constantly tortured and stirred up, appears to me to be not for the glory of Heaven's God, but for the gratification of the Devil—the god of this world. As might be supposed—the devotees of this church, of the humbler ranks, are incapable of thinking—in fact, their priests maintain that they have no occasion to think, all thinking was done many centuries ago for Popes, priests and peoples.

All that need be done in these days is to pay up, and be in the hands of Mother Church, the Infallible from birth, until death; but if they desire a good seat in heaven after they are out of Purgatory—an intermediate place they have provided to enable them to use it as a toll for the sustenance of the priesthood—they must pay up heavily to get in early. Good gracious; can all this be believed in the nineteenth century? Why, if it was true I should be disposed to exclaim with Tennyson who says in his poem of " Despair " :—" If there be such a God, may the Great God curse him and bring him to naught."

The following, which illustrates the ancient and modern position taken up by the Catholic priesthood to the enthralment of their worshippers, is from Longfellow's *Golden Legend*, wherein Lucifer when acting as the Priest says :—

> " And here, in a corner of the wall,
> Shadowy, silent, apart from all,
> With its awful portal open wide,
> And its latticed windows on either side,
> And its step well worn by the bended knees
> Of one or two pious centuries,
> Stands the village confessional !
> Within it, as an honoured guest,
> I will sit me down awhile and rest !
>
> [*Seats himself in the Confessional.*]
>
> Here sits the priest ; and faint and low,
> Like the sighing of an evening breeze,
> Comes through these painted lattices
> The ceaseless sound of human woe ;

Here, while her bosom aches and throbs
With deep and agonising sobs,
That half are passion, half contrition,
The luckless daughter of perdition
Slowly confesses her secret shame!
The time, the place, the lover's name!
Here the grim murderer, with a groan,
From his bruised conscience rolls the stone,
Thinking that thus he can atone
For ravages of sword and flame!
Indeed, I marvel, and marvel greatly,
How a priest can sit here so sedately,
Reading, the whole year out and in,
Naught but the catalogue of sin.
And still keep any faith whatever
In human virtue! Never! never!

I cannot repeat a thousandth part
Of the horrors and crimes and sins and woes
That arise, when with palpitating throes
The grave-yard in the human heart
Gives up its dead, at the voice of the priest,
As if he were an archangel, at least.
It makes a peculiar atmosphere,
This odour of earthly passions and crimes,
Such as I like to breathe, at times,
And such as often brings me here
In the hottest and most pestilential season.

Many and many a time I have walked on to the hill at the back of the town, and wondered, if I set up a "hue-and-cry" that the Devil was in the street, and all the ministers of Bloemfontein had but to go out, and—they knowing full well that the time was come when the Devil had to be chained for that thousand years talked about—whether they would, like old Nelson, look with both eyes shut, and feel that they must not see, knowing that if he was caught and chained, their calling would be gone : for, if the Devil was caught, he would no longer be part of their stock-in-trade. I quite feel that, had I uttered these thoughts in the days gone by, I might have found a home in some dungeon, controlled by what were called God's chosen ministers, but who, for cruelty in using the thumb-screw, racking the body, or dropping water on the head, until madness or death ensued (also fully described in Scott's Rokeby), acted more like ministers of the Devil. Thanks, however, to the efforts and deeds of the men of thought, of light, and of learning, though bought at the price of martyrdom, these conditions are past, and it is now possible, in good faith, to criticise such questions, without fear of being made an inmate of the new Bloemfontein lunatic asylum, to be laughed at by the men I have spoken of as specimens of the inhabitants of the Free State.

I have purposely avoided saying much of the women at the head of the schools, convents, and other institutions, as, in most cases, they are but the creatures of circumstances. The least said about them the better, beyond the fact that, with my universal love for women, I very nearly lost that love by the miserable exhibitions I came across during my stay in Bloemfontein; but, as they are more to be pitied than blamed, one cannot but hope that they will pass on to scenes more congenial to Nature's laws.

Little need be said of the children's fancy ball, beyond the fact that, for once in their lives, they fancied they were part of bygone ages. Their different characters brought up a perfect torrent of historical remembrances, which, alas! so few in Bloemfontein had the slightest knowledge or conception of. One can quite understand that the " Follies "—Tom Thumbs, and the other senseless imitations would amuse and please little minds. I well remembered the observation of Dante, when Della Scala, standing among the courtiers, and the royal jester making him heartily merry—turning to Dante—he said, " Is it not strange, now, that this poor fool should make himself so entertaining, while you, a wise man, sit there, day after day, and have nothing to amuse us with at all?" Dante answered, pityingly, as all earnest men must: " No, not strange, if your highness is to recollect the proverb, ' like unto like '—given the amusers, the amusement must also be given."

Such a man, with proud, silent scorn in his eye, with his sarcasms, and sorrow, and losses, had no resting-place or hope of benefit on this earth. Such was the bitter feeling I had towards the fathers and mothers of these children—parents that could shamelessly get into debt, and skin the widow and fatherless to make their dresses, and then afterwards fail, even to pay the debts contracted to deck out their children, and yet smile and smirk one to another. " How pretty, how tasty, how delightful!" and yet in their hearts a burning jealousy and hatred, that their neighbours' children were better liked, and thought more of, and were, through some more fatherly and motherly care, in better health and looks than their "Nestle's-Food" brought-up, pale-faced little manikins.

"A mad world, this, my masters!" has been often said. No wonder that even in the sanatorium, so lyingly called of the world—Bloemfontein, that they even must build, as an eye-sore, a lunatic asylum—just a part of the town to receive some of these soft and brainless offspring. It was often a marvel to me how men, who had previously helped to bring into existence such unfortunate, puny creatures, had the shamelessness to—keep up the supply. "Truly the lower the form of life, the greater the increase," was here fully exemplified in the many forms you met in Bloemfontein, whether official or otherwise, and human lumber and crippled beings are to be seen, at all times, in the Free State, more especially among its Dutch and foreign population.

Not being a Mason—objecting in principle to belonging to a secret sign society, and not believing that men join such without a belief or hope that some advantage will accrue to them at some time—I did not accept an invitation to join their maze of figures, thinking it undignified for one who somehow has got a belief that he, in sight of so many shams, has constantly to turn Mentor, to take part in such frivolity.

"The mechanics' ball, of its kind, was a perfect success, and compared most favourably with those which preceded it. When the Town Council prepared the programme for the week they acted wisely, and with consideration, by placing at the disposal of what is to our mind the most important section of the community the Hall for their night of enjoyment and dancing.

In every town and district of the civilised and even uncivilised world the real back-bone of all countries are the working classes, and whatever form of Government they live under we recognise no other aristocracy than that of merit. Hence the man who to-day works at his daily duty at the bench or lathe, or any other toil that his hand findeth to do, may aspire to become a leader among men. This is no ideal—because as a fact all great men remind us that they come from humble stock. Our unrivalled singer and poet, Shakespeare, was but a butcher's son; our Cromwell but the son of a mercer, and it will always be true that from the working classes will arise the men among men. It is not now my task to write the biographies of past working men; that is an undertaking I have yet to accomplish; but the truth is becoming a recognised fact that to labour we owe all, and, in this mechanical age, the creators of our wealth are to be considered in all matters.

The last of this memorable week's entertainment was a compound of amusement, instruction, and insolence. The authors of the "Pirates of Penzance" certainly must be credited with great powers of burlesque; they catch at passing events and the actions of many, and portray the dumb feeling in Society in an articulated form.

The "hit," that a pirate's life may be as good as many others, is so true, that one has almost daily recognised as a fact that, with all our civilisation, there are hosts, not only of coast, but of town and inland pirates also; and, notwithstanding the supposed intelligent army of policemen, and other safeguards in the people's midst, thousands are constanly being wrecked, robbed, and murdered.

But when we know that, from the throne downwards, a system of public pillage is consecrated, there is no wonder that so little effort is made to stop such wrecking as is well known to exist among stock and share controllers, the legal profession and others constantly adding, in one form or another, not only to wreck men and women's estates, but their fair fame and name. The bankruptcy trustees, and agents who get control of estates, are another set of wreckers, that, compared with the coast wreckers, are perfect vagabonds.

With smooth face, they will persuade creditors that it is better to place themselves in their hands, and, once so arranged, instead of the 12s. 6d., or even 20s. in the pound, the debtor would fully pay, if time were but given him, the things are sold, wrecked, and destroyed, and perhaps 2s. 6d. in the pound paid. If you ask where the original capital is gone, echo answers, into the hands of a gang of vile blacklegs, such as lawyers, agents, auctioneers, &c., who will wreck honest men's estates, widows, and the fatherless' homes, and their fair fame and name; smirk and smile, subscribe to this charity and church out of such proceeds, and generally be called respectable characters; while the man who does neither,

F

but out of his little store pays his way honestly, helps the widow and fatherless, and occasionally a needy elderly friend, but never goes to church, is not counted worthy to be known.

The tone of amusement all through the piece is so significant of the public feeling, that one cannot but rejoice. The Gregorian church music of the day, introduced as a subject of ridicule, only proves that the time has arrived when people begin to see the folly of the imaginary feeling constantly excited at our churches. Truly the author of the "Pirates" but utters truth when, in comparison, he says, "Away to the cheating world; go all where pirates are well to do." Well do I remember an old Gray's-Inn pirate of the Pottery stock, who, while professing to be a kind of grandfather and grandmother to me, not only robbed me with my eyes open, but even appropriated securities handed to him by another.

Thus he doubly robbed me, and, to this day I feel, may he go down doubly damned, as a warning to others! Duty and obedience, in a burlesque form, is advocated under all conditions. Would that this one fact and idea was made more prominent in all our modes of life and action!

In the Free State, it seemed to be the rule to ignore duties, not fulfil them. This one fact must never be lost sight of, however it may be violated by others—there is no sacrifice when duty is not fulfilled. I do not advocate here what I myself have not carried out. Ten years of self-expatriation at the shrine of duty must testify for me; and to-day I feel a giant, with the strength of an old god, in the consciousness that I have, in my humble way, performed mine.

The insolence in the last scene is too much for my nature. It is a common every-day lie to say that no Englishman hears unmoved the statement, "for, with all their faults, we love our House of Peers." It is with bitter contempt that all true Englishmen look upon such a house of hereditary vagabonds, and to illustrate them by the book through which the bishops hold their positions "they reap where they have not sown, and gather where they have not reaped." After asking us to express loyalty to a Queen that is only a figure-head, and in no case useful, in place of being loyal to our country, rather than to a foreign horde of Germans; with all this, we are to be told that we love this

House of Peers! When shall we have true dignity, freedom, and independence sufficient to remove the whole, and in their place have true heroes and great men, whom we can reverence, honour, love and obey cheerfully, and at all times?

Chapter VIII.

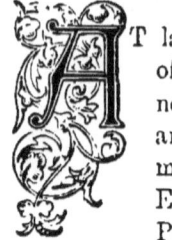AT last, in the early days of June, some of the Members of the Free State Raad discovered that they stood in need of telegraphs, bridges, and other public works; and, in a moment of enthusiasm, they elected a committee to arrange to borrow from one or other of the European Powers, by Debentures as a first charge on Public Revenues, the sum of £100,000, at six per cent. interest, to be repaid by yearly instalments in gold, at the Treasury of the Free State.

No one can complain of the erecting of public buildings; but the modern system of borrowing gold from European countries, is so ruinous to any State—whether large or small—in comparison with the safe and easy mode of each State making its own public, legal tender paper-money, wherewith to pay for the construction of its public works of utility, and so important is the whole question, with all its future possibilities, that, at the request of many friends in Bloemfontein, I here draw attention to a "paper" I had the pleasure of reading at a meeting of the Literary Society, in the old Hall, Chief Justice Reitz in the chair, when my ideas, as expressed therein, were fully approved, and endorsed by a majority of those present, and the "paper" itself I have since had printed.

The same views are advocated in my pamphlet entitled *How to colonize South Africa, and by whom;* also in my *Jottings by the Way in South Africa,* and *How to Construct Free State Railways, &c., &c.,* wherein will be found an explanation *in extenso* of the Money, and other social and political questions, affecting the past, present, and future of South Africa; and the plans I proposed are yet bound to be acted upon by the people of the future in the Free State and elsewhere.

Many and many were the observations on my retired existence and absorption in my business, whilst in the town of Bloemfontein; but to make acquaintances was positively dangerous.

One German failure, whom I had helped considerably, I found out afterwards had been discarded by his countrymen, on account of his dissipation and cruelty to his wife and family. I was, however, desirous of assisting him once more, and did so; but, notwithstanding my kindness, he took most unwarrantable liberties with my establishment, using my name as an introduction and cover, and even borrowed money from my friend Thomas, by the impudent representation that he was my commercial traveller and very intimate with me; and, although he was earning considerable sums on commission at the same time, he never returned the cash to me. This man was a well-dressed libertine, and a disgrace to his nation; and I found at last that isolation was my only safety from such people; to be friendly was to be imposed upon.

It was even so among my neighbours. One German-born Jewish lady—at least she said she was born a lady—constantly maligned me, because in free trade I had made my business on the premises she had formerly occupied; such was her jealousy of my success in business—entirely due to my untiring exertions—that she assailed me with all the fury of a virago; until at last, in self-defence, I had to tell her that, if born a lady, she had outgrown the early conditions; in fact, although I am a man of peace, had it been her husband—a poor hen-pecked, unhappy mortal, that could call neither body nor soul his own—instead of herself who abused me, I certainly should have gone for him.

Although I gave this wretched man and his termagant wife credit, and helped them in various other ways, they did nothing but try to injure me in return for all my kindness; but I forgive even them, for I blame the conditions of life, as arranged by "the powers that be," as the cause of so much uncharitableness and ill-feeling amongst neighbours.

This couple, like many others in times of prosperity, thought a time of slackness would never overtake them. They went in for a large mansion and store, which they erected by means of the

Building Society, and the proceeds of some land which had originally been granted to the husband as one of the old German Legion. This land, in reality, belonged to his colonial creditors, but he had contrived to keep it in his own possession, and ultimately sold it, furnishing their home with the proceeds. But, with all this, they got involved with the building societies, until at last they were eaten up with the enormous interest these associations demand from their victims.

It will thus be seen that the old adage, "fools build houses, but wise men occupy them," still holds good in some cases—although I pitied these people, on account of the losses they had sustained by reason of my competition with them in business; so disgusting was their conduct to me that I felt I could know or help them no longer.

All this was aggravated by the conduct of another German firm, and especially by the half-black compound, who was at the Beck of this man, the well-known Verneuk-Hard, near the Dutch Church.

So intermixed are many of the colonists, that it is impossible to know who have not African blood in their veins, and when they are the outcome of past mesalliances and take it into their heads to injure an Englishman, they—through their influence with the official compounds like themselves—act so that they make it almost impossible for an Englishman to exist among them.

Africa is peculiarly a blackman's playground. An Englishman's sense of justice is annoying to them; cheating and lying is inborn in them.

Well do I remember the Wool Scandal by a German firm, who deliberately cheated one of their customers, which led to blows from their rival black-blooded competitor, and finally landed them in a libel and assault case that cost the cheating firm over £1500, which all said served them right. In fact, Africa is a place for no honest man; to cheat and be cheated is the system all around; honesty is positively unknown. I have met men-Ansell's who boasted openly that they had done their creditors, and were known to live ever after upon the plunder. I have no hesitation is saying that the Boers, Germans and Jews think it smart to lay it on the Englishman whenever they have the opportunity, and I know of no remedy for this evil but to let them stew in their own chicanery, until the rogues so fall out, that there will be a chance for honest men to come into their own and the just reward of their honest toil.

I was often sympathised with over my losses due to the faith I had put in man; but somehow or another, I had in all my walks of life been fortunate in securing affection from friends, and at times great help, and although enemies and those who did me harm, multiplied as fast; still the fact that I had the love of many, would never allow me to lose that faith in my fellow-man —that is as the salt of the earth. Without this ennobling sentiment, we should but find ourselves in the midst of human devils, making it impossible for the pure and good to stop upon this terrestial globe.

I well remember one clergyman, much better than his creed, trying to comfort me in the midst of my annoyances and losses, with the reflection that after all, I had had to bear nothing comparable with what *his* Saviour had suffered for his fellow man. The very fact of drawing my attention to such a case roused me somewhat from my lethargy, and I could not help reminding him that he must never have read the history of Christ out of the authorised version of His life; and that taking the life as there portrayed, was not so bad as our modern lives. The fact of being able to live away from the city—the ease with which locusts and wild honey could be procured—a place with no rent for Him to pay, surrounded by nature in all her beauty, must have made it an earthly Palestine-Paradise to Him.

The fact is we do not get the true life and history of Christ. No wife and children depending upon Him for sustenance, no landlord to worry Him, His wants but few, and in every way and contrast different to our modern life of everlasting "go" and risk. That He had His idea of a higher life, which gave Him the heartache and produced many a bitter hour, when He with His Light would have altered things for the best, must be admitted; but all this was cut so short that it cannot be compared to any of our experiences.

The commercial and agricultural conditions of that age, allowed men great latitude, but all is now so narrowed that men are always being ground on every side to the exclusion of all country-life; and then there is no ending so quietly in these days, as Christ's pain and suffering was. Accusation, trial and death all over in less than a week. Why, compared with modern sufferings and crucifixions, sudden death, if not sudden Glory, certainly was sudden releasement from all persecution.

Far be it from me to repudiate the sufferings of One who was a Hero in His time, but modern facts and experience prove that in the heart of our man-made cities, there is a multiplied torture to the souls of men who think and would act out of the ordinary run of life that positively makes this earth a hell to dwell in.

True it is, there are men who tell us, that it is due to Lucifer, or the devil,—as described in Longfellow's *Golden Legend*—that he is the author of all this sin and trial.

LUCIFER (*flying over the city*).

Sleep, sleep, O city! till the light
Wakes you to sin and crime again,
Whilst on your dreams, like dismal rain,
I scatter downward through the night
My maledictions dark and deep.
I have more martyrs in your walls
Than God has; and they cannot sleep;
They are my bondsmen and my thralls;
Their wretched lives are full of pain,
Wild agonies of nerve and brain;
And every heart-beat, every breath,
Is a convulsion worse than death!
Sleep, sleep, O city! though within
The circuit of your walls there lies
No habitation free from sin,
And all its nameless miseries;
The aching heart, the aching head,
Grief for the living and the dead,
And foul corruption of the time,
Disease, distress, and want, and woe,
And crimes, and passions that may grow
Until they ripen into crime!

Now if these lines indicate a fact, what a horrible state of things it must be that the god of this world, as they say, can commit such havoc. I think I have read somewhere in the Old Testament, that "If there is evil in the city have not I the Lord caused it?" Now, this alters the case again; but if the view is a correct one of the clergyman, then no wonder that men can use the following words of Tennyson, *and with all their heart wish its* ACCOMPLISHMENT.

> But the God of Love and hell ogether
>   They cannot be thought.
> If there be such a god, may the
> Great God curse him, and bring him to naught!
> —TENNYSON.

> What shall I say of those who write or prate
> Of social science and your social state?
> Who draw dark pictures of the ills they see,
> And talk the cant of cheap philanthropy,
> Who rave about the griefs which men endure,
> But never venture to disclose the cure;
> Who never touch the vices of your laws,
> Who never probe the sore, nor show its cause;
> Who either do not know, or will not see,
> Since mischief works, the mischief's remedy;
> Who tell the world the thing it sadly knows,
> Its ceaseless sorrows, and its helpless throes;
> Who deal in sentiment, but never seek
> How to chastise the spoiler, aid the weak?
> The Priest and Levite look, and turn aside,
> The scorn they feel they do not care to hide;
> The poor Samaritan does all he can,
> Stoops to assist and heal the wounded man.
> Those creatures whine a dirge, and scold apace,
> And tell the story of the mournful case;
> But touch and tend him, and their fingers soil?
> No; better save their twopence, wine and oil.
> What earthly benefit do they afford
> To Ginx's baby, and to Bantam's lord,
> Who never strive to place before your view
> Why Ginx's baby is, and Bantam too?

It is the doubts concerning life and existence that make the future so uncertain, and men so despairing—almost creating in every breast a desire for annihilation.

The Religious Orders and churches in Bloemfontein are compounded of idiotcy, poverty and commercialism. Idiotcy may be fairly represented in the persons of the Hon. Little-Town, of Miss Grimes, her "sisters" and associates. A more wretched, shambling, shuffling, canting pair of imbeciles in gait, manner and style than the two named are not to be found in South Africa. They head their respective bodies and homes, and it may be supposed what they are like, to be guided by such a pair. Poverty is the badge of the Sisterhood, but when it is known that not a single institute under their care is out of debt; that the buildings are in a state of decay; that their educational institutions are but poorly appreciated, that they have but one poor student who can tolerate such a home in which to be made into a mechanical parson, all is said that is necessary.

The Theological College is a disgrace in every respect. A Miss German Busybody is at the head of its culinary management—a common cook at ten pounds a year would manage better. It would have been an advantage if the college had missed her so-called services and superintendence.

The commercial element is represented by the Bishop and his Archdeacon, who by their dress, so out of harmony with these modern times, not only make themselves Guys on the fifth of November, but are a source of amusement to the inhabitants all the year round.

The Bishop started with a few pounds in addition to his wife's means, and together they for a time ceased to be shepherds of their Flocks, and amused themselves in sheep-farming, and even set up a mill to grind corn in opposition to a neighbour, entered into keen competition with those in the district as vegetable growers, fruiterers and brickmakers. All this was done for the glory of the Bishop, the associates, and the dearly beloved sisterhood, in more senses than one, if the kiss of sisterhood, and after-pleasures are taken into account, on the principle that carnal pleasures increase their spiritual delights. "How shocking!" I fancy I hear some of them say; but this much may be relied upon, that with the exception of the Bishop, who is a married man, the Hon. Little-town, who is totally incapable, Miss Grimes, whose age prohibits, all the younger ones do it, when the opportunity offers, although they may afterwards rue it.

Another instance of their commercialism is the selling for gold the gifts of clothes sent from England to be given to the Kaffirs and the poor generally, and using the proceeds of these sales for maintaining purposes. Old, and foolish, idiotic women are persuaded to lend money to build institutes to be carried on as boarding houses, in opposition to other private enterprises. Dance parties for juveniles and adults arranged for in front of the Ark of a cathedral so-called, to the inexpressible pain of the pious beholder. Card-playing and even billiards are allowed, within sound of the cathedral bell, to make this commercial speculation succeed, and add to the general funds of the Bishop, who has no need to account for the same, not being responsible to anyone, nobody having the right to demand an explanation of how the funds are gathered or how they are spent.

I know of very little to the credit of the Wesleyans, Baptists, Lutherans, or the ancient know-little, but bigoted Catholic Church; but the English Church, which I did know, is in Bloemfontein a monstrosity. It is but the out-door relief-station for the unfortunates who would not be fit to occupy a decent clerkship in England. It is astonishing what social station the title "Rev." will give, even if possessed by the dullest in some out-of-the-way place; with what unction and persuasion they can influence the middle-aged spinster to give of the wealth she has inherited to assist as they tell them in the Lord's vineyard. They never seek the poor spinster, but the rich widow and sisters, and the well-to-do are always welcome as pillars of the Church in all or any station wherever the bastard English Church is found.

But why say anything of all this? The Cathedral, its Bishop, its "reverends," its clerical and lay officials, Dutch or otherwise, all are but the off-shoots of the system in England, and paraded in all our colonies to the disgust of decent, and the contempt of intelligent men. Their stock-in-trade is the same in all countries, an old but present devil and a future salvation. Without a devil there would be no religion. Once free the world from the fear of the devil, who is called the God of this world, and there will be hope for humanity at large, and the brotherhood of Christ and the son-ship of God will be possible. Peace and good-will then will have a chance among the world's inhabitants.

I had often asked what information these men were prepared to give to the rising generation of both sexes, but could never get an intelligent reply. One man gave his college-life, and being the son of a poverty-stricken peer, indulged in strong abuse of the sons of buttermen and railway contractors, to the delight of his sisters. It was simply an exhibition of himself; of what a "goody-goody" boy he had been, or, in other words, an ignorant sneak and fool; but "what a dear man he was," cried Miss Grimes, to resist such constant temptation; but ask these men to give a lecture on history or any other subject for the instruction of youth, and from sheer incapacity they remained dumb.

The only man who could rant was a Father Douglas, who, it is to be hoped, in his seclusion with his young men, has not the tastes, habits, or the manners of Dr. Twells—a former Bishop of Bloemfonteim—with the young half-blood Beck and his companions. To teach the youngsters the Prayer-book, and who was their Godfather and Godmother was indeed their delight; but how to raise them in manhood, and thus qualify them to become good citizens and good men was out of their power altogether. Their knowledge was a most limited thing, confined within themselves at all times.

July was certainly a most remarkable month in the history of Bloemfontein. Scarcely had the festivities ended, before there arrived one of Rome's itinerant lunatics—a man who in madness had perambulated the world, and brazenly went about proclaiming it as truth that the Church which, three centuries ago, called itself Christian, had then and since been known by reasonable men as a falsehood. In those days of old the Priests of Rome openly preached that sins could be forgiven for metallic-coined money, and these priests did much else then that in face of the wonderful discoveries of modern science they dare not assert or do now.

The Roman Catholic Church, so called, is powerless now for harm owing to its weakness, and as it cannot now apply the fire or shut up in dungeons and immure alive in vaults, as so well described by Scott in *Rokeby*, it raves and struts its knowledge of a place they still call hell. This fellow of a lunatic asylum who had travelled a world so full of light and knowledge, described the devil as so careless, that when walking in hell, he missed his path, and trod on the burning fuel, and even made his audience laugh in church when he described, with a strong Irish brogue, how he jumped and spluttered in pain at his folly in stepping on hot coals. Not content with harrowing up their feelings in an ordinary way, he publicly informed his hearers that there are more women in hell for lying than men, sending many home in a state of terror and half madness. He then, in powerful tones, invoked his listeners to bring each two sinners, and he promised them not only a full account of the lower regions, but even to make them *smell hell.*

Good heavens! what have we arrived at in these days?—that decent men should be harassed by such a sight as this Rome's mountebank, fed by the income that people in fear gave him, to wander about seeing the sights of the world, and adding nothing to its enlightenment, and only fit to sit in a confessional, as below described :—

Edwin Heron on the Confessional.

Here mumbling out his histrionic mass,
His rival chants, here " ass intones to ass : "
Sets up, with folly which is half sublime,
The withered fetish of a bygone time,
States that the priest alone can loose and lock
Who proves his pedigree from Peter's Stock ;
Curses without remorse, or stint, or doubt,
All who don't make the thousand quarterings out ;
And fancying Paradise a strict entail,
Grants hope to those whose lineage does not fail.
Of course asserts that he can ban and bless,
Give or withhold eternal happiness,
Bids women bow before the sacred priest,
Adore his functions and confess at least,
But that this worship of the past should give,
One worthy aim for which to work and live,
Or fancy seek that Empire to renew
Which the strong Saxon smote and overthrew ;
That gewgaws such as these should even be
Anything but a refuge for *ennui*,
That monks can save the world, or ever could,
That anchorite and fakirs do you good,
Is to bring Buddha back before your gaze,
Men do not eat the Lotus in our days.

To be sure that I did not judge this man unfairly, I determined to waste an hour to hear him. I found an excitable, spasmodic man, more intense than strong, with no depth or breadth of thought. One cannot call vehemence strength ; a man is not strong who talks in convulsive fits. We need in these days to remember that shrieking is not indicative of manliness and wisdom, but rather of weakness and imbecility. For three hours did this semi-acting go on; and, to give the audience a change and a something to do and look forward to, they had in the morning been requested to bring with them in the evening matches and a baptismal candle, which, at a given time, they were all called upon to stand up and light, and hold heavenward, while some questions were put, and answered in due form. At length this was enough, and they were told to blow the candles out, and sit down, and then they were solemnly assured that to keep these candles would drive the demons away, and that held in the hands of the dying, they would contain certain virtues. Now, having worked up their hopes, they were regaled with a special rescript— a blessing direct from the Holy Father, used at all times and on all occasions by this itinerant priest; after which, being in a satisfactory humour with themselves and their church, their ordinary priest informed them that this man of God had need of travelling expenses, and their liberality of the morning not being enough, their assistance was once more solicited to help him on his way.

In the old days, priests, to show their zeal and love for their church and cause, thought it not derogatory to their dignity to take their staff and wallet and march on foot to perform their holy mission; but, in these degenerate days, these livers on human credulity must ride in the best conveyances, live sumptuously, and dress in fine linen and black cloth.

This holy man of God!—oh, what mockery!—bitterly complained that the Church was not earnest enough, that Catholics were too quiescent, that the members would fall in love with outsiders, that to such marriages was to be traced much of the coolness to Mother Church, that the youth of both sexes would read the books of men of light and learning, and that in doing so, they would sell themselves to the devil.

I felt thankful for his admission, and rejoiced that at last the writings of men of light and learning were influencing even these people. But what must we think of such members of such a church who could listen to these mutterings? When Lucifer was turned out of heaven and dropped into hell, that alighting upon live coal, he hopped and danced in pain, and that he still so dances, and then to state that was the origin of dancing!

Surely this man must have had the lowest type of intellect or of hearers that they could possibly take all this in, and pay reverence to the utterer as a man of God. Surely the spasmodic attempt and sing-song in the strains of the well-known nursery rhyme, repeating time after time, "This is the cow with the crumpled horn," &c., sending almost all asleep, aided by the incense. But it was truly pitiable to see what is called the house of God, turned into a house of begging. The appeal for money to take this man of God out of the town. at such a time, was a crime and robbery. My sense of justice to myself and the town would not allow me to part with a single coin, although the missionary himself, with the wicked, piercing eye, as some Catholics called him, placed the plate before me ; and it grieved me when I saw a tradesman, who neither properly attended to his business, nor paid his debts, give a donation to help this man to ride out of the town in the best conveyance. Willingly would I have given a crown that he should never have appeared in Bloemfontein, adding one more to the charlatans who play upon the feelings of the women and the terrors of the men.

Did such missions make all more moral, honest, and truthful, one would not complain ; but I, myself came into contact with many Catholics like the Cor-Bitts, who were most particular in their attendance at church, but perfect humbugs towards their tradesmen ; while I must say, that those who were not so anxious to confess, and had lost faith in their so-called and nicknamed holy men of their God, did keep their words, and pay their debts, proving that they were superior to their creed.

Alas! alas! that it is possible in the Nineteenth Century for such shriekers and babblers to go about and talk of a veritable hell, and how so many are in its tortures, and yet teach that the God of the universe is a just God! Surely the time has arrived when such imbeciles ought to be taken care of, and that such simple monstrosities no longer parade our public streets. I call upon all good men to renew their efforts to make known eternal truths, and thus defeat such wretched teachings, for the sake of the rising and unborn generations.

Such works as " Under which Lord ? " by Mrs. Linton, has

exposed the trickery, and the system as adopted by these men to gain their unholy ascendancy.

At the church I noticed one old gentleman hold up his candle the highest, and appear most devout, but this exercise did not make him more human and less grasping : for, a few days after, when a small favour, in the form of the loan of a horse for a sudden journey was needed for an important matter, he would not lend, although I offered to pay most liberally for its use, but, seeing my great need, would sell, and that at an exorbitant price ; and such was my urgent want of this horse for a night ride—for a seventy-miles' journey—that I had to submit to this extortion, for which he deserved Lynch-Ing. Let me here say, that men with no profession of religion, are more considerate, kind, and obliging, to men in need.

The Decline of Orthodoxy.

It has almost become a proverb that the age of miracles is past, and many people suppose that it is a very long time since orthodox people believed that miracles might and did occur around them. But two hundred years ago a man who had denied contemporary miracles would have been handled almost as roughly as an Atheist. Only one hundred and fifty-six years ago a woman was burnt in this country for witchcraft ; and only one hundred and ten years ago the divines of the Associated Presbytery passed a resolution, declaring their belief in witchcraft, and deploring the general scepticism on the subject. Belief in providential miracles was orthodox in the early part of our own century. It disappeared only after a stormy struggle, and then only to hide in many popular superstitions, and to recur occasionally in such movements as Spiritualism. The departure out of respectable orthodoxy of the belief in modern miracles was a much longer stride towards radical unbelief than theologians are willing to admit. Its results have only in these last years begun to make themselves apparent. A Christianity whose deity does not interfere with the laws of Nature or with the government of the world, is only a kind of Deism. It may claim that once upon a time he did interpose in human affairs, eighteen centuries ago, and that, after the lapse of further centuries, he will interpose again ; but none the less are men in the present time left to administer their world without

Divine interference. That is now orthodoxy, but it is unbelief. In is contrary to the faith of the Bible, contrary to Christ's promise of continued miraculous power to his Church. And this unbelief is only bearing its fruits in the wrath and denunciation with which orthodoxy is compelled to defend the faith and the altar which its deity abandons to their fate.—*Moncure D. Conway.*

Protestants and the Bible.

Protestants have committed the truths of Christianity to a theory of their own creation, and when they find themselves in difficulties they fall back on sophistry. The six days of creation are defined precisely by the writer of the Book of Genesis. The period between evening and morning could have been meant only for a day, in the ordinary sense of the word. Science proves unanswerably that the globe has grown to its present condition through an infinite series of ages; and Protestant theologians, entangled with their own fancies, have imagined that "day" may signify a million, billion, or quintillion of years. Construing literally the vehement expression of St. Paul, they have insisted that death originated in Adam's sin. They are confronted with evidence that death has reigned through all creation, through the earliest periods of which the stratafied rocks preserve the record. They hesitate, they equivocate, they struggle against the light; they do anything save make a frank confession of their own error.—*Froude, in " Short Studies on Great Subjects."*

The Triumph of Truth.

In the end, the people who now murmur and ridicule what they do not understand will be grateful for the real manhood that has been revealed to them. In the end, truth alone will command respect, truth alone will prevail; and, in the end, in the far-off time, truth shall make every heart of man its empire and its throne.—*Felix Adler, in " Radical Pulpit."*

The Religion of the Future.

The coming man's religion will have no theology in it. All

questions as to the origin of things, the nature of life, final causes, and the first great cause (least understood), the coming man will naturally pass over. Such subjects have nothing to do with religion. They are questions of science and curiosity, to be elucidated, if at all, by ages of investigation, experiment, and thought. It is not necessary to expound the universe, to assert or to deny a deity. It is only necessary for us to perceive that the question of the final cause is not pressing, not important to us—a matter of curiosity, no more. It is only necessary to agree that no opinion concerning it can be guilty or odious.—*James Parton* "*The Coming Man's Religion.*"

What we Need.

What we need is an ethical movement, a system of moral inspiration, a method of education based on the radical principle that the highest honour is to be a man. What we want on our side is the moral power. That is always supreme. The first thing essential is to destroy the illusion with which the priests and ministers cheat the people. As long as they bow the knee to powers above, they will yield their necks to earthly oppressors and masters. The morality of Christianity must be destroyed. We must cease our submission to the powers that be. We have nothing to hope from poverty of spirit, but everything from wealth of spirit. Out of a blood-stained cross can come for us nothing but misery. " Blessed are they that mourn and weep " must be blotted out of our beatitudes. In the place of this false morality we must put that which is true. True morality is equal and universal rights. Hence the second principle of every true Radical is the right of every man to be and belong to himself. This implies perfect liberty of thought and action, so long as you do not trample on the equal rights of anyone else.—*George C. Chainey.*

Press On!

Struggle, often baffled, sorely baffled, down as into entire wreck; yet a struggle never ended; ever will bear repentance, true, unconquerable purpose, begun anew. Poor human nature! Is not a man's walking, in truth, always that—" a succession of falls " ? Man can do no other. In this wild element of a life he has to struggle onwards—now fallen, now deep-abased, and ever with tears and repentance, with bleeding heart, he has to rise again and struggle again still onward. That his struggle be a faithful, unconquerable one ; that is the question of questions. We will put up with many sad details if the soul of it be true.—*Carlyle, in* "*Hero-Worship.*"

Chapter IX.

HE second and third weeks in July were productive of experiences in the uncertainty of the law. I had been told that there was too much law and very little equity; in fact, no court of equity, and truly I found it so. The Roman, Dutch, and a compound of English, and no-country law, anything and everything to suit the bias of the sitting Landrost, Judge, and the nationality brought before him. With my usual simplicity, I could hardly suppose such acts and deeds could be committed by persons who pride themselves upon being a God-fearing people. In reality I acquit the simple Dutchman of being a party to all this infamy and base iniquity. It is the outcome of the Hollander and German arrangement to fleece all producers, whatever nationality or class they might belong to.

In the case of the manager of a store of mine, stock-taking revealed a deficiency of one hundred and eighty pounds on his part, after being but eight months in my service. This alone was enough to give a shock to any man who desired to pay twenty shillings in the pound. Acting upon the advice of a Maitland Street post-cart-contractor-of-an-attorney, he was urged on, before he rendered any account of his stewardship, or gave any explanation of the loss, to demand of me a certain sum as commission on sales and salary, although dismissing himself from my service on the last day of the month. In the first place a reconvention was allowed, but with the understanding that I, the wronged one, must take my demand into the higher court, where, if I gained the day, I must pay the costs for the benefit of the legal profession and the Government, in stamps (the Dutch Government does believe in stamps).

Now, what respect can men—I say, and mean, *men*, have for such iniquitous conditions, that, if one is in the right, he must pay so expensively for proving it before men, who call themselves judges? Truly it would be well if we knew upon what principle these men were made judges; certainly it is not by acting equitably that they possess the right to sit in judgment. They may argue that they do not sit to make laws, but to administer them, which means that men who swear to act justly and to give no favour, may, like legal highwaymen, enforce black-mail whenever they have the opportunity. The indignation a man feels at being wronged impels him to seek redress rather than submit to being swindled.

The legal adviser of the man that robbed me would have settled all for a certain sum. Accepting this proposal would, on my part, virtually have been condoning the wrong, and publicly saying to my other employees, "Go, and do likewise; you need not take any care of the man's goods, and if you allow them to be taken, and receive the benefit afterwards, no responsibility can attach to you; rob and plunder! your master cannot punish you."

Truly the time has come when all judges must rise above mere considerations of pay, and advocate a cheap system, such as the Code Napoleon, that will enable almost any man to have his case judged fairly, or else let a body of practical mercantile men arbitrate in all cases before an appeal to the judgment seat.

A land without righteous judgments is a piteous sight for the gods, and can only mean its downfall. I feel that injustice is more certain to be done when it is an Englishman who asks for right; and yet it is from England that the Free State owes all its advantages. Much of the food, almost all the clothing, their arms and ammunition, machinery, and, in fact, all that tends to civilise them, is obtained from England. It may be asked, Why employ such men to take charge of stores, or assist in any business? The truth is that it is a case of "Hobson's choice"—these men or none.

The white adult Africander population are lazy, thriftless, and roguish; the climate is calculated to cause them to call upon the black population at all times for the most trivial things. The tropical heat, with its consequent bounteous natural productions, makes them entirely careless as to the future; and when Nature gives of her plenty for seven years in succession, all goes on well, as may be supposed. Wool, sheep, and cattle, are plentiful for all ; but let seven years of drought come, and then starvation and death set in all over the country. Then it is one vast plundering from those who have by those who have not, until Nature is kind once more, and man ceases to be in want. There is no exaggeration in all this ; it is the oft-repeated experience of dwellers in the Cape Colonies and the surrounding States ; and it has been proved that asses, mules, swine and bastards, are the only animals that seem to increase and flourish.

No one can honestly recommend the Cape as a land to emigrate to. It is only a half-way place to India ; and after all it is a question whether, considering the other and more attractive colonies that England has, if it would not be better to simply hold the Coast towns, well guarded as is done by the Portuguese, and letting the natives trade for what they require, and leaving all internal arrangements to them. What have we to do with their fighting and slaveholding ? That is their business. Leave them to make their own terms with each other as older nations have in Europe ; but, in any case, I emphatically say, Africa is not, and never can be, the home of the white man. He may try for many years, and even centuries, to master its climatic conditions, but in the end he will fail. Nature, the mighty, is against him there, just as she would in Europe be against a colony of blacks. It would be well if the English withdrew all protection, letting those remain who so desired, to take their risk with the natives, or find a home in some more suitable place.

The very animals and seeds we send out fail constantly to increase and supply ; all try to run back to their African origin, and such will be the experience in the future. The country cannot be relied upon for the growth even of its own grasses, and it is constantly importing provisions in order to exist ; and, as for its diamonds, man, when wise, will not think it worth his while to barter health and life for them, as they are, after all, only ornaments to feed the vanity of women, and show the folly of man.

But even this is a failure now, and once more the country must depend upon its natural supply, or be doomed to become a howling waste, for what stock the farmer breeds in the summer he loses in winter.

The second demand of this Dutch employee was as bad as the first, if not worse, and in which the post-cart contracting attorney, of Maitland Street, was again the active supporter. Although the plaintiff proved he had dismissed himself, this French-Dutchised attorney, in the hope of getting the expenses of both sides out of me, availed himself of all the well-known legal tricks to secure the same; but my evidence was so convincing that the Solons could not give a verdict against me.

To give an idea of the intelligence of these men: I claimed in my usual way to affirm—to speak the truth, the whole truth, and nothing but the truth; and, while uttering the same, the man, who sat as Chief Judge for his fellow-man shouted out at the end, "So help you God." Now, as I had no help from a god to speak the truth, this was pure ignorance on his part, and could have only been introduced for the purpose of making me say too much, or too little, or to trip me up and prevent me giving evidence. I admit, without shame, that I did not appear to heed him, and, so uncertain was he of his ground, that he failed to grasp the details of the subject. In fear I awaited the verdict, the whole of the judge's summing up being so much in favour of the delinquent, it quite took me by surprise that he accepted my evidence, and gave a verdict in my favour.

It was just at this time that I bought a business in the country, and, after stocking the concern, I engaged the late owner to manage it. After releasing the original bond of seven hundred pounds, I bought the man right out, and, finding that he was no better in management than in ownership, I gave him notice that his services would not be required after three months, as agreed upon. Judge of my surprise, when I found that this man, to injure me, had permitted a summons to go by default, and then allowed the sheriff to take possession of my lawful property, thus compelling me again to employ the lawyers and sharks in making affidavits, costing me the sum of £45. But this was not the worst part of this vagabond's tricks; for it turned out that this judgment being out against this man in February, he committed a fraud on me, in causing to be passed away a considerable quantity of goods in settlement of other people's claims, so that he could give me a general bond upon all at his place. Finding that all did not work satisfactorily, I then, for a further consideration, bought him entirely out. Execution for the judgment got in February was put in force in July upon my property, and then, when I appeared in opposition, I heard, for the first time, that this German had given the bond *fraudulently*, therefore the after sale was illegal, and my goods must pay the debt and expenses. Such was the anxiety and determination on the part of the Dutch authorities at Ladybrand to injure me, that they postponed their decision, in the hope that I should not be able to protect myself, or to stop such public robbery and spoliation. Fortunately, however, in three hours I was enabled to get all things in order and completeness, to stop any further sale on the part of this thief; but to do so, I had to buy an expensive horse to get over the seventy-five miles in sixteen hours, on a moonless night, in clouds descending, and to ride as if one had a reprieve to deliver before ten o'clock the next morning.

This brawling German thief was but the outcome of the conditions surrounding him. When in business in Bloemfontein, he always paid me honestly for all he bought; but going out among the vile horde of his countrymen, who lived in that Alsatia of the Free State, he learnt from them the tricks common to such people, and put into practice the maxim, that it was more profitable to cheat than to be honest. Taking example from the Russians, that all was fair in war, fraud, or marriage, even to stealing your neighbour's land, as was done by them in Europe during the last and present century, and by their fellows in other countries, and thus they and he carried out their nefarious ways over here. I must say here, that they, thinking they had got a simple, honest man to deal with, resolved to take all the advantage possible of him; and, although this was my misfortune, and loss to some hundreds of pounds, don't let it be supposed that it was an isolated case. I give my experience as a warning to others that they may know that the Free State is not a place for honest traders. It is full, and is the home of immoral, dishonest, German traders; and I can almost forgive the simple Boer farmers for their action against those country shops, where they are always taken in by this dishonourable class.

Perhaps some may say passion guides my pen, and that I speak in fierce hate, owing to my losses. Nothing of the kind. I will admit that I feel savage when I see these foreigners take such advantages of decent people under the flag of England and her dependencies. I also admit that, as an Englishman, I cannot allow my country for ever to be robbed and plundered by these roving vagabonds, who as a rule are too lazy to work, but not too degraded to steal, and are to be found in all ranks—from the Guelphs, on what they call the Throne of England, which is a standing shame to an Englishman, and must be wiped away, even to the latest impostor that crosses the German Ocean.

No wonder the Russians wish to get rid of such ruling pests. The time must come when they either must stop in their own Fatherland, or give some security for their honesty, if allowed to make a stay in England or her colonies ; and, until this occurs, up to my latest breath, in speaking and writing, I will urge that these iniquities be abolished, and such monstrosities no longer be permitted to inhabit England's sacred soil, or that of her colonies or dependencies.

That men with honest intentions *could* get a living, there is my own case to prove, but it was only by constant, hard, toil from morn until late at eve, and strictly following the advice given me in Aliwal by an old Bloemfontein trader that I was able to do so. That advice was to stand behind my own counter, and look after my own till, and then all would be right. Immediately that my business increased so as to need assistance to carry it on, virtually making me a prisoner in my front store, then I became subject to the jumping proclivities of Free-State-born assistants, for I can testify that, neither for the home nor for the store, could I find persons possessing common honesty, notwithstanding the fact that I paid higher salaries than was usual.

The inhabitants were no better in other respects ; to get into debt was the rule, from the President, members of Parliament, &c., downwards ; in fact, I was delighted to leave the capital of the Free State, as a nest of polite and unpolite robbers. They would get into your debt, rob you, and afterwards laugh at you, or trek into the next town to repeat the process all over the State ; when they could not secure credit, they slandered you in no measured degree. It was truly laughable to notice with what unction they (finding that they could not steal your purse, not that they considered it trash) would steal a character, as described in immortal poetry by Shakespeare, till at last, in self-defence, one had to act on the old advice of the Greek philosopher : " live it down."

The slanders were not of the old women's gossip type only ; for when the little satellite of the mongrel church got to know that I did not "swear," but acted on their advice repeated Sunday after Sunday, not to take the name of the Lord in vain, and I " affirmed" to speak the whole truth and naught but the truth, I was immediately christened without godfather and godmother the "atheist." Although they were repeatedly assured that they were in error, I being a positivist and an all-round protestor ; such was their enlightenment, that the names of Auguste Comte, Lewis, Congreve, &c., were unknown to them, much less did they know what true religion consisted of.

Then I found the town was puffed up in England as the healthiest spot in Africa, to inveigle invalids suffering from pulmonary disease to end or spend some of their days in—to enrich the doctors of the town where even quacks, made respectable by long residence (as mentioned in the *Express* of May 22nd, 1884) charge a guinea for a visit, and seven and sixpence for a box of pills. The genuine doctors at Bloemfontein did profess to believe that it was a veritable health resort, as described, and offered to accommodate the sick for a stipulated sum per month, as they do at Malvern, Torquay, and other places in England, and I know that when these well-to-do wretches read this they will call a meeting and pass condemnation upon me, and maintain that I must have murdered my grandmother, or committed some other heinous crime ; for what they all lack in intelligence, they make up in spite and dog-like cruelty. My own experience proved, as all can testify, that Bloemfontein is a most unhealthy spot.

The " Queen City " of Cesspools, Cow-Kraals and Pigsties.

Bloemfontein, March 8th, 1881.

To the Editor of the *Friend*.

Sir,—For some time past so much has been said by the leading English Medical Journals, and others, about Bloemfontein, as a "Health resort and Sanatorium," that no wonder so many persons, ourselves included, have been anxious to avail themselves of the great advantages held out to delicate constitutions if they could only get here. We therefore made an effort a few months ago and did get here ; but if, in describing our disappointment in the place, and attempting to describe it fairly, we should displease those who hold opposite opinions, we shall only be too pleased to be corrected in our judgment ; hear the other side of the question and, if possible, be convinced that this place is all that has been represented. Upon entering the town by the Monument we were surprised to find it situated in a hollow which naturally must be anything but a salubrious position, for, during the summer months, the sun pours down with an intensity, having no chance of the heat being counteracted by the breezes around, and in damp seasons there is a fœtid miasma arising from the town in such an insanitary condition that the wonder would be if it were not the fruitful source of blood poisons of every character. You have recently informed us that diphtheria and scarlet fever have made their appearance in the town, but let us be warned, for these diseases admonish us and tell us of typhoid lurking in the back ground, and no wonder, for lately we breathe nothing but the poisonous fœtid exhalations from filthy cowkraals, stinking pigsties, and old standing cesspools. Whilst medical and scientific men are at present engaged in enquiring into the meteorological changes of the atmosphere in the locality, I would suggest that they immediately set about to ascertain how many cows, goats, sheep and pigs sleep every night in our midst,—to say nothing of the dogs and cats innumerable. In the present defective state of our sanitary arrangements it is more than difficult to get rid of the filth necessarily made by the human population ; but when there is unnecessarily added to this the abominable filth made by the above-named animals it is a problem how to keep disease out of the town. There is, within six yards of my own windows in the centre of the town and a closely populated neighbourhood, a yard, converted into a cow kraal ; here, every night, there are between thirty and forty head of cattle sheltered. During the late rains the place is some feet deep in filth—issuing a most abominable stench—and the only way the owner drains it is by surreptitiously making a hole at the bottom of the yard wall, so it runs into the neighbouring yard, and from thence into the back street—his own street, of course, being too aristocratic for him to venture upon such a mode of procedure. Then there are the pigsties always to be met with in the most thickly populated neighbourhoods. If you can't see them you may always smell them, and these wretched animals are allowed to go about the streets rooting up every bit of garbage, and adding filth to filth. Goats innumerable also add to the odour of the town ; so what with one animal and another we are nearly reduced to a sort of animal existence ourselves.

It is not sufficient to expect that one man, a sanitary inspector, can properly see into and arrange these matters. Generally speaking, one man don't care—even though he may be well paid for it—to be looked upon as the obnoxious individual prying into the privacies of every home ;—besides, a sanitary inspector might perhaps be a cow-keeper himself, and, in such a case, it certainly would not be to his interest to interfere with cow kraals. What really is wanted is a sanitary committee, consisting of several men, who really, thoroughly understand the laws pertaining to hygiene and have some power to enforce them. The town really is about one of the best doctored in the country, judging from the number of medical men ; but then, in these places, it pays far better to cure disease than to prevent it, and we must not look to them for suggestions.

I have seen cases of typhoid in this town, and only one common cesspool between two houses, with a wooden partition at the top only, and the poisonous evacuations thrown down the cesspool. Can we wonder how fever is generated ? But is it nobody's business to look very deeply into these matters ? How dirty water is to be got rid of, is another question. The Sanitary Inspector very properly tells us it must not be thrown into the street, and we very properly tell ourselves it must not be thrown into our yards, and the landlord informs us it must not go down the cesspool, so where is it to be got rid of ? But everyone does get rid of it, somehow, nevertheless, and the town and spruit is often in a very unpleasant condition. I would therefore urge that the Municipal authorities take means to prevent any filth being made in the town that is positively unnecessary, such as that which is accumulated by allowing kraals and pigsties of any kind.

When Bloemfontein is spoken of as a resort for Pulmonary

invalids, I often ask, wherein lies the advantage? But suddenly I remember what an old woman in England told me many years ago viz., that "cow-dung and milk" was the sure and only cure for consumption, and, nasty as I then thought it, and much as I laughed, I can begin to see there must be some truth in her state-

nt, i,e., if Bloemfontein really offers, as it is stated, a specific for this disease—it must be its "cow-dung and milk :" very large and nauseous doses of the former and sometimes very little of the latter. But to this "Queen City" of cesspools, cow-kraals, and pigsties, I must soon bid adieu, and look in another direction for a "health resort"—a "Sanatorium."—Yours, &c.,

HYGIEA.

Its extremes of cold and great heat, want of rains, dirty erfs yards, and kraals in the town, and a most foul sluit in the centre —all breeding diphtheria, scarlatina. and other contagious diseases, —drove me at last, for fear that my own family should become victims, to send thom once more to the Colony.

In my bachelorhood I was compelled to engage assistance to keep my rooms and linen clean, but in doing so, I was subjected to all kinds of inuendoes. Living in the heart of the town, and many of the fair sex being my customers, gave the opportunity, when I would not give them my goods on credit, to call me names, maintaining that I was a Mormon in heart and a Turk in practice. Truly through all the petty wars, Bloemfontein became the home of the vilest and most contemptible set of wretches it was ever my lot to fall among, and in very joy I shook the dust off feet, and was glad to bid such a spot a last farewell.

"Good gracious!" I hear some say, "what an unfortunate man." Stay, my friends; I was not more so than others. I but give an experience that many could, but dare not. To plunder, cheat, and lie was the every day practice, and if not to be done in the light, then in the *dark*.

The cruel wrong that I had suffered in the Colony through putting faith in human nature forcibly brought to my recollection my dear old mother's words, when I was in my early manhood and releasing myself from the swaddling clothes of my early religious training—and emerging in light through my reading and studying nature and life, with its many vicissitudes, and thinking out the problem of existence. She told me then, my unbounded faith and confidence in human nature would be my constant ruin. Truly (as all will feel if ever I do write my autobiography) I have been the sport of many in whom I have had faith, and yet with all this I always seem to be perpetrating some Quixotic blunder, from the belief that men are only waiting for a guiding light, in order to climb to a grander and nobler life ; and strange to say, no experience, however bitter and discouraging, seems to shake this faith or make me feel in the words of the poet Heron :—

> " Make it a golden rule, and keep it so,
> Trust none you know not, and trust none you know."

Many were the sympathisers and even opponents who, like all others who are wise only after the event, expressed their surprise that I should be so taken in ; to whom I could only reply by shrugging my shoulders and expressing myself to the effect, that if they were so wise why did they not tell me *before the event*—it was a known thing to all *after* it had occurred.

I was momentarily pained by one with whom I had had many a confidential chat and even taken counsel over all my transactions. This man had always expressed his unbounded confidence in my customer's honesty, if not in his ability, yet he had the courage and impudence to say, when I expressed my indignation that a countryman of his—in whom he took such interest—had failed in such a manner, that it was not owing to his own independent judgment that he had faith in him, but because I reposed confidence in the man. Good heavens ! What desertion from his previous views. I felt, after such a statement, a bitter contempt for this former friend.

Truly a man's friendship is proved if he helps in time of trouble, and proves a friend in deed or counsel when a man is in need thereof ; but then, as Carlyle says—when speaking of the wretched mistakes which different ages make concerning the best and greatest—" Why the Jews took Jesus for a scoundrel, and thought all they could do with Him was to nail Him up on a gallows. Ah ! that was a bad business ; and so He has returned to heaven and the descendants of the murderers go wandering about the streets buying old clothes ! Is was truly a bad business that the working out of a Divine plan, so stated, of Salvation, should depend upon a wretched mistake committed by such Jewish fiends and yet we must press on, struggle on, often baffled sorely—baffled, down, as into entire wreck. Yet a struggle never ended, ever will bear repentance, true unconquerable purpose, begun anew. Poor human nature! Is not a man's walking in truth always that—a succession of falls? Man can do no other. In this wild element of a life he has to struggle onwards :—now fallen, now deep debased, and ever with tears and repentance, with bleeding heart, he has to rise again and struggle again, still onward. That is, struggle, be a faithful unconquerable one. That is the question of questions. We will put up with many sad details if the soul of it, and man be but true."

In this age when the true Gospel of man is well known—and which, if acted upon, would make all feel their existence to be a much richer, and grander and more valuable inheritance, if properly used, than ever dreamt of, and if believers in such were scrupulous in their engagements, loving fathers, faithful husbands, honourable neighbours, and as just citizens as are to be found in other creeds and beliefs—let us advocate the brotherhood of man and the fatherhood of God, and all will be well, and notwithstanding the general laxity of faith, which is the characteristic of our age, the moral sentiment of our day is growing broader and better. There is more charity, more sympathy, more love and tenderness, a greater desire to know the truth, and be guided by it, a stronger hatred of injustice, tyranny and wrong, and a deeper love of the true, the beautiful and the good than ever was known before.

But morality is not Christianity. It is common to all religions. The fundamental principles of morality are everywhere, and at all times the same. The coming man's religion will have no theology in it; all questions—as to the origin of things, the nature of life, the duration of life, final causes, and the first great cause—the coming man will naturally pass over. Such subjects have nothing to do with religion.

Self-Improvement.

Whoever improves his own nature improves the universe, of which he is a part. He who strives to subdue his evil passions, vile remnants of the old four-footed life, and who cultivates the social affections ; he who endeavours to better his condition and to make his children wiser and happier than himself, whatever may be his motives, he will not have lived in vain. But if he acts thus, not from mere prudence—not in the vain hope of being rewarded in another world, but from a pure sense of duty, as a patriot of the planet upon which he dwells, then our philosophy, which once appeared to him so cold and cheerless, will become a religion of the heart, and will elevate him to the skies ; the virtues which were once for him mere abstract terms will become endowed with life, and will hover around him like guardian angels, conversing with him in his solitude, consoling him in his afflictions, teaching him how to live and how do die.—*Reade, in " Martyrdom of Man."*

The Morality of the Future.

Of one thing we may be perfectly sure : the coming man's religion will inculcate and actually produce a genuine and high morality. Much more is requisite, but this is preliminary and indispensable. Philosophers and *littcrateurs*, who survey the scene of human life from a library window, may not know that the practice of the homely moralities is the first condition of all welfare and all excellence. It is the fact, nevertheless. For my part, I avow my conviction that the most blind and bigoted religionist, Catholic or Protestant (Buddhist or Mohammedan), who performs with loyalty and diligence the duties of his sphere and home, is not only a better man, but, in truth, a more intelligent man, then the most brilliant philosopher who does not.—*Parton, in " The Coming Man's Religion."*

I had once more from compulsion—not in love or confidence—to apply to the lawyers for legal assistance to prove my case —knowing but too well that like crows or dasvogels smelling a carcass, they would help until they had devoured the meat, and then, when no more flesh in the shape of gold could be found in my clothes or on my bones, they would leave me to dry up. It has often been said that very few lawyers ever get to heaven. Certainly my experience tells me that they are only fit for that period of torture described by Dante in his *Inferno*, if being paid beforehand and then getting incapable through the luncheon, &c., indulged in, or forgetting a duty—or how to defend—when the liberty of a man is at stake, without taking into consideration his prospects of the future, deserves punishment; then many have my best wishes for some punishment, in a warm place, as a warning to their brethren.

I witnessed conduct on the part of legal gentlemen robbers, during the Transkein war that was perfectly shameful. After taking all the money they could get from their clients, and smirking and bobbing their assurances that nothing should be left undone to maintain their rights, when it suited their purpose to do so they deserted their victims in the most heartless manner; and yet these men were afterwards made judges of the land, and even sat in Parliament to make fresh enactments giving them additional facilities to rob and plunder; and what makes the matter more disgusting is, that it is all done in the name of justice, truth, and right.

Napoleon the First! If for naught else, I remember thee as a hero for thy "Code, Napoleon." Would that we had such in our country, and the same opportunity for asking and getting advice and help before it was possible for any fool or rogue to drag us into the meshes of what is called the law. Gilbert and Sullivan! your names must go down to posterity for describing so nicely how much of modern law is fudge, and how so many in similar ways become judges.

By way of illustration and in corrobation of my views I submit the following extracts from the *Express* and *Mercury*:—

A great deal of feeling has been evoked by the discussion of the Draft Ordinance which deals with the prosecution or punishmen of legal practitioners and other professional men who carry on their business under the provisions of Ordinance No. 6—1884 (Tariff Ordinance). It is held by this new measure that a legal practitioner, who has drawn up a summons in a careless manner, causing absolution from the instance; or who has brought a trumpery case into any Court, or neglected a defence, causing thereby loss of suit to his client; or who has advanced silly exceptions to delay the case, shall be mulcted in the costs of the case, with the right of an appeal to a higher tribunal. Further, that any person practising under the provisions of Ord. No. 3

H

1880, shall be bound to the tariff fixed therein, and shall not be allowed to enter into a private contract for the purpose of evading such tariff. Those acting contrary to this provision shall be deprived of their licence, and shall have no legal redress to recover the amount of such private contract. A defendant in any case shall have the right to demand from plaintiff's attorney security for costs in the case. If any moneys shall have been collected by or entrusted to a legal practitioner, and he shall fail to render an account when called upon, he shall be brought up for the embezzlement of trust moneys. The above provisions are severe, and in some instances unduly so, and we have every hope that the feelings of our legislators, outraged as they have been by innumerable instances of carelessness, over-charges, and embezzlement, will not carry them from one extreme to another. For this would result in a defeat of the good the Raad aims at, and which in the public interest is moreover indispensable. At the same time there is no use disguising the fact that the iniquities, that have been perpetrated upon an unprotected public cry to heaven for redress and protection. Who is there in this State that cannot point to some abuse, by means of which he has been robbed of hard-earned gains? To instance cases would require volumes. Who, again, has not the knowledge of the fact that the medical profession (so-called only in many instances) counts amongst its members men who have abused the ignorance and helplessness of their patients to a most fearful extent? Before us lies a Doctor's account for £78 1s. 6d·, for work done in one of our towns during fourteen days! How many such accounts are there? Is their number not legion? And will any *real* professional man say, that he has a right to such a charge—to a charge of £11 1s. 6d. for one day for visits and medicines? We should like to know the gentleman who would come forward to claim it. And the legal profession? In our own experience we have smarted under treatment that deserves no other name than theft, and how are we to protect ourselves? By employing only honest people? That's just what we did in the instance that stands before our minds' eye, when we had occasion to employ an agent, but our opponent was not what we should have desired, nor had the Magistrate much idea of law. As a result we were on trifling exceptions mulcted in a much arger amount than was represented by our claim, and we had to bear it, in the hope that one day the legislature would think of these things and make an end of them. Thus, as we say, there can be no question of the necessity for some means by which the public shall be protected, as little as there can be that these enactments should not take the form of provisions calculated to drive honest and able men out of the country. There is no country on earth, certainly no civilised country, where the various professions are not bound down by law to remain within the limits of honesty and reason. At the same time it is left to any able man to either fix the price of his work, or refuse to do work, and why should he not? A man's brains are as much his own as his house or lands, consequently he can make his price for either; and a law prohibiting good men from making the most of their capabilities drives good men out of the country. By this means we return to a state of things such as we had in the early days of this country —when anyone became a lawyer and anyone a doctor. Besides, there is another difficulty in the matter, and it is this: If a person going, or dragged, into Court has to give security for costs, the rich man has all the chances, and the poor man none. With the aims of the law we have all sympathy; with the means very little. For the indifference and stupidity of the public, no laws can be made; and it is a fact which stands out prominently in this discussion, that in spite of all the swindling, no doctor has yet been brought before a Court (at least not to our knowledge) because he attempted to swindle his client. It is just as rare an accurrence to see a dishonest lawyer figuring before a Judge to answer for his misdemeanours. What should be done is, that the legal and medical professions obtain a status and legal enactments, enabling *them* to take cognizance of the abuses, and to remedy them by the expulsion of the offender. If the general public co-operates by giving due notice of the abuses to which they are exposed, there is little doubt but that this remedy will be effective.

We were unable to make any reference on Friday to the very remarkable charge delivered by the Chief Justice on opening the last criminal sessions in Cape Town; but the address deserves careful attention. It is in part an answer to Mr. Froude's last article, but we agree with much that is in that article, and also with a good deal that Sir Henry de Villiers said. Mr. Froude thinks that in this Colony justice is not often by white juries to natives, but that the charge as he makes it is by far too sweeping. There is often occasion to complain of this, but it arises very frequently from the absence of newspapers. In most of the circuit towns there are no journals, and in these courts the press is not represented. Occasionally a barrister will supply reports, but these are such as lawyers would make, and the jury do not feel that their conduct will be made public and commented upon when the court rises. At other times the fault lies with the presiding judge who shows that he is in a hurry, that he is not well, that he has lost his temper, or that he has made up his mind as to the verdict, and means to have it so. Ordinary citizens know very little about the rights and privileges of jurymen; but they have vague ideas of the tremendous powers of a judge, and when he bullies a witness, or shows his temper to the jurors, they submit under the impression that it is their duty to do so. It is true, as the Chief Justice says, that the Supreme Court has been adorned by a succession of judges who were both lawyers and gentlemen; as it is true that Sir Henry de Villiers sustains the reputation of his court; but there have been judges of but slender fame, and there still are judges who would benefit the country by attempting to adorn the life of common citizens. If it were necessary we could find a number of cases in which the injustice that has been done nominally by juries, is due to the conduct of the judges.

While waiting at the Court House I had an opportunity to note how the Landdrost treated a case of trespass and assault preferred against a man who had reason to suppose that another trespassed on his conjugal rights, and in the attempt to find this out, walked into the yard of the house where this wife dwelt. The man had, as I afterwards learnt, committed himself, while in the colony, and had to flee from the punishment that his employers—the Government—would have meted out to him, and left his wife and children to the mercy of a cold world, and in the immediate care of his mother-in-law—a hard-working body, who did her best for all this family. Now, unfortunately, this man was a human cripple: once out of Government employ, he was physically and mentally incapable of recovering himself, and, instead of being a help and a breadwinner for them all, he simply underwent a caving-in through his intemperate habits, and at last became a nuisance. In a fit of generosity the wife allowed him to dwell in her mother's house, and thus, to her misfortune, she gave light to a child, and in consequence became reduced to a wretched state of poverty, which was so degrading an experience to her as a sensitive woman, that she determined never to live with him again, unless he could provide for them, and had an assurance that she was not to be only a child creator without the means of being properly supported.

For a long time, in conjunction with her mother, they kept a roof over their heads, and clothed her children, but the income and profits did not enable her to pay all, and, therefore, it was a loss to the tradesmen of the town. Now this human skunk having failed to find means of subsistence for his family, and, having learnt of the death of his wife's mother, at once returned, and claimed conjugal rights. To this the woman very properly objected, and, to prevent violence, a young man, in a moment of chivalry, protected her from his repeated annoyance. The assumption that the husband rushes at is, that his wife must, of necessity, be encouraging immoral attentions on the part of this young man —a position by no means certain.

I grant that the Free State is not the most moral; its farmers are like the old generation called " Bucks "; their constant eating of dried and fresh meats, without a fair proportion of vegetables, increases the animalism of the Free State burghers, and the same may be said of the women. Animalism is rampant all over the State, and, strange to say, the Dutch pretend to be ruled by Roman-Dutch law, and they carry this out so far as to lend their wives to each other; but not as the old Romans did—as a token of respect and regard for their special friend, and a proof of their esteem, inasmuch as it enabled them to part for a time even from what they held most dear.

Whether it is due to some climatic influence in the tropics or not I cannot say, but that warm climates do produce a looseness of life and disgusting immorality is undeniable, and the polygamy of the natives, and the giving of their women simply to be mothers, has intensified the lustfulness of the Dutch farmers, and it is no uncommon thing, as in the old slave states of America, to find likenesses on the farm, in the shape of two-legged bastards, but of a darker colour.

To bear this out as a truism, and an indisputable fact, the

Griquas, whom I met fifteen miles from Kokstadt, and who were on the point of slaying me while passing over that district, on my way to the Colony, at the time I took a sea passage to Natal, and returning by way of Kokstadt and Uemtata to King William's Town, with the families of Garbutt, Smith, and myself, mustering in all, three women, four men, and twenty-seven children.

These people, who were living among the Bastards of the old Cape Dutch colonists, who were called Griquas, with Adam Kok as their chief, and who, becoming a constant peril from their numbers and general intelligence to the Dutch of the Free State, were eventually persuaded by the Colonial Government to sell their possessions in Philippolis and trek over Basutoland, into what at that time was known as No-Man's-land, and at the foot of the Drakensberg, near Natal. After twenty years, fearing that they again would lose their all, and be absorbed by the white man, they rose suddenly under the leadership of one Smith Palmer.

Now, it so happened, that I was in the immediate neighbourhood of their principal town, called Kokstadt, and, on the advice of their chief magistrate, Captain Blyth, hastily retraced our footsteps to Harding for protection and certainty. It was never expected that we should pass out of No-Man's-land alive, and I fearlessly say that, but for the coolness of Mr. Garbutt, who came out of Natal to settle there, we should never have had a tale to unfold. I then, and often since, have felt for all who in after years were surrounded by savages. The horror that one felt when in the presence of naked men with assegais in their hands, cannot be described, and only one false move at that time on our parts, would, in all probability, have ended in a general massacre of our little party.

Captain Blyth, after three hours' fighting at Kokstadt, was enabled to drive these Griquas away, but not without a heavy loss in killed by the blowing up of the magazine in the town. Three days after Smith Palmer was shot, and we were once more enabled to return over Pondoland to the Colony; but I have often thought since what little incidents prevent us getting into positive danger. There was I, a perfect stranger, in a No-man's land, and bewailing my fate that I was unable to get on. Now, had I entered Kokstadt before the engagement, so few were its defenders, that I should, of necessity, have been pressed into service ; and who can tell but what I might have been one of the blown-up victims ? Truly, at that time, I passed through the bitterness of death, and that at the hands of the unfortunate descendants of Dutch and native *liaisons*.

Afterwards I never saw a " Bastard " or Griqua, either in the Free State or the Colony, but a shudder ran through me, and when I came to know the true history of this people, I often felt that animalism and lust on the part of the Dutch had produced a fruitful crop of active agencies to bring about a fearful reckoning on the innocent and weak. At the present time the Dutch are increasing their " Bastards " as fast as the half-breeds are begotten in America, and the time must come when they will be a scourge to the Dutch themselves.

I am not exaggerating when I say that the Dutch are both immoral and vicious, and that they look upon all black women as mere instruments or beings for their lustful delights, and then afterwards treat their progeny as slaves for their profit. This is, perhaps, a fearful thing to say, but it is only too true, as could be proved in all the Dutch districts of South Africa.

I am no advocate for women leaving their homes, even though they may be unhealthy spots to live in, unless under some special pressure, and I feel that a man so left is placed in an unfair position ; he is tempted of all who do not hold the Seventh Commandment in awe, but the many many evidences I had of the cruel treatment, by lustful men, of women who, in many cases, worked and supported the families that the men should have sustained, compels me to give credence to a woman's word rather than to that of the men-husbands ; let a man once get lustful and drunken, and he becomes brutal, so that the sacredness of woman is for ever lost.

Will the day ever dawn when men and women, calling themselves Liberals, shall understand the issues at stake in all these fights for larger liberty, and comprehend the principles of purity and justice for which you are so gloriously labouring, and cease discolouring by their own perverted mentalities, thus representing white as black, and purity as filth ? Oh, for a race of men born of free mothers, conceived in love, and because desired ; gestated in knowledge and observation of natural laws ; reared in the sunshine of happy homes; nourished on a diet of pure and simple food; supplied with air to breathe, free from the contamination of alcohol and tobacco; educated according to the laws of evolution; body and brain developed in harmony! Such a race would know no sickness, misery, nor crime, but would bring the kingdom of heaven down to earth, where it belongs, and usher in the Millenium morn. To bring about such a consummation it were the greatest honour to suffer persecution, scorn, or ostracism from a society too corrupt to perceive purity and recognise self-sacrifice But glory will in the future crown the noble workers who, with bleeding feet, clear away the brambles and make easy the pathway for future generations.

I do not speak without having well observed, and I am sure that England and other countries will bear out this view. I have said somewhere that women should not be the breadwinners; they are far more helpless than men, and are far more tempted by men. I have met men who would be horror-stricken with their wives if they went astray, but who, in their very lustfulness, would think it no sin to set traps for other men's wives. I know it may be argued that men love women for themselves, while women love to know that men love them; but, so long as man remains the stronger, it is his duty to curb his passions and lusts, and guard and protect the weak.

Marriage to me is a holy and sacred condition; and in such a state for men and women to forget themselves, is a prostitution of the word Love. Let us at once call it by its right name—Lust! and on whichever side it is shown, call them wild animals, that, for the sake of the morals of others, and of rising generations, should be kept in check, even to confinement or isolation, if necessary. Parties, when married, should regard the agreement as sacredly binding, should guard its sancity, and seek to carry it out; and in another way men should band themselves as of old, to guard the helpless, the widow, and the orphans from the libertine and devourer. While I uphold the sacredness of the marriage tie, I cannot forget there are conditions in marriage that make it desirable to disunite; and, while condemning the loose way divorce is carried out in the United States, I must admire the conditions recently proposed by the French Assembly, and which I here annex for the reader's information :—

"The French Senatorial Committee on Divorce have agreed to M. Eymard-Duvernay's scheme, which allows divorce for desertion, adultery, or scandalous misconduct, and an attempt on the life, health, liberty, or honour of the husband or wife. It likewise admits divorce after three years' judicial separation, but forbids the respondent to re-marry in the petitioner's lifetime, unless with the consent of the latter."

Whilst supporting such a rational system of divorce, I protest against any sympathy being given to men who do not protect or guard themselves from committing violence against, or fail to provide for, their wives and children; and it behoves us at all times, if we have any chivalry in us, to specially hesitate to condemn a woman without positive proof.

The man whose conduct led me to write these rambling remarks, did not deserve the slightest sympathy; he failed in all that denotes true manhood, and would have lived upon his wife's earnings, and enjoyed, in his way, his sensual appetites. Such men are better buried, and that their children know them not—their acts and uncertain conduct. But alas! they too often leave their nature in their children, and it is for this reason I preach these lessons. May their shadows grow less, and may the true protection of all women continue to grow greater in pure love and unselfishness.

I may here mention that this woman kept a house that was visited by some of the most particular of her sex. She was also scrupulously particular in the education and bringing up of her children, and in no way was there positive proof that she at any time misconducted herself, and, under such circumstances, I felt it incumbent to protest against the inuendoes and statements of her husband, who was well known to be most unreliable in his walks and habits of life. Lustful, drunken, and unreliable men are not the best judges, and cannot be expected, therefore, to look aright, and should be the last, without positive proof, to destroy the reputation of their wives, and bring everlasting disgrace upon their offspring.

Chapter X.

HILE penning these thoughts I had hoped that my application for a board of arbitrators would have been granted, and that the possibility of being dragged into court, and thereby partially ruined in the attempt to prove my rights, would have been prevented; but alas! here, as elsewhere, victims must be had to fatten the lawyers' trade union—one of the vilest combinations against the life, liberty, and property of the subject ever allowed to exist.

Although, time after time, a demand has been made for a confidential public servant, who could advise a man how to act, with power to stop litigation until he had investigated the cause of dispute; no such man or friend has been appointed. The absence of such a person might be tolerated if lawyers were held responsible for the advice they charge for; but, as matters stand at present, if they are wrong, a man may be ruined in endeavouring to prove he is right; and yet we are told that justice is open to all—to poor as well as to peer.

What vile untruthfulness! the facts are all the other way. The liberty of the subject is constantly threatened and violated, and the victim has no redress. Let a man but speak the truth, and a conspiracy will be formed to convict him of some misdemeanour, outlawing him from all civil rights, and the very conviction used against him to prove that he is a vile scoundrel. Many and many a time have judges been proved drunken and idiotic—(see *Mercury* reports on Fitzgerald), and yet they will sit, and (as they say), dispense justice. Good heavens! when shall the earth be covered with righteousness, and such impostors be impossible?

The late cruelties in connection with the victims of the Blasphemy Laws—Foote and others—feeding the pretentions and cruelty of one class to satisfy the cant and hypocrisy of another, is proof positive that, in England, the judges are not always appointed on account of their capability, but in consideration of their political party services; and thus it is we see such injustice flourish.

The same my be said of many of the judges of South Africa, in the Free State. The Chief Justice made a journey into the Colony to stir up strife between the races, as a party "move," for, in reality, the Dutch and English are but a part of the great Scandinavian race, and, in conjunction with a Mr. Hofmeyr, they desired Africa for the Africanders. The Dutch and English could live side by side happily; but it is German, the Hollander, and the Jew that cause strife, as I will show before this history is finished.

They say the Dutch cannot read the printed reports of Parliament because they are in a language they do not understand (which says little—worse than little—for the *Zuid Afrikaan*, and the three or four gentlemen who so diligently report for Dutch papers); but English journalists may well complain to Mr. Hofmeyr that they cannot read the reports of his "Bestuur" meeting, as they are in Dutch.

We do not know what part Chief Justice Reitz took in the debates on the resolutions that England should leave Basutoland to the colonists; that unnecessary trains should be stopped; or in advocating protection for Colonial industries; but the Chief Justice of the Orange Free State was present, and must be held responsible for such resolutions. What he has to do with Colonial industries we do not know—though, when a judge becomes a party politician, he may also be interested in trade; and we cannot quite comprehend what it matters to a judge in the Free State whether trains run on Sundays or not.

It has been asserted, with some authority, that the President of the Free State informed the English Government that he looks to them to fulfil the Treaty of Aliwal; and, that treaty being fulfilled, Sir John Brand, in his opening speech to the Raad, gave it to be clearly understood that the State he presided over had nothing to say about the future of Basutoland. Is Chief Justice Reitz to be allowed by his own Government to come into the Colony, and assist in carrying a resolution, which, if accepted by the Home Government, must involve the Free State in a Basuto war? This question is one that might very well be asked of the English Secretary for Foreign Affairs. Possibly he may be questioned about it in the House of Lords; and we agree with the *Argus* in thinking that some enquiry will be made in the Colonial Legislature when it meets.

Mr. Hofmeyr has recently been telling some friends in Bloemfontein how far advanced in civilisation the Free State is as compared with the Colony. Cape Town has not such Houses of Parliament as adorn Bloemfontein; the senators do not dress themselves as elegantly, or as sombrely, as do the members of the Raad, and more in the same after-dinner style. When running down his countrymen, Mr. Hofmeyr might have added that the Cape Colony had not a Chief Justice who would so far forget himself, and so besmirch his ermine, as to visit the Colony to assist in organising a "Bestuur," with the object of disturbing and, perhaps, of destroying its established Government. There are some things done in the Colony that are not altogether to its credit.

As far as we know, all the English organs of public opinion in the Colony have of late years given expression to the most kindly sentiments towards the Orange Free State. They have drawn comparisons most favourable to the Republic, and have held up its example as one which, in many respects, deserves to be followed. Whatever unplesant things may have been said about the Free State by a section of the Colonists in times past, in those days we feel confident that Mr. Hofmeyr would have to search long for statements derogatory to that State, and, if he should succeed in finding them, he will only succeed in proving the rule by the exceptions.

The second statement of Mr. Hofmeyr, which calls for notice, is that, "The Rules of Order in the Free State Volksraad are superior to those of the Cape Parliament, and are better observed than is the case in the Cape Legislature. As to the superiority of the Volksraad Rules, we can express no opinion, not having seen them. Mr. Hofmeyr, who attended the Volksraad deliberations on one or two occasions, is, of course, in a position to judge; but to the assertion, or to the insinuation, that in the Cape Parliament the Rules of Order are but indifferently observed, we must take exception. Hitherto we have always been told, and we never have seen anything to persuade us into the belief that it was meant as an idle compliment or mere flattery, that the Cape Parliament is an exemplary body among colonial legislators ; nay, when we call to mind the scenes which in the British House of Commons have made the *Cloture* Bill a necessity, we do not see why we should not plainly say that, as to orderly conduct, the Cape Legislature is not inferior to its great model. Mr. Hofmeyr, who has been several years a member of the House of Assembly, may have noticed flagrant breaches of decorum and disregard of the rules of the House ; we must admit that they have altogether escaped our attention.

Then a comparison is drawn between the dress of the Volksraad members and that of our members. "The members of the Volksraad," says Mr. Hofmeyr, "are all properly dressed in black, while members of Parliament appear in fancy costumes, ornamented with neckties, which display the colours of the rainbow; nay, some even enter Parliament House in buttermilk trousers" (whatever this may mean).

It is certainly a novelty to have a legislature judged by the garments of its members ; and if there was any reason for presuming that a man is in a better position to vote for or against a new bridge, or for or against a Municipal Bill, when clothed in a black coat than he is in his every-day suit, then we also would declare in favour of black coats ; but, in our abject ignorance, we fail to see the connection between a black suit and a clear brain, and we, therefore, are profoundly indifferent about the colour of a legislator's wearing apparel.

"If, in the Free State," Mr. Hofmeyr goes on to say, "an election is going on, burghers come and they vote for their candidate. With us, in the Colony, it is not practicable, when the utmost trouble is taken, to bring the farmers to the polling place." This was the case in the years gone by ; but a vast change, for the better, has in this respect taken place during the last few years, and Mr. Hofmeyr, of all men, knows this. He has, therefore, been most unfair to his countrymen, when, in a neighbouring state, he painted them as so callous and indifferent. He surely must remember all the recent elections, that, at Oudtshoorn, the two at Swellendam, the one in the Midland Circle—where was the apathy with which he charges the farmers of this colony? If at Montagu, for instance, on an occasion when two gentlemen, who are both members of the Farmers' Protection Association, contest a seat, 261 out of 263 registered electors think it worth while to record their votes, we may safely challenge the Free State, or any other country under the sun, to compete with us in political activity.

And Mr. Hofmeyr proceeds to give the reason for this political torpor. "It is the language," he says. "The Boer in the Colony receives a notice, in English, at his residence to vote. He does not understand it, and he does not think it worth while to have it translated. He begrudges the money which he would have to pay an agent for translating." It is not clear to us what Mr. Hofmeyr means by the "notice" left at the Boer's residence? In the *Government Gazette*, these election notices are published in Dutch as well as in English, and though but few farmers ever see the *Gazette*, they are informed in the Dutch newspapers when the election takes place, and who the candidates are. The notice sent to their residences, referred to by Mr. Hofmeyr, can only mean notices sent round by the candidates themselves. And surely these men have sense enough not to send English notices to Dutch Boers!

When men are anxious to obtain votes, they are obliging enough as a rule, and they will be particularly careful not to offend any prejudices. But even supposing there were such fools in existence, will Mr. Hofmeyr seriously contend that there are any Dutch farmers in this country who will require a translator to tell them what "Vote for Barry" means? Really the Colonial farmers have little reason to feel flattered with the picture which Mr. Hofmeyr has seen fit to draw, and with the small modicum of intelligence with which he has credited them when he addressed an audience in a neighbouring state.

Inexplicable to us again is the next sentence. "The farmer takes not the least interest in the politics of his country! What then is the meaning of the numberless meetings of the Bond and of the Farmers' Associations? What means the innumerable resolutions discussed and passed at those meetings, dealing with every imaginable political question which now engages the attention of Parliament and of the public ? The farmers of the Colony are represented by the leader of the farmer party as taking " not the least interest " in the politics of their country ! Are " visions about ? " And then it is said they do not take that interest, because the Parliamentary reports are published in English ! Is there no *Zuid Afrikaan*, and is there no *Volksblud* which inform them in the vernacular of what takes place in Parliament ? And does not every Dutch newspaper in the country republish these reports ? Nay, are not even the laws passed by Parliament published in Dutch also, and obtainable by every person who desires to purchase them ?

We must conclude. Mr. Hofmeyr's peroration is devoted to the " United States of South Africa, extending from the Cape of Good Hope to the Zambesi." We must co-operate to bring that about, he says, and for that purpose the population must be reconciled and work in harmony. But we fear that if the men of the Free State do not take this after-dinner speech with a grain of salt, they will feel little inclined to ally themselves with so miserably ignorant and backward a lot as their Colonial brethren are, on the authority of Mr. Hofmeyr, M.L.A., the reputed leader of the Colonial party.

Time—the tyrant of us all—will wait for no man ; no, he would not even wait for the virgin Queen Elizabeth, though she offered to bribe the venerable scythe-bearer with pounds of the earnings of her subjects, for one day more, in order to enable her to satisfy her mind, and to put her affairs, as she called them, in order—a warning to us all not to put off till to-morrow what we can do to-day.

I was summoned by a stern demand to appear on the 16th of August, to resist a claim of £32. Although the man who made this claim had, as he himself swore, in his possession more money than the amount of the claim—money that I had entrusted him to collect for me—I was compelled to take him before three judges, in what is styled a High Court of Justice, to demand an account of him for a deficiency amounting to about one hundred and eighty pounds.

These judges, as in most other countries, turn what they designate their High Courts of Justice into halls of injustice—plenty of senseless form, ceremony, delay, and expense, but very little regard to the comfort and convenience of plaintiff, defendant, or witnesses. Why are magistrates and judges so unjust (seeing that they are not the masters of the people, but the servants of the inhabitants of a country that pays them enormous salaries for doing but little in return) as to allow a day to be named for the hearing of a case, and, when that day arrives, to hear actions of all kinds that could be disposed of in Chambers, thus causing delay, and multiplying the expenses and anxiety of both sides ? Many other questions might be asked, such as, Why don't the judges move for the expenses to be reduced, and security given for the costs by all who will rush into litigation, regardless of consequences, thereby encouraging lawyer-sharks to take up cases in the assurance that their expenses will be met by the man who defends his right, who, unlike his assailant, is not a man of straw, and who cannot disobey without fearful penalties the mandate of any court ? Why don't they move to allow merchants, or other competent inhabitants, with one judge or legal assessor to preside over them, to go into all commercial disputes and questions, with power to decide whether or not there exists any cause of action, and to take security for costs before any action can be brought in any court of law or equity whatever.

Of course, to all these questions, if I paused for a century, I should get no satisfactory answer. If they did answer, and truthfully, I should be told that they did not wish to prevent litigation ; that, in reality, it is their business to increase it, if possible, for the benefit of their numerous relations and the land monopolists in general.

To this I reply, we must reduce, as speedily as possible, these legal confiscators of our wealth ; take away their power, and the possibility of their ruining any man, who, by industry and carefulness, may have saved a little money, and who, in the present state of things, becomes a mark for all the lawyer-sharks who scheme to compass his ruin. Pass a law to make it compulsory to arbitrate outside the court of injustice, and give men of business a chance to settle commercial disputes, and a jury of inhabitants to arrange causes of quarrels before proceedings are allowed to be instituted elsewhere to incur expenses, and, it may be, ruin the defender of the right. Then there would be less wailing and gnashing of teeth from robbed merchants, and, as a possibility of getting rid of land and lawyer-sharks, and the numerous exploiters who so readily assist the land, money, mercantile, agricultural, home and share-making monopolists to confiscate, by a legal *ruse*, the producers' wealth, and, in so doing, reap where they have not sown, and are the main causes of the poverty which we find side by side in our midst, with the so-called rich, who are but living upon what they have stolen from labour's ranks. Once remove these unnumbered monopolists, and there will be a chance for the wealth producers; but I trust, in my *Political Economy*, to elucidate all these questions to the entire satisfaction of all who want to know the truth.

The disproportionate increase in the number of men who make a living by " business " other than that of productive industry, is beginning to be recognised as one of the greatest evils of the modern economic and social system. It is seen, of course, in its fullest development, in the United States, and fresh statistical instances of it are always coming to light. In 1856, for instance, there were 23,939 lawyers in that country; in 1870, 40,786; in 1880, 64,187; a supply quite out of proportion to the needs of the population. Once past a certain point, and the more lawyers the worse law. It it perfectly obvious that the object of a large number of these men must be not to do business, but to make it. We see the same phenomenon in other directions. The number of bankers, brokers, agents, and other auxiliaries of productive industry is out of all proportion to the regular army. If the time ever comes, as at the present rate of income it will come in half a century, when the States boast 200,000 lawyers, this new army of locusts will have become an even greater pest than the host of monks and friars who infested Europe on the eve of the Reformation; and the reforming of them will be no easy matter.

At last, after one day's waste of time for all parties concerned, and the best part of another, occupied in hearing motions, &c., I was called upon to give evidence. Wishing to affirm, to speak the truth, and not to swear, the judges referred to the law on the subject, but found no exemption clause, except for those goody, goody people, the Moravians and Quakers; so I had to give evidence in the usual way.

The Chief Justice said that the law upon the subject ought to be altered for the benefit of all, and I have no doubt that when the

I

Free State comes once more, by request of its inhabitants, under the control of the English, the law will be so modified as to meet all requirements; but certainly not before, for it seems, in this Free State, nobody's business to see that they keep pace with civilisation. The Dutchmen don't want change, so long as they can live on their farms, tax the commercial classes, forego paying for years their quit rents, enslave or apprentice their blacks, or shoot them down as thieves for taking cattle, because they had not paid them their wages. Living like Africanders, which means—eat, drink, and be merry with the women, they are content ; and so long as the foreign judges and officials can rob and plunder in the name of the Dutch, all things have, as the Cape Town President says, " to right come," and no change is desired. A change, however, *must* come ; but the intervening period will be short or long, in proportion to the poverty of the Free State in general, and its officials included.

On the 20th, the mountain, with its three judges, brought forth its mouse, in the form of the following decision, to the surprise of everyone who really expected a compromise to please the Dutch element :—

" M. J. Boon *v.* V. Van Reenen.

" After hearing counsel on behalf of both parties, the Court decided that, after allowing for natural waste, and deducting the amount for which defendant had given credit to customers, contrary to orders, and for which he acknowledged his liability in the present case ; there still remained a deficiency of some £110, in the amount of stock in the business not accounted for ; and that the defendant was liable for such deficiency, whether the loss arose from his having giving other credits, or from errors, thefts, and the like ; but that there was no reason to suppose that the deficiency was due to any dishonesty on the part of the defendant ; and gave judgment in favour of plaintiff to the amount of one hundred and fifty pounds, with costs."

The Court dismissed the claim in reconvention, with costs ; but, as the man was not worth a farthing, the costs fell upon me, and, as I was supposed to be able to pay the lawyer, he did not forget to charge me. It is this and other experiences that compel me to demand that no one should be allowed to bring an action into

Court unless he or they can give satisfactory security for costs. I know that the law is as uncertain in England and in other countries, as will be shown by the following extract from an English newspaper :—

"We are occasionally having striking examples of the certainty, cheapness, and charm of justice, as administered in our law courts. Perhaps the following is about the most striking : A Mr. Smitherman was killed in 1878, in attempting to cross the South-Eastern Railway, in front of a passing train. There were some circumstances which tended to show that the Company was in fault. The widow brought an action for compensation, and recovered £900 at the Assizes. The Exchequer Division thereupon granted the defendant Company a new trial. This decision was reversed by the Court of Appeal, and their decision was reversed by the House of Lords. Thus the matter had been four times before a judicial tribunal. This, however, turned out to be only a beginning. A new trial, in accordance with the decision of the Lords, was held in London. Again the jury found for the widow, but this time with only £700 damages. Unfortunately, wanting, as juries do, to seem very wise, they appended to their verdict an expression of opinion that both the Company and the deceased had been guilty of negligence. This opened a nice little question of what lawyers call 'contributory negligence.' Application was therefore made—first to the Queen's Bench, and then to the Court of Appeal, to enter the verdict for the defendants on the finding of the jury. This failed. The matter had now been seven times in a court of law; but the Company were not daunted. They attempted to set aside the verdict, as being against the weight of evidence. The Court of First Instance would not help them, nor would the Court of Appeal; but the House of Lords has taken a different view. Hence, after ten arguments, before I don't know how many judges, and thousands had been spent in solicitors' bills of costs and counsels' fees, the matter is—to begin all over again!"

A friend, who had lived in the Free State, told me that after twenty years' experience, during which he had had twelve cases in the Law Courts, and in which he always ought to have been the gainer, he lost, owing to bad law, lawyers, agents, the poverty of his assailant, or to the ante-nuptial cover of his opponent. The

following illustrates the ante-nuptial arrangements generally :—
"In our country," said the Englishman, as he leaned back in his chair, "before we marry we arrange to settle a certain sum upon the wife." "Yes, I know," replied the African, "but with us it is different. It is after we are married that we settle everything on the wife, and arrange to beat our creditors." "Haw, I see. And how do the creditors take it?" "They never find anything to take!"

And such was my experience, after this decision.—I came across the proprietor and editor of the *Dutch Express*, who, after expressing his sympathy, assured me that after all my "cases" and unpleasant experience, there was the silver lining to the cloud in the knowledge of the Free State *Express*. I smiled, and passed on; for at that time, I was not disposed to combat any argument or statement; but a few days afterwards I had an opportunity of knowing that the Press can be a power to harass and injure as well as to support; but I protest against this common cry and agree with the subjoined words of Edwin Heron :

> Perhaps it may be thought you could discern
> One other means by which to serve your turn,
> And while these natural forces all confess
> Are grown too weak, too sordid, try the Press,
> If you believe the voice is talking still
> Out of an honest heart and fervent will,
> As when men spoke their thought, and when their word
> Sounded like thunder, and the people heard;
> If you conceive that in the latter days
> There burned one flicker of that ancient blaze:
> When like a beacon on each lofty height
> Each nobler spirit caught and gave the light;
> If you imagine that the hackney's pen
> Can win its wages, and win also men.
> Or that these sightless leaders of the blind
> Can keep the trust, or gain it, of mankind;
> Dismiss the fancy, scout the idle dream,
> And learn that things exist not as they seem.
> I grant that men at the present hour,
> The faded echo re-unites its former power;
> But just as trembling savages adore
> The fetish worshipped by their sires of yore.
> So though your fourth estate affects to rule,
> Its bluster only serves to scare the fool.
> Distrust the moral that it fain would tell :

It does not write to teach—it writes to sell.
Trust me, a nation's teachers never stoop
To act the sycophant, to catch the dupe;
Nor would they, if they held their vaunted power,
Retail the gossip of the passing hour;
Nor in a sea of soft sensation splash,
Nor vend a racing prophet's slangy trash.
Nor scribble cockney talk of fells and streams,
Nor dribble science and its airy dreams,
Nor twaddle on the marriage of a peer,
Nor meet stern anger with a clever sneer,
Nor always wait upon the " upper ten,"
Nor write as " gentlemen for gentlemen,"
Nor chatter to a city of the dead,
And never touch one heart or teach one head.
Give me a man that loves, a man that hates,
And I may think he means the thing he states;
What leisure or what patience serves to heed
The idle chat which languid quidnuncs read?

CHAPTER XI.

OME days after this, I learned that my own expenses, in the form of a lawyer's bill, were over £77 and, by way of "adding insult to injury," the defendant's lawyer, after putting me to this expense, had the impudence to ask whether I would not pay *him* the amount of ten pounds odd, as expenses incurred. Really, I was so disgusted at his mercenary begging disposition that I felt convinced the Maitland Street would-be-lawyer for everybody would not be above stealing, if he ran no risk of being found out, seeing that after urging my opponent to sue me for what I did not owe, and then after putting me to such an outlay for costs, yet had the audacity to prefer such a request. Truly the Free State lawyers were, as one woman had the courage to say in open Court, only legal swindlers, thieves and black-coated rascals.

Such was my indignation at this mean wretch that if I dared I would have slain him, and the difficulty of burying such human carrion alone stayed me from removing him from the midst of that humanity his very existence disgraced and polluted.

Just on the eve of my leaving for the Colony, I experienced another loss. I had a horse, that cost me £25, to dispose of— wishing to sell rather than feed the animal during my absence. Picture my surprise when, after handing over to two men the horse to test its qualities, they simply cleared out of the town without paying me; and, to my further astonishment, I found that they had lived upon the hotel-keeper for two months, and had got deeply in debt all round the town. This was quite a common thing out in that Free State, whence, after taking all they could get hold of, they passed on to steal the land and goods in Stellaland; and the corn-lanky Dutchman was no exception to this eating upon English importers.

Feeling outraged by such a bare-faced robbery I, acting upon the advice of the Landdrost's clerk, declared that under a pretence of examining the animal and an agreemsnt, if they approved of it, to pay me the cash at a certain time, instead of which they ran off with the horse, and having failed to pay their just debts in town it was a fair inference that they had stolen the horse. The clerk thereupon at once made out a warrant for their apprehension, and owing to their being in debt to others—but from no desire to help me on the part of the black-blooded Dutch Sheriff—the warrant was executed. The men, however, took the precaution of providing the amount of cash, so that when in town—having explained that they had paid it in Ladybrand—they were released. A second warrant was at once issued against them upon another charge, but this not being my business I dismissed them from my mind. Judge then of my feelings, when I was threatened with a law suit, for a £1000 damages, for—as they called it—false imprisonment.

This was the information I received on my return to Bloemfontein, and at a time when, to make me still more enraged, I had to suffer from the robbery by the German villain at Paradise. Truly this trading-place, called Paradise, was a Hell to me; for I had to make a claim against him for £1,042, and when other incidental expenses were added bringing it up to £1,200—which, however, was a total loss to me; for although there was £600 in bad debts due to him—which was never collected—and anything else that remained was eaten up by the lawyer-sharks.

To make this matter even worse, the friend who had so mismanaged the business, availing himself of the looseness of the Dutch conditions, threatened me with a claim for damages, etc., which fortunately—like the threat for damage for false imprisonment—by sheer doggedness, on my part, came to naught; but only after months of annoyance to me in the attempt to still further rob me of my small possessions.

The Judgment against my employee for £159 and costs, was the finishing stroke to my patience. The lawyer-shark in defending this case brought me in the following bill of £77 11s.:—

In the High Court of Bloemfontein,
In the Orange Free State.
In the case
F. Van Reenen ... Plaintiff, in Reconvention
against
M. J. Boon ... Defendant, in Reconvention.

Account of Disbursements made and salary earned by H. Bier, Defendant's Attorney, in said case for the payment of £100, real injuries, etc.

	Disbursements.			Salary.		
	£	s.	d.	£	s.	d.
Instruction to draw out Defence				0	5	0
Attending to hand over Defence to contra party				0	4	0
Drawing out Defence				3	3	0
Original				2	2	0
Two copies at £1 1s. each				2	2	0
Drawing up Notice to make out taxation				0	5	0
Copies, at 2s. 6d.				0	2	6
Attending on receipt of claim in Reconvention				0	2	0
Do. to hand in pleadings				0	2	0
Do. with resumption of documents				0	7	0
Do. to consult with Client				1	1	0
Do. to be present at Taxation of Account				0	4	0
Do. pleading case, first day				0	4	0
Making out account				0	10	0
Duplicate				0	10	0
				11	3	6
Taxation				0	9	0
[Stamp 9s.] Total				£11	12	6

Agreed,—Eleven pound, twelve shillings, sixpence sterling, against the Plaintiff in Reconvention.

The 27th day of August, 1883.

(Signed) JAMES A. COLLINS,
Acting Registrar of the Court.

In the High Court of Bloemfontein,
  In the Orange Free State.
    In the case
  M. J. Boon ... ... Plaintiff
      contra
  F. Van Reenen ... ... Defendant.
Account of Expenses and Salary earned by H. Bier, Plaintiff's Attorney, in said case, for account to be rendered to, or payment of £180 7s. 10d., etc.

	Disbursement. £ s. d.	Salary. £ s. d.
Letter of demand		0 5 0
Copy		0 4 0
Drawing out Power		0 5 0
Attendance to have the same signed ...		0 4 0
Instruction to Sheriff about serving of Summons		0 5 0
Do. to pay Sheriff for serving Summons		0 4 0
Attendance to take out Summons ...		0 2 0
Do. for handing same to Sheriff ...		0 4 0
Do. to pay Sheriff for serving Summons		0 4 0
Do. for looking over his Return ...		0 4 0
Drawing out Summons		1 10 0
Original		1 1 0
Two copies at 10s. 6d. each		1 1 0
Paid to Sheriff for serving Summons ...	0 7 0	
Notice requiring Defence (made out) ...		0 5 0
Two copies at 2s. 6d.		0 5 0
Making out Notice of Documents to be handed in		0 5 0
Two copies at 2s. 6d.		0 5 0
Making out Notice of domicile		0 5 0
Two copies at 2s. 6d.		0 5 0
Making out Notice requiring Rejoinder		0 5 0
Two copies at 2s. 6d.		0 5 0
Carried forward ...	0 7 0	7 13 0

	Disbursements.	Salary.
	£ s. d.	£ s. d.
Brought forward ...	0 7 0	7 13 0
Making out Notice of Documents to be handed in		0 15 0
Two copies at 2s. 6d.		0 5 0
Making out Notice of Taxation		0 5 0
Copy at 2s. 6d.		0 2 6
Instruction to draw out Replication ...		— —
Do. to Sheriff about serving do. ...		0 5 0
Attendance to hand over Replication to contra party		0 4 0
Making out Replication		3 3 0
Original		2 2 0
Two copies at £1 1s.		2 2 0
Attending to receive Defence		0 2 0
Do. do. Notice of documents to be handed in by Defendant..		0 2 0
Do. to receive Notice of Domicile...		0 2 0
Do. to hand in Pleadings		0 2 0
Do. with resumption of documents		0 7 0
Do. to consult with Client in Convention		1 1 0
Do. with two witnesses at 7s. 6d. each		0 15 0
Do. settling with two witnesses, at 4s. each		0 8 0
Do. case heard—twice postponed...		1 1 0
Do. settling with Defendant ...		0 4 0
Do. to be present at Taxation of Account		0 4 0
Do. and Pleading case—1st day ...		5 5 0
Do. do. do. 2nd day ...		6 6 0
Do. Sworn Translator for translating one document ...		0 4 0
Do. to pay Sworn Translator ...		0 4 0
Copies	11 2 0	
Carried forward	11 9 0	33 3 6

		Disbursements.	Salary.
		£ s. d.	£ s. d.
Brought forward	...	11 9 0	33 3 6
Translations	...	5 12 6	
Making out Account	...		0 10 0
Duplicate	...		0 10 0
Stamps	£1 13 0		
Power	0 1 6		
Document ...	0 4 0		
		1 18 6	
Paid to witnesses:—			
H. Drinkwater, three days...		1 10 0	
C. G. Hudgson, three days...	...	1 10 0	
		22 0 0	33 13 6
		33 13 6	
		55 13 6	
Taxation	...	1 7 0	
Total ...	...	£57 0 6	

[Stamp 7s.]
[Stamp 20s.]

Agreed to—Fifty-seven pound, — shillings, and sixpence sterling against the Defendant.

The 27th day of August, 1883.

(Signed)

JAMES A. COLLINS,

Acting Registrar of the Court.

In the High Court of the Orange Free State,

At Bloemfontein.

In the case

M. J. Boon

v.

V. Van Reenen.

Account of Disbursements made and Salary earned by H. Bier, Attorney of Plaintiff, in said matter regarding the Exception :—

	£	s.	d.
Instruction to Defend against the Exception ...	0	5	0
Drawing out Defence against Exception	3	3	0
Original do do.	2	2	0
Two copies at £1 1s.	2	2	0
Attending consultation with Client on Exception ...	0	10	6
Attending Taxation	0	4	0
Notice of Taxation, with copy	0	7	6
Attending to the settlement	0	4	0
	£8	18	0

Taxed at £8 18 0

(Signed)
JAS. A. COLLINS,
Asst. Reg. High Court.

From this my readers will have an abundant opportunity of convincing themselves of accuracy of my assertions, borne out—as they are—by the following remarks in the *Friend* of the Free State :—

"It did our hearts good when we read your leading article last week, anent the monstrous charge a client is put to to have his rights upheld by the law courts of this State. I am sorry you did not express yourself in stronger terms. It is an admitted fact that to obtain justice, in this State, costs money; and the Courts as constituted in Britain really give our law-makers in this State, if they wish to follow it up, an easy mode and cheap means of getting rights upheld. To give you an instance of what recently took place here in the Landdrost Court. A plaintiff appears. He has two cases against the defendant, respectively £25 and £36 sterling. The Landdrost of Jacobsdal gave judgment. Plaintiff's Attorney takes out a writ, and in each case the defendant has to pay £22 sterling and £18, together with costs: £40 to recover £60. Suppose now that the Sheriff brings a return of *nulla bona*, plaintiff has then to pay costs—which otherwise defendant had to pay. In case of no *nulla bona*, what does the plaintiff actually gain? for in these cases he has to pay all the attorney's travelling expenses, which will no doubt at the lowest come to £10. Execution will follow, proceeds of sale amount to nothing at all, simply costs to pay the Sheriff for work, publication in the *Courant*, &c."

So that my legal robberies and my business robbery—mainly due to the shark who drew up the bond, who misled me as to its value, and which being written in Dutch gave no light to guide me—cost me in a few months as under :—

Paradise-Hell robbery	£1042
Employee in business	227
Personal and sundry expenses for the whole ...	330

In all £1500 odd, the cost of Private, Legal, Parliamentary, and Public Robberies.

Now if, after this, anyone wonders at my condemnation of the Free State managers, they need indeed eyes to see, ears to hear, and brains to understand. I have written strongly of the man who so deceived me in the management of the business at Paradise; but when I mention that he knew of the bond that was given to me fraudulently—a judgment having been given against my original debtor, but not executed until an opportunity occurred to put a claim against my property—and that he was drunk at the time of the Sheriff taking possession, and thus helped to rob me ; being in hope, as I afterwards learned, of an opportunity of helping himself at my expense, did not protect my interests, although in receipt of £20 per month ; and thus my original desire to save about £250 was frustrated owing to my need of depending upon outside help, and the impossibility of relying upon honest legal help—and the hasty legislation of its Boer Parliament at £2 a day, headed by its incapable President at £3000 a year, in allowing such legislation in a hurricane, to the injury of its English supporters. The mere fact of writing strongly in the face of all these facts, can be understood and felt for ; more especially when it is known that it could all have been prevented if ordinary arrangements, as in England, were followed out.

"Complaints are continually being made of the expensive machinery of our Free State Courts. The rooted horror of law induced by the fear of a lawyer's bill, often accounts for people paying any moderate claim made on them, so long as it does not amount to extortion, rather than run the gauntlet of an action-at-law. And some do not care to press a just claim against a person who may be of little means and of doubtful honesty, because the expenses of the winning party are often more than the sum in dispute. We believe in the Colony there is a small debts Court. In England there are County Courts, which are the machinery for collecting a great number of small debts, and thousands of cases are annually disposed of by these Courts. A judge presides and business is carried on very expeditiously. Sometimes a jury of five men, substituted for the traditional twelve, is called to the Judge's assistance, especially if the case, being too trifling for the higher tribunals, has been sent down to the Court below. An appeal lies from the decision of a County Court Judge, if it can be made out that a question of law is involved. The County Court Judge not only gives judgment against a debtor, but he generally breaks the blow of his judgment by allowing the defaulter to satisfy the claim in easy instalments. We cannot help thinking that something of this sort should answer well in the Free State. The tariff is now so high as to be well-nigh intolerable. We have heard of people suing a debtor for a few pounds in our lower courts and being mulct in about £25 for law costs! We are no well-wishers to the lawyers and agents, and we think the line should be drawn somewhere. It appears monstrous that justice should not be often obtained simply because the costs in a case are so high as to deter creditors from suing debtors. We are not aware of the tariff of the Colonial lower courts, but we are led to believe that it is considerably lower than ours. We shall proceed to give a few of the charges for bringing, say a claim of £5 to £10, in our lower court. There is first 12s. for the stamp on the summons; 1s. 6d. stamp on every subpœna; 1s. on every translation, abstract, or other document, delivered in; 1s. 6d. on every special power of attorney; retaining fee for agent 10s.; letter of demand, 5s.; making out power of attorney, 5s.; drawing summons, from half a guinea to a guinea, for defending a case if witnesses are heard, three guineas for the first day and two guineas for every subsequent day; and 2s. to the messenger for serving the summons. Besides these there are the thousand and one little charges and costs for stamps and salary, which anyone who has seen a lawyer's bill of costs can readily understand. Now we consider this tariff altogether too high for the lower courts. If parties have thousands and thousands of pounds at stake they must expect to risk a few pounds in recovering their own, but we maintain it is not only monstrous, but the ends of justice are defeated by the tariff being so high that no one can sue a debtor for a small sum without risking more than double the amount in doing so. We should have thought it might have been possible to set apart one day in the week for the hearing of cases similar to those brought before a County Court at Home. There you do not require to be much of a lawyer to carry your own case through, as there is not, as in the High Court, any of the 'preliminary skirmishing of pleadings.'"

Draft Ord. No. 1,000. A1.

(For consideration by the Triumvirate, &c.)

The Volksraad being mindful of the provision in the now existing Constitution (adopted from the earlier Constitutions), that "the law is for all equal," and desiring to compensate the sufferers from the injurious consequences of contraventions of that principle, enacts as follows :—

1.—That henceforth each stock farmer shall pay yearly, as licence for freedom to earn his bread, the sum of ten pounds sterling for each thousand morgen, or less, which he possesses or uses.

2.—That henceforward each agriculturist shall pay yearly, as licence to be allowed to work, the sum of ten pounds sterling for each acre or less, sowing or garden ground which he cultivates.

3.—That as stock farmers and agriculturists have hitherto (for 30 years) escaped payment of licences to carry on their occupations, each stock farmer and each agriculturist shall within one year pay thirty times the sum claimable from them respectively, under the foregoing articles; and the sum to be collected under this article shall be equitably divided among the shopkeepers, canteenkeepers, and others who formerly paid licences contrary to the provision that "the law is for all equal," to compensate them for all the licences heretofore paid by them. Where such licence payers are already deceased, their shares can be claimed by heirs and creditors.

4.—That whereas hitherto has been exacted from practitioners in the law, contrary to the Constitution, four per cent. on the amount of their bills of costs for their earnings, henceforward to make all square the same rule will be applied to all officials, stock farmers, agriculturists, and others who have hitherto escaped taxation upon their income, and they shall now pay four per cent. on the amount of their yearly income, while practitioners in the law shall be freed from the tax alluded to for thirty years.

Draft Ordinance No. 1,001. AA1.

The Volksraad, desiring to do right and justice, enacts as follows :—

1.—The Judges, high and low, including Landdrosts whose decisions have been, or shall be, set aside, or altered in appeal, shall respectively bear the costs of suitors in the original and appeal cases, and on non-payment they shall be immediately dismissed from office and cast into prison for the term of their natural lives and no longer.
2.—All markets are abolished, and all stock and produce shall be sold only according to valuation by a jury, consisting of the person who wishes to buy and two of his friends. Contraveners are to be hung without form of legal process.
3.—Any stock farmers or agriculturists, who shall be caught in presenting for sale any deceased or crippled animals, unwholesome oat-sheaves, emaciated fowls or ducks, unripe potatoes, rotten tobacco, unserviceable butter, dirty and sandy wool, and such scandalous things, shall be banished from the country and their property confiscated to the State.

Draft Ord. No. The Last. AAA1.

The Volksraad, considering that it is expected from the Legislature that it shall make, repair, and patch laws, enacts as follows :—

1.—That all laws regarding which any difference, in regard to the interpretation or meaning thereof, can arise, are hereby repealed and declared of no effect, and the makers of such incomprehensive laws, as far as they may be come-at-able are fined each in the sum of one hundred pounds sterling in favour of the treasury of this State. Such fine to be levied without any form of legal process in execution against the persons and properties of the guilty.

2.—That to obviate any further clashing in regard to the remaining laws (if any) the Judges are commanded, on a penalty of banishment in case of non-compliance, to give within one year *one* unalterable interpretation of all remaining laws. Such interpretation shall be printed in the *Government Gazette*, and thereafter no earlier law-book shall be taken into consideration.

3.—That as probably all earlier judical sentences, civil as well as criminal, were faulty, all decisions of Courts or Judges are hereby repealed, and parties are invited except those who have undergone capital punishment, to proceed at law *de novo*.

4.—That as it is advisable that legislators should study, and as enough laws have been made, no further Ordinances shall be discussed for one hundred years.

Supported by various Colonial organs of public opinion, extracts wherefrom I have somewhat liberally quoted, I have in the immediately preceding pages endeavoured faithfully, although—I am painfully conscious—inadequately, to portray for the edification and enlightenment of my readers the scandalous and disgraceful condition of all things pertaining to the judicial office and the legal profession generally—I had almost, and without any great breach of propriety or veracity, might have said universally—in that morally, socially, and *professionally* pestilent Republic known as the Free State. With regard to the three Draft Ordinances—1000 A1., 1001 AA1., and AAA1.,—the reader will experience no difficulty in grasping the satire therein contained, and he will I feel satisfied unreservedly admit its force and appropriateness to the circumstances. These Ordinances were proposed by—satirically, of course—and printed in the *Friend* as a "perfect cure" for all Legal, Clerical, Commercial, Agricultural, Legislative and Presidential Rascality.

K

All these small matters can be settled by a Judge and at a little cost in England, and why not in the Free State? Echo answers, that for the sake of plunder the President, the Judge, and all the Officials wink at such deeds, and sanction such bare-faced actions and robberies in a "Free State" where a man should have full faith in his fellow man. What a libel upon a Free State Republic; and I fear this state of things will continue until the horror and fear of losing all, the Boer and other inhabitants of the Free State —like the Boers of the Transvaal—will cry out to the English to come over and save them from their Presidents, Hollanders, Germans, and other robbing officials.

Chapter XII.

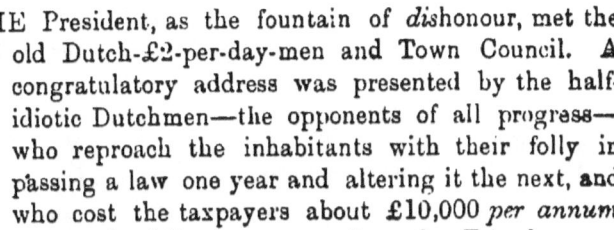HE President, as the fountain of *dis*honour, met the old Dutch-£2-per-day-men and Town Council. A congratulatory address was presented by the half-idiotic Dutchmen—the opponents of all progress—who reproach the inhabitants with their folly in passing a law one year and altering it the next, and who cost the taxpayers about £10,000 *per annum* —as will be seen by the following extract from the *Friend* :—

" *Our Dear 'Landvaders.'*—Last year these ' precious gems ' cost the country £9,153. A memorial will, we understand, be sent in to the Volksraad by the 'Landsmeeders,' offering to do the talkee-talkee for a third of that amount. That retrenchment is imperative, is indicated by the debit balance of £84,000. Therefore let the ' mother ' try their hands at making both ends meet, and permit the ' Landsvaders ' for a while to enjoy their *otium cum dig.*"

These men are not elected for any ability, but simply because they possess lands that they or their fathers stole from the natives. This President, with his speeches of fulsomeness and " bunkum," only needed the services of a scene painter to make the whole thing look thoroughly ridiculous. If the Council had made the necessary arrangements for the amusement of the existent and all future inhabitants, the artist might have painted a scene depicting the President, with a well-worn shamboc in his hand, in the act of conferring the honour (?) of knighthood. With a flourish of the shamboc the President slashes across the back of the kneeling old-fashioned God—Hard (for the time being the God-head of the town), and ere the blow descends upon the postulant, he promptly resumes the perpendicular in response to the President's command "Rise, Sir Knight of the Trowel and Fumigating House ;" to Stock—a low-born German ostler—" Rise, Sir Knight of the Brandy Bottle ;" to little Arthur—the mean dog of Petticoat Lane—"Rise, Sir Knight of the public Agapemone ;" to Bloemingtone, "Rise, Sir Knight Panderer, Flatterer, and Tom Noodle of my Court ;" to Clarkson, "Rise, Sir Knight of the Deal Box ; may you, for this honour, bury me for nothing when I cease to be an encumbrance upon this long suffering English people ;" and so on for the noble vote of not to exceed £10.

This disgusting aping of the miserable customs of older countries is simply so child-like and idiotic that one wonders how the hard In-Man can tolerate it. He may explain it on the principle that he never, after dessert, would expect to be paid for being Court Milliner. It is said that the President flatters the Dutch on the one hand, while he takes their money and that of the English on the other, for fear that—at some future time—the Dutch, finding out what an old woman they have had at their head so long, should give him and his family their sudden discharge, and that then being pensioned, like President Burger, he could go to the English for support. Perhaps it may be said this is awfully strong language. True, and I admit it ; but when I witness such base crawling to a man of no genius—yet at the head of a people that dare to insult Englishmen, after all the advantages reaped by them from English capital and enterprise, both of the mother-country and her colonies—I am filled with such loathing that I feel the time has come to expose them in all their deformity.

I don't pretend to write gracefully, or to spare the feelings of these heartless, cruel, mean Boers. I have felt degraded as an Englishman, at the rough bully swart Dutchmen, who never knew or wanted to know their mothers, but who had the audacity to tell Englishmen that they—the half blacks with Dutch names—were better than the Saxon ; and that it was only through pity for our families that we were not turned out homeless ; and when a minister of the Dutch Church in Smithfield urged the Dutch to give notice to what they—in their impudence and insolence—called *uitlander* to clear out, my blood boiled to know that much of this was due to the folly of a Colley and the weakness of a Gladstone.

The following from the *Friend* will doubtless prove interesting.

A Modern Daniel.

"We hear that the Rev. Mr. van Niekerk, of Smithfield, preached on the occasion of Independence Day a most spiteful sermon against all Europeans in general, and the English in particular, and that the 'discourse' gave great offence to the public. It is said, he expressed himself to the effect that no Europeans ought to have a seat again in the Volksraad or in the Cape Parliament; and that, in a couple of years, the prayer that every *uitlander* should be out of office—or words to that effect—would be answered and his prophecy fulfilled. This is the same reverend gentleman who did his level best to bring our Dutch Reformed Minister into hot water at the Synod, in May last, for using the English language in the pulpit; and he would no doubt have made himself conspicuous if he had been among those degenerate *uitlanders*—Peter and the Apostles, on the day of Pentecost—by 'mocking' because they spoke other tongues than the mellifluous *landstaal*! This reverend gentleman draws a salary from the State Exchequer and then uses his pulpit for political purposes and to vent his hatred against Europeans generally. We think it is high time that the Synod or the Volksraad took notice of his desecration of God's house. He should not forget that millions of Europeans belong to his Church, and that the good old faith was kept pure by the *uitlanders*, who finally planted the Church in this land—the Church of which he is a minister."

Perhaps some one will say, "all this language will help to bring on a civil war among the white races in Africa." Granted; so much the better, I am not one to ask for the deluge in our children's time, and "Peace in our time, O Lord." The time has arrived when the English, representing all that is grand, enterprising, and loyal to law and order, must not be spat upon by the bastards of the Colonies, who dare to reproach and use even our own weapons against us. This is not a work of love on my part; it is the work of necessity, the outcome of watching and of facts.

The time has come for no more pandering to prejudices, and fawning upon Germans, Jews, or Hollanders, with all their blatant loud-mouthed impudence. It was not possible for an Englishman to be treated fairly in any sense, and at last it was considered legitimate conduct to plunder and annoy any Englishman, until through very want he failed to express his manliness and nationality. These results were mainly due to the outrageous folly in the Transvaal and of the fools in power at that period. It may be said that my self-esteem has been wounded. Granted; I feel, as an Englishman, we should hold the front place on the Continent of South Africa, by virtue of the many, many sacrifices made by the English nation, individually and collectively, as all history proves; and are we to be driven out of our Colonies, as we have been out of England, by the Germans, Jews and other foreigners? I feel that I must, at all times, expose these impostors at English expense, aided by the folly of our Premier Gladstone, &c.

Idolatry.

John Bull is very much addicted to idolatry in one shape or the other. His present weakness is the Right Hon'ble. W. E. Gladstone, better known in the Colony as the "Wizard of the North." We have the idol at Leeds, and the calves of the bull sucking in every frothy utterance, as children suck honey. A man in his position must speak, and that plentifully. He has to study his audience, and coin sentences to suit the hour and the people. A very pleasant game of excitement to play, especially to a man fertile in resources, and mentally endowed with great and versatile gifts. But even this picture has an opposite side The man who is constantly haranguing people as to what he has done, and what he intends to do, speaks advisedly of the future, and plays fast-and-loose with the interests of a great empire, such a man I say, has much to answer for, because his listeners, as a rule, have more tenacious memories, and are more or less impressed with the idea. The man means what he says, and intends to fulfil what he so unctuously promises. As time wings its flight, and events occur exactly opposite to what was predicted by the idol, then the multitude, by some process known only to themselves, gradually come to the conclusion that they have been bowing to a false idol, and immediately the people who were so lavish in their praises of the said image, forthwith merge into iconoclasts, and down goes the great idol, amid howls and execrations. The people, as a natural rule, then cast about for a new thing to worship. Idols have ever been plentiful, and the void is presently filled, to end in the same result. The present British idol came in with a great flourish of mob music and much eating of humble pie. I allude to his wild assertions anent Austria, when in Midlothian, and to his ultimately eating the largest leek ever swallowed by an English prime minister in London. It has ever appeared to my obtuse faculties something of the marvellous that a man should be convinced, and then convince his audience that such and such things pertain to Austria, and when he is questioned, after a few miles of travel to London, distinctly pleads previous ignorance, and forthwith abases himself in "sackcloth and ashes." The least that can be said is that it is good evidence of an intemperate-minded man. A chilly unbelief steals over one, when one contemplates such a man being at the helm of the State ship. It would be too lengthy a subject to follow the idol through all the tortuous, word-twisting casuistry, sophistry, cajolery, &c., which he has displayed since assuming office. I shall content myself with airing a few of the remarks made by the idol at Guildhall. The idol was safely delivered of a long speech on things in general, and nothing in particular. Amongst other golden sentences which fell from this most wonderful piece of clay, was the following, in relation to African affairs: "He was happy to say he had initiated a policy which would reconcile all the conflicting races and blood in that hitherto unhappy country." Then later on, he assured the mayor and audience " that he could not speak with certainty as to the future; in fact, he had no control over the future." This is about equivalent to a schoolboy saying he could not control the sun. The view I take of the matter is this; When the idol takes so much credit to itself and party for the great good they have vouchsafed to the people of Africa, and becomes eloquent on the lasting peace which is to settle over the land; that it never occurred to the idol and satellites that the very great and good work they have accomplished here is but the foundation of the fabric which is to rise in the future, over which the "People's William" confesses he exercises no control.

The utterances, both wild and reckless, about "reconciling races" and "lasting peace" are taken by Colonial-bred men to mean an immense mirage, interwoven with gross delusions. It was a saying of the late Abraham Lincoln that "you should not stop to swop horses in the stream." Unfortunately for South Africa, that is just what has occurred. When we had one of the most eminent Colonial statesmen that England can produce among us, a man with a comprehensive grasp of mind, and a varied experience amid the native races of the earth, with a Colonial prime minister in accord with him, and a great Englishman statesman at the head of affairs in England—when the horizon appeared to indicate that peace, formed in stability, and not the phantom of of jugglers, would serenely lie like a morning cloud over this country,—who, but the party now in office, with their belongings and hangers on, clamoured for the recall of Frere and the installation of peace. And it must not be forgotten that the said party in England was ably seconded by a large part of the Press in South Africa. When I say the Press I include the many abortions that the name of Press covers. And to "what complexion have we arrived?" The question is easily put, but it requires careful thought to answer it. The outlook to an African or Colonial born man, is not by any means assuring It cannot for a moment be supposed that we can take the *colcur de rose* view that the English people do. Colonial wars with them mean taxes, with us they signify supremacy—life or death. When the idol tells them that he has settled the Colonial bill, and assures them there will be no wars, and they will not be constrained to dip into their purses, it is only natural that they will believe such a golden statement in preference to a statistical argument that Great Britain must disburse thirty or forty millions to put African affairs on a firm and safe basis. To the Africans we are forcibly reminded of Æsop's fable of the "Boys and the Frogs." After much stone-throwing between political parties in England, during which each side appears to have enjoyed it immensely, we are very apt to say, "What is sport to you is death to us." But is time to nutshell the whole matter? War in Africa has not ceased; it exists among the black races at present, with power to extend to the white ditto. The Basuto peace is still in the purchase stage, the bargains so far being all on the one side. Loyalty has had the most crushing defeat at the hands of the Gladstone Ministry that loyalty ever received from any ministry, barring the Scanlen Ministry. The Transvaal peace hinges on how much the idol will allow them yearly to behave themselves, and also how much he is prepared to wink at, supposing the Boers think fit to sweeten up our black brethren. To my mind, it appears very doubtful, whether if a collision took place between the Dutch and blacks, "which always was and always will be," Gladstone would interfere. His genius would most assuredly point out that the Dutch had no other course to pursue, that for the very existence of the Republic it was necessary to subdue the natives. He (the idol) would call them rebels in this case. Certainly Gladstone would not send troops. That would mean expense, and he kindly tells Britons every day he won't put them to such horrible suffering. And after the exhibition of the British army in Africa, it would, no doubt, be to our benefit to keep such luxuries (useless as they are expensive) at home. In the meantime, who is to allay the storms awaiting us in the dim future? Are we, the people of Africa, shivered into atoms by prejudices and jealousies, to rule coming events? Are the political mountebanks, now in office in England going to hush the elements? Query. I want Free Englishmen to chew the cud of reflection, and not call each other ugly names

Chapter XIII.

O N August the 5th Sepinare, the Free State made Chief of the Barolongs, arrived in Bloemfontein to complete a Treaty of Amity with the Free State; the said Treaty to be broken, and advantage taken of the same, whenever it might please the Dutch Government, Hollanders and Germans to do so. This Sepinare was not the rightful heir: but simply made the Chief for the time being and to be removed at the will or caprice of the Free State Governors.

To give to the proceedings an appearance of legitimacy, a Resident was appointed at a salary of twelve hundred a year, paid by the Barolongs and levied by this Sepinare. One bully of a lawyer was silenced on behalf of the Barolong Government by having given to him the use of a sheep-farm, which, when the end of this Chief arrives, will be made over in due course— another mode of plundering the natives. In proof that this was all arranged for we refer the reader to the following extract from the *Friend* of September 20th, 1883:—

The Barolong Commotion.

There has been no end of rumours afloat during the week respecting a threatened invasion of the Barolong territory by some of Samuel Moroka's partisans. One account was that some of the Barolongs over the Vaal-river had crossed that river armed to the teeth, with the intention of succouring Samuel and deposing Sepinare. It may be true that some of Moshette's or Montsioa's men, who are geting tired of being pushed from pillar to post by the gentlemen volunteers who fought for those chieftains, are trekking to either Samuel or Sepinare with no hostile intentions to the one or other, and that some people have ascribed this movement on the part of the Transvaal Barolongs to the intrigues of Samuel. Another rumour current was to the effect that some of our burghers were behind Samuel, and were egging him on to try conclusions with Sepinare. We understand that the Government received information that a rumpus was brewing; consequently, steps have been taken to secure the neutrality of the State. Sepinare is also not asleep. He has, we are assured, strong armed parties out on the watch on the border, and has entrusted the defence of his whole territory to that well-known officer, Commandant P. Raaff, C.M.G.; so a warm reception will be given to any who may have the temerity to dispute the authority of Sepinare by crossing the border with any hostile intention. It is said that some of our burghers, who are suffering from earth-hunger to a considerable extent, are anxious to set the Barolongs by the ears, in the hope that a partition of the country would soon alter take place. And it is even asserted that some farmers who live not many hours from the Barolong border, have promised Samuel something more than their good wishes in the event of a scramble taking place. Material support is wanted, and farms are to be given as payment. We do not think for one moment that the Government would ever consent to Free State soil being made the base of military operations against the Chief with whom have just concluded a Treaty of Amity. The Free State Government have always been mindful of the good turn done by the late Chief Moroka to the Emigrant Boers when they were spoiled by Moselekatse, and will support the reigning Chief in his lawful undertakings. Besides, the President is far too wise and sagacious a statesmen, and too amenable to public opinion, to allow any part of the Free State to become a " Palfontein " or " Rooigrond," as did the Transvaal authorities about eighteen months ago. If it is true that any of our burghers are inciting Samuel to abuse the hospitality of our State, an example should be made of them. And if Samuel, whilst living under our protection, is proved to be scheming to overthrow the authority of the Barolong Chief Sepinare, he should be banished from the State. It is so difficult to get at the truth of all the rumours abroad that

Samuel is moving at all. So far as we know, it may be only a concoction of lies by interested parties to create a bad feeling between either Samuel Moroka or our Barolong allies and ourselves. When men hunger and thirst for farms what will they not do! A Commission of Enquiry should be instituted by the Executive; for these rumours do a great deal of harm to the country, and place the Government in a wrong position. We understand, too, that the cost of maintaining a force on a war footing is a severe strain on the revenue of Sepinare, which has already many claims upon it, for the Barolong Chief is governing his country with more expensive machinery than is usual with native rulers.

Since writing the above we have seen Mr. M. Steyn, Member of the Executive Council, who left town on Thursday last to make enquiries into the cause of the commotion prevailing in the neighbourhood of the Barolong boundary. He reports that the rumours are much exaggerated, and brings evidence that several of the farmers of this district have openly sympathised with Samuel Moroka, and that one or more have called for volunteers, *a la* Moshette and Mossouw, to assist the Pretender. Mr. Steyn, who took with him, for the sake of distribution, copies of the Treaty of Amity recently entered into between this State and the Chief Sepinare Moroka, warned the partisans of Samuel that they were violating the laws of the land, and would be held responsible for the consequences. He states that Samuel is at present at Kruidfontein, some distance from the line; but that about thirty Barolongs, with passes from Moshette, were outspanned in three or four wagons near the boundary of Moroka's territory. Their passes, which were for Kruidfontein, had been countersigned by the R. J. P. of Bultfontein. Mr. Steyn complains that the Pass Law, so far as Samuel Moroka's Barolongs are concerned, is a dead letter. This shows clearly that many of the border farmers are siding with the Pretender. Mr. M. Steyn, on his way back, passed through Thaba 'Nchu, and found Sepinare fully prepared to give a warm reception to any one who attempted to dispute his authority. Mr. Commandant Raaff has white officers under him, and has enlisted a corps of Bastards, so that things are pretty snug in Morako's territory. We are of opinion that things will blow over; and commend the action of the Government in nipping the affair in the bud. His Honour the President, who has been on a tour to Ladybrand, will, we understand, pass through Thaba 'Nchu to-morrow or Saturday, and will, doubtless, give confidence to Sepinare and his tribe.

Thus we have the testimony of one of the Executive, that Dutchmen were doing their best to get the rightful heir to the seat of the Chieftainship ; and if successful, to take farms as payment for services rendered. Now mark what happens. It was well known that efforts would be made by Samuel to drive out Sepinare, whom he and many other Barolongs knew to be an usurper, who would be upheld by the Free State authorities so long as it suited their purpose.

For some years (as I have explained in my *South Africa* and *Jottings by the Way*), it was well known, that Sepinare had given farms to lawyers, missionaries, and to the Bishop of Bloemfontein to use, on condition that they would support him at all times ; but he did not give them liberty to sell the land.

It is also a fact that some thousands were extorted out of the Barolongs to pay the Resident, and the white forces with Commandant Raaff at their head to uphold Sepinare's power ; but the time having arrived when the users of the farms, with the religious bodies at their head, desired to sell the lands as private property, they winked at all that was done to get rid of Sepinare ; and thus it happened, that when the attack was make upon Sepinare at sunrise, and for hours afterwards, not a white—Commandant, Missionary, Resident, or trader—helped in any way to defend him.

Now what happens after the chief and his head councillor were slain ? The Free State burghers are summoned by President Brand, and—to show how insignificant was the whole affair—he, with a force of a hundred men, takes possession of Samuel and his followers ; and then, without taking counsel with the Raad, this man—who so loudly protested against the English Government taking possession of the Transvaal without the consent of the inhabitants—immediately annexes the whole to the Free State, notwithstanding the fact that there was a son of the Chief Sepinare living, and under the care of the Free State Government.

Although this was one of the most barefaced robberies of native lands on record, it surprised nobody. Of course not ; because in various ways it was known to have been arranged for, and all the parties implicated were acquitted—the whole thing being settled in the hope of (as I stated in my "Jottings," while passing through this spot the year before, would come to pass) the Dutch obtaining ownership of the land, which, if sold, would defray the cost of constructing the Free State railway ; or if not sold, but let, would pay the interest of the Free State Debt. Under the circumstances can anyone doubt that the whole was an official and unofficial arrangement ?

For confirmation of my views I again quote from the *Friend*, of July 17th, 1884 :—

The Barolong Disturbances.

"The unexpected," says Beaconsfield, "always happens." Little did any of us think that Sepinare—to whom had been awarded the chieftainship of the Barolongs by the President, some few years ago, on the death of the old Chief Moroka, and who had been recognised by our Government, which entered into a defensive treaty with him in August last, which treaty was ratified by the Volksraad in February at its Special Session—would now be no more and that the country he used to govern would be Free State territory. Sepinare not only at the time of the last disturbance managed to defeat and scatter his enemies, but secured the goodwill and amity of his surrounding neighbours. It will be remembered that the claimant to the Chieftainship, Samuel Moroka, failed recently in getting his claims acknowledged by the British Government, to which he applied *in propria persona* in England. Thus Sepinare seemed likely to "live for ever." The fates, however, decreed otherwise. A plot was so secretly and quietly hatched, that none of his councillors and officers, or any Free State officials, knew anything about it until it was carried into execution. Viewed in the light of a successful undertaking, it was simply perfect. Bogachu, the Councillor and General of Samuel, it is supposed with the assistance of some petty chief of the Basutos, and aided by a handful of white men, managed to enter the Barolong territory from three or four points and ride across it a distance of three or four hours, and strike a blow at the Head of the country. To prevent suspicion, Samuel, it is said, remained on the farm where he has been located for some time, and only repaired to Thaba 'Nchu after the *coup d'etat*. Although we cannot in any way approve of the deed committed by Samuel and the conspirators who acted in his name, some allowance must we think be made for the way in which the acknowledged Chief by the great majority of the Barolongs was despoiled of his goods, and the heartless manner in which the followers of and sympathisers with the Chief had been literally " eaten up " by the, to them, Usurper. No doubt Samuel had been goaded on by his people, who became outcasts in the land, especially when they saw the country of their fathers portioned out to strangers—men of another race—for bolstering up the Usurper. It is not for us to say who was the rightful chief : that has been decided by competent judges ; but we have only to state facts, and they are, that the Samuelites far outnumber the followers of Sepinare, who by his harsh treatment of " suspects " rendered his name an abomination to a great portion of his tribe. White men who love to fish in troubled waters, lent their aid. The consequence is we have to chronicle what is considered by Europeans as " a most unnatural murder." No one who knew the two men, Sepinare and Samuel, could have the least doubt who was the most fitted to govern. The late lamented Chief Sepinare was born to rule. He was a man of much dignity, and although, we believe, of little or no education, was possessed of great information in history and in the art of governing. He was commanding in stature, straight, well-made, and handsome, and had a most kindly presence. He was brave in the field and a leader of men. Samuel, on the other hand, although educated in England, is a man of far inferior caste of mind and body. Moroka shortly before his death, it is said, pointed Sepinare out as his successor. No doubt the sagacious old Chief knew he was far more competent than his son Samuel. The evil has been that the common people among the Barolongs thought differently. Sepinare, from a young man, has taken part in the councils of the tribe, and has led his men in the field. During the last Basuto war, he commanded the Barolong contingent, and was present at the conclusion of peace in April, 1866, at Thaba Bosigo, and his name appears among the witnesses to the signature of that important document. All Europeans who came in contact with Sepinare were much impressed with his dignity of manner and his gentlemanly bearing. He was of generous disposition and liberal as became a chief, and many poor people of the Caucasian race were recipients of his bounty. There is no doubt that the attempt to govern his people on enlightened principles was one of the causes of his sudden downfall. The system was too costly, and his people were heavily taxed to bring up the revenue required to carry on a government with expensive white officials. The consequence was that many of his people were compelled to leave the territory, and many more would have left but passes were refused them. Those who had nothing—or next to nothing—to lose, left the country, and many others were eaten up for going without leave. The country about here is full of Barolongs, ninety-nine out of every hundred of whom tell heartrendering tales of how their cattle have been taken from them by the deceased Chief. Many whites, who were well-disposed towards Sepinare, advised him to be more lenient. His Honour the President, in speaking with the Chief, requested him to deal more humanely and leniently with his people. The Chief replied that the President did not understand a native as he did, saying that a Kaffir would not listen to smooth words, but could only understand a strong hand. We sincerely regret the death of the late Chief, for he was in many ways a noble specimen of a Bechuana chief: and we fear, too, that the tribe, by his removal, will be scattered even more than before, for the territory is now Free State soil, and our burghers are not likely to allow natives to congregate in any great numbers without working for them. We take it Sepinare will be the last of the Moroka, or Seleka, line of the tribe of Barolongs.

The Annexing of the Barolong Territory.

It has been said that " the days of small States are over." The Barolong Territory, ever since the close of our last Basuto war, has been an anomaly. It was surrounded by this State, and retained its independence simply because it was always felt that Moroka, who had been a faithful ally to us through the whole of the war, was deserving of very great consideration at our hands on account of the way he treated the Emigrant Farmers in their hour of need. After his death, when Sepinare was awarded the Chieftainship by His Honour the President, the Volksraad and people were intent

on honouring the memory of the good old Chief, and of protecting
the tribe so long as they behaved themselves well. Since that
time there has been so much plotting on the part of the claimant,
Samuel—and more by his pseudo friends—that it was becoming
well nigh intolerable. So much was this felt by the Raad in their
special session in February last that it almost refused to ratify the
Treaty entered into by the President in the preceding August.
The events of the past week have proved to be like the "last
straw which breaks the camel's back." It was not only vexatious
to us that our burghers should be every now and then called into
the field to act as policemen in preserving the peace of our sable
neighbours, but there was the constant danger of the territory of
our ally becoming the theatre of a war in which other tribes than
the Barolong might take part. There was also the constant danger of our burghers enlisting themselves on the side of one or other
of the Chiefs. No doubt some white men (citizens of this State)
were among the ringleaders and actual leaders in the late disturbance. It has been a too common practice in South Africa of late
for white men to espouse the cause of some native chief, and, like
the cuckoo who kicks the young sparrows out of the nest when it
gets big enough, or the nest is too small, they turn the natives
out, and possess the land. There have been far too many free
lances and freebooters in this part of the world lately, and we are
glad that this State has put its foot down and refused to counte-
nance any such evil. We hold this State guilty of allowing the
late Chief of the Barolongs to employ white mercenaries to
"slaughter" his kindred. What that Chief sowed he unfortunately reaped. We pointed out at the time that the policy of
allowing any Chief to employ white men to fight for him was as bad
as bad could be, for the end of it would be that white men would be
found fighting against other white men—as in Bechuanaland.
Besides it is very lowering to the character of white men, in the
eyes of the natives, to hire oneself to be shot at by their enemies.

The territory of the Barolongs has been occupied by that tribe
a little over half a century. At the close of 1833, the Wesleyan
Missionary Society bought "all that spacious country designated
Thaba 'Nchu, with all that extensive range of hills on the north,
south, east, and west, with all their plains, extending on the
north to the ford called Farmer's Ford, or Boeredrift; on the west

L

to the summit on the mountains on the west side of Modder-river, or River Khaba ; on the south to half of the distance between Mount Moriah and Thaba 'Nchu, and forming a circle to join the western limit ; and on the east to the river passing through the mountains near Maquatling, and called ———, and passing along the hills in a circular direction to Boeredrift, the northern limit," from Moshesh and one of his subordinate Chiefs, named Moseme, for the price of 7 young oxen, 1 heifer, 2 sheep, and 1 goat.

In 1849, Major Warden fixed the boundary with Moroka of his territory. Before that time many of the Barolong kraals were between here and Modder-river, being many miles on this side of that stream, and others as low down on the other side of Modder-river as Doornspruit. The tribe at that date was estimated to number 14,000 souls. This boundary was confirmed in 1862 (in Pretorius' time) by this State, the late Mr. Allison having been instrumental in settling what was then a rather vexed question.

Diplomatic Relations.

The unfortunate tragedy enacted at Thaba 'Nchu ; the arrest of Samuel Moroka, together with a number of his coadjutors, both black and white ; the unusual undiplomatic manner hostages from Bering Letsea were taken over by a commanding officer of a Burgher Force ; and the fact that direct communications took place between His Honour the President and His Excellency the High Commissioner—have all had their share of criticism. The action of our Government has been much extolled by the Natal and Colonial press for annexing the Barolong territory and for dealing out summary justice against the raiders. In these days of vacillation and temporising of the British Government, the ready action and the strong hand are much admired. No doubt men like to see the leaders of the people take the bull by the horns, and exhibit a firmness, especially in dealing with natives. There appearing to be Basuto complications connected with the raid, the authorities of the State had to deal with matters of very grave, moment. The decisive measures taken to prevent a Basuto raid thought then to be imminent, commended themselves to Colonial men, who are used to witness a vacillating policy ; and the ready sponse of our Burghers to the appeal made to them by the Executive is deserving of all praise, and naturally is contrasted with the tardy action of the Colonial burghers when they were wanted to subdue the Basutos during the late war. While fully approving of the vigorous policy pursued in the matter of the late raid, we quite think some of the minor details are open to criticism. In saying thus much we think the suddenness of the attack, the very imperfect information to hand, and the great difficulty of obtaining reliable news from the scene of the disturbance, all made it exceedingly difficult to grasp the situation. As a party of Basutos had just previously been implicated in a cattle raid on one of Sepinare's posts, and as Commandant Peter Raaff brought the news that the Basutos were mixed up in the affair, the President and others naturally thought there was *prima facie* evidence that the "Nation of Thieves" was making common cause with Samuel Moroka. Even the missionaries and the white inhabitants of Thaba 'Nchu, although witnesses of the disturbance from a distance, thought the whole of the morning and a part of the afternoon that the Basutos were taking an active part in the affair. The Executive naturally thought that Samuel was not strong enough to oust Sepinare without assistance. The consequence of all this was, that as time went on, the plot thickened. Men who had been to Thaba 'Nchu, we believe, assured His Honour that the Basutos were implicated. As we have before stated, the Basutos, rightly or wrongly are thought by certain people in this State to be plotting the destruction and spoliation of our frontier country. The wire was put in motion. A Field-cornet on the border made himself extra officious, sent spies into British Basutoland, interviewed Bering Letsea, and received hostages from him that no Basuto force should cross the Caledon River to take part in the affair at Thaba 'Nchu. It is, no doubt, in times of emergency a great thing to have good men on the border equal to any occasion which might arise; yet it is hardly respectful to our neighbours, with whom we are on such good terms, to go past the head of that Government and treat with understrappers who have no authority ither from the Government or from the Chief. This is doubtless what Colonel Clarke feels. It will be seen from the official correspondence that the gallant Colonel thinks that he has been snubbed by the Free State authorities from His Honour the President down to a Fieldcornet. This all comes from the miserably weak rule of the Colonial Government. Since Colonel Clarke has been at Maseru, we do not think there have been any just causes of complaint against the Administration being too weak ; but as the Resident Commissioner has no force at his back, the people of this State naturally fear he has not sufficient moral power to restrain the Basutos if they had made up their minds to make a raid on this country. The President, who is usually the most cautious of statesmen, and who generally errs on the side of being too extra-diplomatic, was carried away by the reports, and appeared to forget for the nonce that there was any Resident Commissioner at Maseru. This is a venial mistake, and under the circumstances an allowance can be made for the excitement the country was in—partly caused, we fear, by the spreading of lying reports. As we pointed out in our issue of the 17th instant —the massing of men on the border, nevertheless, made the Basutos restless, and was anything but a good policy. The worst of it is, the position of affairs on or about the 10th or 11th instant, was, that the Basutos may or may not have contemplated joining hands with Samuel. This is a debatable point, and, perhaps, will never be satisfactorily cleared up, as it is difficult to go behind a man's or people's intentions. But what is certain, is that eleven—some say more—burghers of this State deliberately plotted and carried out what the poor Basutos are accused of contemplating ! So far this Government—although innocently—is to blame ; and if Sepinare could rise from his grave, he would accuse *us*, and not the Basutos, of his death and the partition of his country. We grieve to write thus, but the truth must be told, for some are making capital out of things which actually reflect shame on us as a people.

The Beginning of the End.

The surrender of Samuel and his councillors on Saturday last has put an end to a threatened calamity which appeared to be assuming great proportions. This day last week, a false move on the part of the head of the State might have caused blood to be spilt. And if such had taken place, who knows where it might have ended? The misguided followers of Samuel vainly imagined that they had only to get rid of the Chief whom the President had made, and then they would live in peace and security under the protection of this State. But they reckoned without their host. Deplorable as a raid by a party of semi-barbarians on a friendly territory may be, it is nothing in comparison to the complications which might ensue if the Basutos and others were allowed to take part in the struggle for supremacy. For good or for evil, the Barolong tribe of the line of Seleka are now dispossessed of their territory as far as they understand the tenure of land. It must have come sooner or later, and the death of Sepinare gives this State a chance of stepping in and annexing the territory, and so restoring peace and order there.

It is well-known and street talk that several burghers of this State took an active part in the disturbance at Thaba 'Nchu. Many natives and several white men, it is said, saw some of the prisoners, and spoke to them soon after the killing of Sepinare. Will the authorities allow these men—and others who are said to be quite as guilty as they—to be only tried for breaking into a shop ? If so, the *raison d'etre* of the annexation of the Barolong territory is not such a good one as we were led to expect. The looting of Abraham's store is a small matter compared to the attack on Thaba 'Nchu and the slaying of Sepinare. It may be that the authorities will bring other charges against the prisoners. If so, there is, we understand, plenty of evidence to prove that if they were not with the deceased Chief of the Barolongs, they were against him. With regard to the complicity of white men in the Thaba 'Nchu affair, an esteemed correspondent in this State writes: "I suppose Samuel would never have acted as he has done unless he had white backers. The whole affair is the result of the unpunished action of our burghers helping Transvaal *v.* English Government, Freebooters *v.* Chiefs in Stellaland and Goschen, and Dinizulu *v.* Usibepu. The interference of white men in native disturbances will, I suppose, go on to the end of time ; or till there is no chance of loot of land or stock. The Governments will, it is to be presumed, condone such action while it is profitable." We fear there is much truth in these observations.

Aiders and Abettors.

Eight white men are said to have led the Samuelites. Some of them are known, and were seen at Thaba 'Nchu by the white residents, who spoke with them. Warrants are, it is said, issued for their apprehension. We trust for the sake of law and order that an example will be made of these men.

" Is it Peace ? "

A man bearing a white flag came out about a thousand yards distance from the village, and met the commando as it was proceeding to the scene, shouting, "Vrede! Vrede!" (Peace! Peace!) He was immediately referred to His Honour the President, who detained him until the camp was formed and our cannons placed in a position ready for action. He then gave the flag-bearer a copy of the proclamation requesting his messenger (Harry Hanger) to accompany him to his chief and read and explain to him that he was about to annex the country. After waiting some time the messengers returned with a letter from Samuel to the President, stating that he wished to see the head of the State. His Honour replied verbally : " I will see him on Monday, and at the same time will require of him the delivery of the murderers of Sepinare."

At four o'clock the President read the following proclamation annexing the country, and the artillery fired a salute of three guns as the flag was hoisted :—

Proclamation.

Whereas the Chief Sepinare Moroka was murdered in a treasonable manner on the 10th July;

And whereas the territory over which he ruled is now without lawful government;

And whereas, for the maintenance of law, order, peace, and safety, it is necessary that a regular government should be established without delay ;

And whereas this can best take place and be facilitated by annexing the Barolong territory, over which the late chief Moroka

—and after him Sepinare Moroka—ruled at Thaba 'Nchu, to the Orange Free State ;

Therefore I, Johannes Hendricus Brand, President of the Orange Free State, hereby annex the said territory to the Orange Free State, and proclaim that the above-mentioned territory shall form a portion of and fall under the authority, government, and laws of the Orange Free State.

Everyone is hereby requested and commanded to take notice hereof and govern himself accordingly.

This done and given under my hand and the Great Seal of the Orange Free State at Thaba 'Nchu this 12th July, in the Year of Our Lord, One Thousand Eight Hundred and Eighty-Four.

J. H. BRAND.

By order,
THOMAS F. BRAND, Private Secretary.

> In our presence :—C Van der Wath, member of the Executive Council ; Jan A. Prinsloo, Commandant of the district of Bloemfontein ; R. Albrecht, Captain Artillery ; P. J. Fourie, Fieldcornet Boven-modder-river.

Thus at last the one hope of the Dutch of Bloemfontein was realised, and by a Treaty of Amity *and Treachery* the lands of the Barolongs were stolen by violence, to the everlasting disgrace of the President and the Orange Free State.

CHAPTER XIV.

HE year 1884 was a most unfortunate one for the Free State. The inhabitants had exhausted all their cash and even their credit. In December, 1883, it was a disgusting experience to pass through and notice many, who would or could not pay their legitimate accounts, freely expending money in luxuries and for fireworks with which to usher in the new year.

Trade was at a standstill; money, like the old year, seemed to have passed away for ever; and to drive hope still further away from the Free State. the loan sought for from England was refused; a salutary rebuke to the insolence and impudence of the Dutch, who thought the English would run to throw their cash at them. However, the news came (to lower the pride of the Hollanders) that the English knew not the Dutch, and refused to advance them cash for their needs; and then to make the blow still heavier, the financial particulars threw the officials into a perfect fright and placed them in a contemptible position; for the Free State had hitherto boasted that they not only had no National Debt, but could always show a large balance to their credit.

It was a pitiable sight for the gods, to see all heads nodding at this juncture and in fear whispering one to another "What next?" Then, to add to their discomfiture, the Government lost their heads, and in alarm called the members of the Raad together at an expense of some thousands to decide the future arrangements. On examination it was found that—like a fool that tried to raise a loan on his estate without consulting his lawyer—the President had had the temerity to attempt to float their loan personally, instead of consulting and paying some Banks to do so; and to show still further the utter ignorance of the President—after twenty years of official life, with his communications with the outer world and particularly with England—he was mad enough to tell the hoped-for lenders that they could get the interest for their money in Bloemfontein. Then, of course, all discovered the blunder that the high and mighty Raad, with the "wisdom of years" at their head in the person of the President, and their Treasurer-General, assisted by the Executive, had committed; and which resulted in bringing upon the people at large the discredit of official folly.

The *Express* Editor, fully believing in the gullibility of John Bull, was simply astonished at the common sense displayed by Englishmen in not lending their money to a bankrupt Dutch State simply for the asking of the same; and then, with the howl of a mad dog, he charged all the officials with want of foresight in not knowing better,—a charge which was as applicable to himself as to any of the others, as will be seen by the following paragraphs from his own paper:—

An extraordinary session of the Hon'ble Volksraad has been called for Thursday, the 21st of February, 1884, to discuss matters which, if only a serious attempt is made to deal with them, will keep the members of the Legislature at least a month in our midst. The reasons which prompted the Executive to call the Raad together—notwithstanding the difficulties of the times, and the serious expenditure necessitated by that step, are manifold. In the first instance, the settlement of Basutoland (at least the official announcement of such being brought about) necessitates with regard to Art. 9 of the Aliwal Convention, the enforcement of a Pass Law. Article 9 stipulates that no native living in Basutoland shall be allowed to enter the Free State, and no Free State burgher Basutoland, except under conditions and regulations than already in force, or later to be enacted by the two contracting Governments. Ordinance No. 5, 1866—which provided the terms of a Pass Law—became unworkable, however, through the Basuto war, and the President has for some time been anxious to replace that Ordinance by one suited to the altered circumstances of the situation. The hon'ble Volksraad has thus far refused to place this country, by means of a stringent Pass Law, in the position of a policeman to another Government. In how far the present settlement of the difficulty alters this conception we are anxious to learn, as we feel little inclination to change our very decided opinion on this point, remaining, as we do, of opinion that any Pass Law on our side must be preceded by an *actual* Government in Basutoland, for the evidence of which such clear proof must be given as has hitherto been entirely wanting. The next, and undoubtedly the main question the Raad will have to deal with in the ensuing session, will be the financial position of the country. This, we regret to say, is by no means a satisfactory one—comparatively speaking, and from a Free State point of view we are in duty bound to add. The fact that our debentures were not taken up in London has naturally thrown our Budget out of gear—the public works, to be paid out of the loan, having been entered upon, thus obliging the Government to defray their cost out of a Revenue already seriously embarrassed by the state of agriculture and trade.

There is little doubt that the debentures—which the Government failed to float, and which the National Bank is now attempting to place on the money market—form the very best investment that can possibly be offered to European capitalists. Four causes militate against their finding favour. The first is that the country is little known, and as a Dutch Republic suffers under certain prejudices; the second, that the amount is somewhat small for a State loan; the third, that a rate of interest of 6 per cent. prejudices the transaction in the eyes of capitalists who are accustomed to pay 4 per cent. to $4\frac{1}{2}$ per cent. for the very best State debentures; the fourth and main reason, that the capital and interest is payable at the Treasury in Bloemfontein. It is asserted by the very best authorities that Mr. Scanlen damaged the credit of the Cape Colony seriously by offering 5 per cent. on the new loan, an argument which is most likely to be brought forward in the matter at issue.

It is thought here generally that principally through the above-named provisions of the Ordinance—which made both capital and interest payable in Bloemfontein — European investors were deterred from entertaining the loan. Be this as it may. the National Bank has certainly no light task to perform, especially if it is taken into consideration that a venture which, through whatever cause, has—so to say—failed, requires careful handling to gain the public confidence necessary for success; and we cannot refrain here for an expression of regret that the Government did not, in the first instance, avail itself of the agency of a monetary institution—a course pursued by every Government in existence.

Without some connection, agency, or reference in London there can be no question of any such transaction, (certainly not, if the money, as was expected, is to be found there), and that our London Consul is about the most unfit person to represent this Government, inspire investors with confidence, and generally negotiate a loan of this description, requires not our assurance. On its merits, the loan without doubt should be a successful one; however, there is no saying what reasons may weigh with investors in England, and the Volksraad will at all events have to devise means to provide tht Executive with the necessary funds to carry out the existing contracts until such time as the loan, even if successful, will be an accomplished fact.

Besides the small-pox epidemic and the means employed for the prevention of the introduction of the disease into the State, the treaty with Sepinare requires confirmation; the appointment of an Assistant-Landdrost at Wepener must be considered, which appointment, for certain reasons, has not been made; and the establishment of a bi-weekly post between Bloemfontein and Colesburg. There is also a deal of arrear work which, according to its own resolution of the 7th July last, the Volksraad will have to deal with.

Finally, 15 memorials on sundry subjects are proposed to be submitted. As we stated at the outset, the budget of the work is a heavy one; yet it is to be hoped that most of it, if not all, will be done, so as least to give the country value received for an expenditure which, however necessary, it can ill afford.

The Volksraad.

This honourable body had two very important subjects under

discussion at the end of last week, viz ; the Report by the Commission on the Diggings, and the Allowance made to Members of the Raad. The Raad very wisely, we think, refused to interfere with the tenure, or to do away with the compulsory working of claims. Although, if the diggings are any good, no compulsion need be required to induce men to work the claims, yet if there be no penalty, speculators would buy claims and allow them to lie fallow —with the hope of their becoming one day valuable on account of the others being worked by industrious and go-ahead owners.

We believe it has been the practice in all countries to compel diggers to work claims which had been originally granted on application. Indeed, the title, so to say, is embraced in the fact of working. In California and Australia, where " Diggers' Law " for the time took the place of the law of the land, this was always acknowledged by everyone to be the only fair, just, and equitable way of dealing with the question of claim-rights. In those countries, the individual digger stood in the place of the rich—or supposed to be rich—companies here. It would have been too intolerable for the poor hard-working digger to have borne the injustice of a monopolist, or speculator, appropriating claim after claim to himself to the injury of his fellow man. The injustice was too self-evident, and as it affected the majority, the law being on the principle of the axiom, *Vox populi, vox Dei*, no one questioned it.

It is a thousand pities that our Diamond-fields ever got into the hands of the speculators ; for if they are payable at all, the poor, industrious, hard-working digger ought to be able to make a living out of working his claims. If, on the other hand, they will not pay the individual digger or the companies, the sooner they are shut up the better. More good money has been thrown away at Jagersfontein, for instance, than there seems any chance of getting out of the Mine for many long years to come. We are quite aware that the "original shareholder" is an amiable fool, who has done his work in his day and generation in other ventures and in other parts of the world, yet there appears no hope of breathing life into the dry bones of any of our Diggings. Time, of course, will tell. Although this question affects the mining population more directly than any other section of our community, yet nearly everyone in the State is, more or less, interested in the issue. We therefore hope, when the whole question of our Mines comes on at the annual session in May next, the Raad will not "listen to the voice of the charmer," but will strictly uphold all diggers' rights, and do everything which will conduce to the benefit of the Diggings generally.

The second question more immediately affects the whole of the burghers of the State ; for it must be admitted that the means taken to secure good representation of the people in our Volksraad is of paramount importance. Although there are certain property qualifications required for those who are born out of the country who were not burghers in 1866, yet seeing that every person who was born in the State has a vote on attaining his majority, Manhood Suffrage may be said to prevail in this Republic. The property qualification for a member is also exceedingly low—the being owner of unencumbered fixed property of the value of £200 being quite sufficient to entitle one to a seat, if duly elected.

We thus see that our Constitution has made every provision for the election and seat of the comparatively poor man. It has gone further, and provides for the payment of our legislators. This being the case, the only question to be considered is, What is a sufficient remuneration to our representatives?

There can be no doubt, we think, that sufficient remuneration is just so much that the members are not out of pocket by attending the Raad, and compelled to spend more money in living than they receive from Government. We take it, then, that £1 1s. per diem would be quite sufficient to keep a member in any of our hotels or lodging-houses, and have a little over for calls on his charity on account of his position. We quite deprecate the idea that the office of a member is an office of profit. It is not. It is an office of honour, and an honourable office solely. We believe that most people feel that £2, or even £5, per day would not be too much for thoroughly competent men, but that 15s. is a waste of money when paid to incompetent members. We for our part think that the Chairman of the Raad should receive at least double as much as ordinary members. He is known as the Chairman of the Volksraad wherever he goes, and it is not too much to expect that he must spend some of his private means in keeping up the dignity of the office. Our present head of the Raad is, we believe, a wealthy man, but provision should be made for the time when one may be elected, who is the fittest for the responsible situation but who is not so well-to-do that he could afford to keep up the position of Chairman of the Raad.

Although in England, where most of the members of Parliament are wealthy men, who would scorn to receive a few pounds a day for performing what they consider honorary duties, no compensation is allowed for their services, yet the Constitutions of the Colonies, to which we can be far better compared, provide for the payment of legislators.

When the Constitution of the United States was drawn up, there were not, of course, a tithe of the wealthy men in that country there are now. The framers of that important political instrument took care that good men should not be excluded on the score of poverty, so the Constitution provides that "Senators and Representatives shall have a compensation for their services, to be ascertained by law and paid out of the Treasury of the United States." This system of payment for legislative services, which prevails throughout the whole of the Union, has produced a class of professional politicians, whose probity in some cases has proved unequal to the strain put upon it by the power of dealing with the public money and the public possessions of what will soon be the wealthiest community in the world.

We think no one can doubt that we can pay far too much for our representation. Perhaps, a good way out of the difficulty would be, as suggested by some during the debate, to reduce the number of the members. Two members for a district would be ample. That would reduce the number of the members by half. It is almost certain all the present good members would be returned, and there would be more expedition, and we think better laws, at half the expense to the country.

At the present moment we have about one member to every thousand inhabitants, including men, women, and children. If we had one member to about 2,500 or 3,000 inhabitants, it would be ample. It will be easy to augment the number of members as the population increases. We are afraid that the Raad, although they have left this matter of allowances to members as it was before, did not give the proper reasons for doing so. "The labourer is worthy of his hire"; and we trust *Raadsleden* will not be found wanting when weighed in the balance of Public Opinion.

The Raad was closed yesterday, but before the members were dismissed they passed the Debenture Ordinance, which will enable the Government to float the loan of £100,000. We think the country at large will commend the action of the Raad in this matter. The talk about Bluebacks has subsided, and business will have a heatlhier tone now that all fears of a forced paper currency have been dissipated by the line taken by our *landsvaders*.

We are sorry to say that some valuable time of the Raad was taken up with tinkering with Ordinances. Nothing does so much harm to the State as this eternal amending of our laws. The want of finality shakes the confidence of the public. No doubt some laws require revision, but the privilege accorded to private members of proposing alterations to old-established laws, or to Ordinances hardly yet promulgated, has the effect of making the public think that our laws are the reverse of those of the Medes and Persians. A few years ago, when everyone felt himself well-off, a ridiculously high tariff was passed.

Now everyone is down in the dumps, retrenchment being the order of the day, the tariff must be reduced. If the country were governed by a party Government, there would not be so many changes, for the political parties would support and oppose particular legislative measures, and we think this would give a greater sense of finality to our legislation than at present obtains.

The way it "should" be done.

We direct the attention of our Government to a telegram which appears in another column respecting a loan floated by the Standard Bank for the Capetown Municipality. It makes us, as citizens of a Republic, feel very small to think that an insignificant and by no means flourishing corporate body can command a large credit in the London money market, whilst, through gross mismanagement, the Free State has not only not succeeded in raising a loan, but has had its credit seriously damaged. We trust the Government will ponder well over this matter, and next time it attempts to float a loan, discard all private individuals from a participation in its monetary affairs; success will then be assured.

Patent Law.

It is with regret that we notice the passing of the "Patent Law" by the Hon'ble the Volksraad. Supporters of such laws may fairly be called men who ride their principles to death without just and proper application. We quite concede that an inventor should have the full benefit of his enterprise and perseverance; and so he has, considering that there is hardly a country in the world where Patent Laws do not provide for his protection. But in a small and young country like ours—without rivers or forests —water or wood—without regular rainfall—thousands of miles from the seats of manufactures, and hundreds of miles from our own sea-border,—it seems an utter farce that our Legislature should waste £50 to pass such a Law. It is a senseless apism of circumstances utterly foreign to ours, a waste of money, and an injury of all the greater weight to the country, when it is considered that useful legislation might have been undertaken in the place of this "useless play." The next thing to be brought before the Raad will be a law punishing "Railway Excursions to the Moon!"

I had previously given him chapter after chapter of my *National Paper-Money and its Use*, in which I had shown how easy it was to make Imperial or Republican paper-money for all purposes of Government, to pay all their servants' salaries, and for the construction of Public Works of Utility: but of course this plan, not feeding the class of robbers that live on usury, was passed by as being of no account.

It was not for want of knowledge on the part of the Editor of the *Express* that my proposals were not appreciated by him. Like so many others, being in the hands of the ferneuk Hards, he dared not call his convictions his own, much less a thing he pretended to own—called his soul—even if he had believed in the right. He was on a par with the well-known legal thief who began to ask for works on political economy to enable him to argue on the subject at the forthcoming meeting of the Raad. This individual was a generally recognised counterpart of the notorious Old Bailey legal black-sheep, who was up to every dodge, equal at all times to any trickery, one who could manufacture a witness to support his case by swearing without compunction, and who if promised a handsome premium—as in the great Will Case of Jajersfontein v. The Company of the Sluit— he (the legal thief) would go to any length to secure success for the side on which he happened to be retained. This man was a perfect buck animal; no woman was safe from him at any time, and his very blood relations were contaminated by his immorality. Alas, he was not the only Black German Buck who sat in that Assembly at £2 per day. That the lawyers, conveyancers, auctioneers and doctors were a curse to the town and State may readily be gathered from the following from the *Express* :—

"Following up our remarks regarding the position the legal profession occupies in this country in the public estimation, we pointed out the necessity of steps being taken to remedy this abnormity. In alluding to the principal remedy, we referred to the establishment of a Law Society, the members of which would be called upon jealously to watch, that the reputation of an honourable profession should not be dragged into the deepest mire of public indignation by the constant malpractices of men, who should occupy quite a different position towards Judges and Juries than they do at present. The *esprit de corps* now wanting, and thereby supplied, would, however, not be the only gain achieved by the establishment of such a Society.

"A still greater advantage would be afforded by a Society—a corporate body, taking upon itself, and that 'officially,' a duty which individuals shrink from, firstly, because they dread the personal animus that might be suspected of them, even if it did not exist, and secondly, because they look to the head of the Bar for the performance of certain duties which are calculated to affect the whole body. Not only, has the Attorney-General not displayed overmuch anxiety to merit public and general applause by the display of that jealousy, which would prove that the interests and good name of the profession he leads and represents, are dear to him, but we are given to understand that the official in question has displayed a good deal of indifference, when the idea of co-operation was mooted to him by individual members of the bar. We regret this very much.

"Certain offices and positions impose certain duties and obligations, and whatever Mr. Vels may think fit or unfit, the Attorney-General has the distinct duty to lead in a matter of this kind. We say this with the more emphasis, and the more freedom, because we are conscious that the Attorney-General has enjoyed so much forbearance at the hands of the press, that exactness in this very matter cannot be considered, even by him, as severity The times we live in, and things as they are, are unhappily not what they should be, but we bear in mind, that the virtue 'patience,' is engraved upon our coat of arms, and calls upon us, to wait and bear, in the hope that if 'alles zal recht niet komen,' many things will advance and improve with the *gradual* advancement of the country. But, though we are ready to use such an amount of patience, as will make us doubted in the eyes of men, whose principles of right and wrong are not affected by circumstances, there is an end even to our patience, at the stage we have arrived in the question at issue.

"Were the dignity of the legal profession alone at issue, we might use, even now, more patience, and confine our emotions to a strong feeling of regret, that men of conspicuous position are so indifferent to what they owe to themselves. But since public considerations are involved as well, we trust that the Attorney-General will exercise the prerogatives of his position, and lead in a strong effort to resuscitate the legal profession from its present moral dilapidation. Extravagant as the various popular remedies may seem, that have been suggested for the purpose of confining the sphere of the lawyer to the smallest compass imaginable, we could, ourselves, not be expected to resist the ideas that have been advanced, if, in the case of nothing being done by the members of the Bar, the next Volksraad decided to follow up its actions of this session, for the purpose of placing work that is now done by lawyers, in the hands of officials, paid by the State, and whose earnings would, besides covering the amount of their salary, benefit the State Exchequer."

The summons to the Raad in February to meet in Bloemfontein upon serious and urgent business gave such a shock to the nerves of the country members that even to this day they feel it in all its intensity. Through very fear that before they could meet, some earthquake might swallow up the Free State, they grew thin and cadaverous in appearance ; and when they did meet over their " talkee talkee," they were but skeletons of their former obese selves, such was their horror at the audacity of England in refusing their loan.

Picture then, if possible, their chagrin and vexation when they found that England readily offered to advance to Cape Town over £500,000, when only £100,000 was asked for—although she had refused to furnish a single farthing towards the loan asked for by the Free State. Fearful of the results that might accrue from their loss of credit in the financial world in consequence of England's refusal, the Government made another and final appeal for help to the amount of £200,000. This and some other law-tinkering occupied the Raad during the months of February and March ; and then with the few pounds they had received for doing nothing, the members ran away in haste to their Vrows and Kinders with the fear in their hearts that the last days of the Free State had arrived—a fear yet to be realised in sad and sober truth, as this History will prove, and in support of my opinion I append the Free State Balance Sheet :—

Our Balance Sheet.

The financial statement published by the Treasurer-General in the *Government Gazette* of the 6th inst. indicates but too clearly the severity of the monetary crisis through which the Free State, in common with the whole of South Africa, is passing. The receipts for the third quarter of the current fiscal year amounted to £38,033 11s. 6d., whilst the expenditure reached £61,798 8s. 5d., —thus showing a discrepancy on the wrong side of the ledger of £23,764 16s. 11d. The revenue estimated for the year was £222,360, or £55,590 per quarter, but the actual receipts will probably not exceed £45,000 quarterly, or £180,000 per annum. The disbursements, however, will overleap the estimates by at least £20,000. This is a gloomy outlook ; especially when it is taken into consideration that, on 31st December last, the Government owed the National Bank £32,000, the Bank of Africa

£20,000, and the Administrator of Funds £11,000—altogether, £63,000. By the close of the fiscal year on 31st March proximo, we shall have outrun the constable to the tune of £100,000, which the contemplated Debentures, *if ever floated*, will just cover. We say advisedly, "if ever floated," because if the interest of the debentures is not made payable in London, or some other European capital, we may whistle to the winds for £100,000, or even 100,000 pence. Men of substance know as little about Bloemfontein and the Orange Free State, as they do of Jerusalem the Golden or the Mountains of the Moon. Therefore it is not to be wondered at that they are chary in subscribing for debentures, the interest on which is payable in this city. When the Debenture Ordinance, No. 17—1883, was passed, we pointed out the gross absurdity of making the interest payable here. Consequently it is not surprising that we are no nearer obtaining the much-needed £100,000 than we were eight months ago. We have acted like goats, and been punished for our folly. The successful issue of two Colonial Loans in a single week for an aggregate amount of nearly eight million pounds (£8,000,000), indicates that there is no lack of money seeking investment in England if only the right kind of security is offered to the public. The Cape Colony has been borrowing of late years with startling rapidity. Little more than ten years ago its debt was only a few hundred thousands, and now it will reach to nearly twenty million pounds. As the London *Standard* truly observes, there has been no corresponding increase in its population, or its realised wealth, in the course of that short time; but Mr. Scanlen knew how to "work the oracle," and readily obtained nearly £5,000,000 for his bankrupt government; while our Volksraad, understanding nothing respecting the routine to be pursued in matters pecuniary, made a dreadful mess in attempting to raise a paltry hundred thousand pounds, and thereby impaired not only the credit of the State, but every importer residing in it."

The truly and almost hopelessly deplorable position of the Free State as regards its financial condition is so justly and tersely described in the foregoing article that my readers will not only be enabled thereby to take a complete grasp of the gravity of the situation—bad enough in all conscience of itself without taking into consideration the even more disastrous results quite within the bounds of possibility—brought about by the incompetence or corruption—perhaps both—of the Executive ; but they will, I feel satisfied, admit that I had abundant justification for drawing public attention thereto in the manner I have, and that although I have expressed myself with more force than elegance, I have " nothing extenuated nor aught set down in malice."

In dismissing this subject—at any rate *pro tem.*—I commend to the reader's attention the subjoined sound, common-sense letter of " T. C." in reply to Mr. Higgo's suggestion for a Day of Prayer and the article immediately following under the heading " Hard Times."

Mr. Higgo and his Day of Prayer.

" ' T. C.' writes with reference to Mr. Higgo's communication which recently appeared in our columns :—Just a word to express surprise that one said to possess ' a vast fund of shrewd common sense' should rush into print to point out the urgency of setting apart a day for prayer to get us out of our present crisis. Instead of praying, we must set to and work, observe the inevitable laws of nature, and act in accordance with them. By praying to God to remove our dire distress, do we not inferentially blame our Creator instead of ourselves ? No matter how deep and strong our faith may be that we shall succeed by trusting to the efficacy of prayer, we shall soon be in the Bankruptcy Court unless we avoid bad debts. Let us hear no more of setting apart a day for prayer, but manfully facing the perils of our country, investigate, discover, and get rid of the effect by removing the cause."

Hard Times.

" In these days of complaining, and that too with some show of cause, of the scarcity of money and food, one is frequently led to think whether there might not be some method or other to allow the money to circulate more in the country, and thus to be kept more in the hands of the people themselves, and, at the same time, to strengthen and improve the agricultural interests upon which so very much depends.

"Firstly, with regard to the circulation of money, one is naturally led at once to inquire, where is this money you are going to circulate amongst the people? There is none in the hands of the people themselves. True, and who is to blame for it? No one but the Government, not for inconsiderate recklessness of expenditure or for thoughtlessly incurring debt, but simply and solely for too much and ill-timed precaution.

"Let us look at the facts of the case. Money was growing daily scarcer, when, to improve matters and put affairs on a firmer basis, debenture bonds were put forward by the Volksraad to start reproductive public works, such as bridges, telegraphs, &c., with this result—that they fell through—and why? There was no money to be raised in the country: Well! England and Holland have money which they would be perfectly willing to lend at a moderate interest; but no, 'Out of debt, out of danger!' said the sages, and there they erred grossly, for no one can deny that money makes money, and the countries that have the largest National Debt are universally the greatest, most powerful and most wealthy, for if a country has nothing it can gain nothing. 'Nothing venture nothing win.' It were therefore far better to seek help where it could be obtained, and do the best possible to raise the status of things in the country than to sit with folded hands trusting, like Mr. Micawber, that something may turn up. Nothing can be proved worthless till tried, and we must confess that the very many instances of countries raising money for public works have been universally productive of public benefit—the rates, being proportionate to the amount raised. (Observe, we use the term Public Works, not money raised and then recklessly and uselessly squandered as in the case of Turkey; or as in the case of Russia, Spain, and the South American Republics—countries groaning under heavy National Debts incurred, almost solely, through expenses in the constant wars in which they are engaged, and which for ever wrack the mind and harass the peace of the inhabitants without benefiting either the public or private purses; but money raised to enable works to be put in progress for utilising the latent wealth of the country and encouraging the energy and skill of the people.)

"To prove the above statement, let us compare the young, though highly prosperous, colony of New Zealand with the Cape Colony financially, and tabulating results, we find that New Zealand has :

Area	106,000 square miles.
Population	530,000.
Public Debt	£30,000,000.
Exports (1881)	£6,000,000.

Whilst Cape Colony has :

Area	240,000 square miles.
Population	1,250,000.
Public Debt	£13,000,000.
Exports (1881)	£4,000,000.

And here we must also note that New Zealand has had the full benefit of her loans, the minor-portion only having gone in expenses for the carrying on of war ; whereas, in the case of the Colony, by far the majority has been used to defray expenses incurred in the continual struggles carried on between her and the native races ; so that, in reality, her debt, with regard to the extension of public works, becomes even still less in comparison with that of New Zealand.

"Now this is how matters stand at present. Money is scarce in the country, and two bad seasons succeeding each other swallow up any overplus that may have lain accumulated, this money not even circulating in the country itself, but being, for the most part, sent out, directly or indirectly, to other countries, in payment for goods imported thence, together with any product of these two years, and losing, in its circuit, a large percentage. Inexperienced men, too, thinking by speculation to better their affairs, borrow on the security of their estates comparatively large sums ; their speculation fails and they become bankrupt with great injury to themselves, and, most probably, to a large proportion of their neighbours. Continuing in this manner, it is easy to foresee that in the end a country must either take a step (and that no inconsiderable one) backwards in the course of civilisation, or put forth all its combined energies, as speedily as possible, to seek measures for a bettering of its affairs. 'All things come to those who wait' may be a very wise old saw, but it is much better to remember that 'God helps those who help themselves.' Money! money! is the cry. Well, raise it by loans, raise it anywhere, but only raise it.

"Now, in the second place, let us consider the best methods of using these moneys when obtained, so as to benefit the majority; and, certainly, amongst these the construction of public works and the promotion of home productions stand highest.

"How often do we hear people complaining of the difficulty of obtaining articles they require at stores and blaming the storekeeper for it, who, already holding a large stock owing to the distance from the ports and the slowness of transport, is utterly unable to keep it well sorted up owing to his inability, except by some rare chance, to get transport for the comparatively small quantities of goods he needs from time to time. Again, what delays occur to up-country storekeepers in obtaining their goods (to mention nothing of the risk of damage incurred) through drought or sickness among the oxen; or the inability or unwillingness of transport-riders to load on account of their own crops or flocks requiring attention. All these hindrances and difficulties are so many checks on trade and advancement of the interests of the country. What is the remedy for them? There is but one. It is the extension as widely as possible of railways, so as to open direct and speedy communication between the ports and the interior, thus enabling goods to be readily and in any quantity obtained, and also dispensing with heavy stocks and consequent risk, loss, and expense to the storekeeper; and at the same time allowing him to keep pace with progress and civilisation, and also enabling him to sell his goods at a lower price.

"There is no doubt, too, that the railway would be a great social benefit, introducing greater energy into the country, and replacing listlessness and carelessness with briskness and ambitious emulation; for there is no doubt had more energy and determination, in a right groove, been exercised in times of prosperity, the present distress and scarcity might have been much less. Knowledge too of other places and other people, and contact with the highest branches of civilisation, cannot be without its effect. Man

—if he be worthy the name—always seeks to be better, nobler, to do, at least as well, if not better, than other men have done. Again, steam once in use, must eventually extend in use, and become of inestimable benefit to the country, making present impossibilities possible. And, lastly, turning to the question which at present agitates itself, the construction of railways throughout the land increases the demand, stirs up energy to supply that demand, and at the same time spreads money over the tract it traverses in construction as a foretaste of the rich results to follow.

"But some may argue that railways do not benefit a country, and quote their apparent failure in the Colony. If they do not succeed as was expected, why is it? Simply through want of patriotism, through striving to benefit the few to the neglect of the majority. Had there been two grand trunk lines from Capetown to Port Elizabeth, say to some such centre as Colesberg, and thence to the Diamond-fields; instead of, as at present, Capetown having its line to Beaufort West; the Bay it's, to Graaff-Reinet and Colesberg, and East London with its to Queenstown, with the consequent increased expense, whilst the goal (in all cases the Diamond-fields), is still unreached, we should then have seen a different phase of things; smaller and cheaper lines could have been opened up to the other towns, and communication established far more widely and with much less cost than under the existing circumstances is possible, to say nothing of its being far more remunerative. What we want is a trunk line through the State, from the Orange-river at Colesberg, through Bloemfontein, to Harrismith; thus gaining, so to speak, egress at both ends: for in matters of public welfare the greatest good for the greatest number should ever be the first consideration, and will ever pay the best in the long run.

"But we would not advocate the spending of these moneys alone on railway extensions; there are other things equally worthy of attention. Why should a country like the Free State import its breadstuffs, its starch, its jams, its tobacco? Decidedly not because it cannot itself produce them—it has done and still continues to do so, but in unpayable quantities. Why should we not have our own manufactories for these things, and men competent to carry on the work be encouraged to come into the country, men with capital and energy and skill? Let us no longer go to other countries to seek what we ourselves are in every way supplied with, let bonuses be given for home manufactures from home products, as an example of which take the amount of peaches that are yearly wasted and given away in this country, which, prepared as a jam, could find a market in any country, and be made most remunerative.

"We say distinctly let bonuses be given, not monopolies granted, we decidedly do not advocate protection ; Free Trade is the thing to promote the interests of a country. What has the Transvaal gained by allowing Nellmapius to monopolise the manufacture of brandy from anything but grapes for instance, with several other things of a similar nature of a general use ? Monopolies simply benefit the person who holds them, and who can thus ask what price he likes for his goods, knowing there can be no competition.

"The demand for manufacture necessitates a greater supply being ensured, and as this season has shown us in this country that nature, unaided by art, cannot always render the due reward for toil ; and, after the warning we have thus received, we cannot help but see that to insure success in agriculture, the water supply must first be ensured, and for this purpose we would advocate the expending of a portion of the promised loans on Government irrigation works, or in loans to farmers as bonuses for the erection of dams, and for the best plans for watering the soil. At present tons of water are daily being wasted, and, in fact, doing just as much harm by forming bogs, &c., as they might do good, if only conveyed into proper channels and used for agricultural purposes, thus nullifying, to a considerable extent, the severe effects of such a dry season as we have experienced. There are many Boers to-day who, if they had sufficient capital, would carry this out—they see the evil and its remedy, and are willing to undertake the latter. Let them be encouraged and helped, and not only they themselves, but the whole country will be benefited, its value will be increased ten-fold, its products more than doubled, its people far more healthy, wealthy, and contented, and we shall hear ' no more complaining in our streets.'

"In point of fact, in these days, when everything progresses at express rate, and the old saw as to the building of Rome occupying more than the space of four and twenty hours seems, as it were, but a slur on the irrevocable memories of the past; when men fly along upon one, two and three wheels, and hold communion as easily with a friend half-a-dozen miles off as if he were at their own fireside, and when the barren wilderness, almost before our very eyes, assumes the joyous garb of a fruitful field, to succeed—whether as a State or an individual—one must be ever in the van of that fierce struggle now raging amid the shouts of Progress! Science! and Civilisation! When once fallen back to the rear, the difficulty becomes an hundred-fold magnified to take a foremost stand, continual striving is the only way; the strife brooks no cessation. We are behind the times, things are now at their worst, and we must now, once for all, make a grand rush for the front, banish 'Failure' from our lexicon, and with 'En Avant' as our motto follow where Progress leads."

At no time within the memory of the oldest inhabitant had trade been so bad as in the first three months of the year 1884, which culminated in the downfall of many, notably of the Criterion and of the Swindle and Thomas—the unbelieving one—in conjunction with the Sell the Hand, an old deserter from a Penge regiment, who turned insolvent in a most shameless way. His friends had duped a Port Elizabeth house and even boasted of the trick and lived on the proceeds of the robbery for years after. He also appropriated some diamonds entrusted to him to sell by a Rossshire man, saying that he had lost them; and as they were the property of an illicit gang, no procedings could be taken against him. This kind of thing was repeated time after time, and the man lives by such means to this day and the outcome of a Cameron Estate.

This Jew then helped another Jew (the Moss) to raise among his spirits the Fire King, and while taking his walk in the Market Square he made a Fire Dragon, and but for the appearance of a few Bloemfontein watchmen would have burnt down the timekeeper. Finding fire would not succeed, he sold all his stock by underhand means and then called his creditors together but paid no dividend. In the meantime he visited his brother Jews —who were introduced to him at the time he stole the wool money from poor Bee——les—and then acting as the go-between and receiver of the illicits of Kimberley, accumulated his thousands out of his dupes; and at last, in fear, drew a draft for £500 on Cape Town, sold his furniture for £20, and hastily assuming the guise of a Rabbi, once more hid himself from all his victims and ever after lived on the proceeds of his plundering by means of the usual cent. per cent. business.

Truly has it been said that no one could understand the ramifications of a brotherhood of Jews. If ever a Race deserved the hatred of mankind, it is the descendants of the Impenitent Thieves of the Roman Era. These two instances, added to by the rottenness and fraudulent tricks of the Old Sons from a fountain of rascals, with the culpable insolvency of the Company of the Crash—— Wells, gave a shock to the commercial morality of Bloemfontein that it had not recovered from up to the time of my departure, and which was of so foul a nature that I feel it my duty to chronicle the same as a beacon light of the future to the path of the honest merchants of England and South Africa.

CHAPTER XV.

THE wisdom of the Bloemfontein Town Council was so apparent that they ceased to be respected, and became the subject of many a "skit," one of which I here reprint for the amusement of my readers from the *Friend* of December 21st :—

Meeting Bloemfontein Council, in the Year of our Lord, 1881.

Present :—

Dramatis Personæ.

MAYOR (*Unrobed.*)

COUNCILLORS.	COUNCILLORS.
Muttonhead.	The General.
Beefchops.	Goathead.
Muddleton.	Catchup
Bungleman	Gaspipe.
Hazybrains.	

Resolved by Councillor Beefchops and seconded by Councillor Catchup :

" That we are the people."

The speaker then proceeded to point out to the august assembly that were it not for the Municipal energy displayed in this city, and the unique subtlety of their engineering plans, together with the patriotic feeling shown by the members in their arduous duties, Bloemfontein, ere this, must have died from mere debility and " dry rot," trade would have languished, the clergy would have left, women would have eloped, and the Queen of the Prairie would by degrees have become the habitat of the owl, the bat, and apostate members of the Africander Bond. (The speaker was immensely cheered during the safe delivery of this marvellous oratorical display.) This resolution was carried *nem. con.*

Resolution proposed by Councillor Goathead and seconded by Councillor Hazybrains:

> "That the building of culverts proceed on the plans laid down by the Council, and hitherto carried out, with such improvement as the Council may suggest—always keeping revenue as the lode star in view."

The speaker then thumbed his waistcoat under his arms and essayed to enlighten the members on the culverts. It had been said that culverts ought to be arched and built by good tradesmen instead of the genus "Mahowa." He could prove that he had superintended the building of more culverts than any member present; and he was further prepared to prove that were it not for said culverts, the financial difficulties of the Council would before this have reached that state that even Gladstone, or a Rivers Wilson, would have failed in any endeavour to elucidate them. There were members present he knew that from personal dislike to himself advocated arched culverts, as they were stronger and more scientific. He (the speaker) didn't believe in science: he left science to the doctors, and they pursued it so well that our undertakers' "eyes were standing out with fatness." The reason he advocated the present style of culverts was this—firstly, a "Mahowa" could build them cheaper than a mason; secondly, they were attractive to *kurweyers*; thirdly, the carrier paid for them. He had a good deal of experience in culverts, and he could safely say that as soon as a culvert was finished the "hour would bring the man." Some carrier would arrive with five tons on his wagon, he would naturally make for a culvert, and certain as his wagon covered it, the fabric would give way. Assuredly that man was fined sufficiently to enable the Council to carry on public trust. Councillors, he said, argued as St. Paul did against Alexander, and no doubt wished as Paul did; but he was resolved to go on with his work, as his motto was the Corporation "expects every man to do his duty." (Sensation.)

The General assumed the perpendicular and assured the members he entirely agreed with the resolution of Councillor Goathead, providing that a culvert was built near his corner and gravel laid on the approaches to his emporium. He did not care for the argument used out of doors, that the Councillors only looked out for themselves. How was the stranger to know, when he visited the city, who was a "Roman of the Romans," unless he had a culvert and "et ceteras" near his premises? "Fair play" was a characteristic of Britons. He might point out that Muttonhead, Beefchops, and Muddleton had culverts near their winkels. Why should he be left out in the cold? Were they more patriotic than himself? Did they burn the midnight oil more than himself in solving Municipal problems? Then why, in the name of Justice, should he not have a culvert? The resolution was carried by a majority of four.

Proposed by Councillor Bungleman and seconded by Councillor Gaspipe:

> "That the Council do appoint another Sanitary Inspector with the title of 'Sub-Sanitary Inspector.'"

He (Bungleman) was proud to assure the Council that during twenty years' residence in the city it had never been privileged to him to witness such monuments of dead cats and such a varied assortment of dead dogs, romantically varied with dead pigs, as now adorned the purlieus of this Volksraad city. The present Inspector had been scolded for collecting the departed in heaps and placing them in pyramids opposite the houses of favoured individuals. It was said the hygienic arrangements were disturbed and people suffered. He was not prepared to dispute with the members as to the public health, but this much he could assure them, that in the vicinity of the said pyramids peaches were found to measure nine inches in circumference and pumpkins nine feet. It was obvious that the market was improved and thereby the revenue. He quite held with Councillor Goathead that revenue was the cardinal point to keep in sight. A family or two disappearing might inflict pain on a few, but a fat revenue brought comfort to the many. He hoped the Council would appoint a man to assist the present rabbit-faced Inspector, as he seemed to suffer in health owing to his exertions in preserving the health of others.

The General again rose and plainly told the members that he did not wish to be indicted for manslaughter.

Councillor Catchup said pyramids were no doubt essential to gardeners, but he opined "chloride of lime" ought to be used on these displays of architecture.

Councillor Hazybrain was of opinion that pyramids in a town prevented small-pox and cholera, and he would vote for an Assistant Inspector.

Councillor Beefchops was determined to take a more exalted view of the situation. If a family was carried off by the collection of cats before the front door, it was clear to his mind that it was undoubtedly a moral wrong. If cats improved peaches and pumpkins, then he was willing they should be ridden to his farm adjoining the town lands. (Cries of "Don't you wish you may get it?")

The Mayor suggested that the resolution be delayed *sine die*. He stated that he had received information that people were sending their dogs and cats to the country; and if so, an Assistant would be unnecessary. Agreed to.

Proposed by Councillor Muddleton, seconded by Councillor Muttonhead:

> "That in the opinion of the Council it is highly necessary to light the city after sundown, more especially the main thoroughfares."

The speaker stumbled through a speech which ran as follows:— He would not suggest an expensive system such as brush light, electric, gas, or any of the modern lights. He held the Council was bound to "creep before they could walk." A few blue-bush poles and a requisite number of lanterns would answer all requirements. He was not a very fluent speaker, but he hoped the Council understood him. He then sat down to the immense satisfaction of the Councillors.

Councillor Gaspipe called attention to the fact that Muddleton had a large lot of lanterns, which he had been obliged to take for a bad debt, and that was why he advocated that system. He himself didn't believe in lighting the town. If people were nervous to travel in the dark, let them get home early and stay there. If men would stay out and drink brandy and soda, let them stay there and take the consequences. Lighting the city would be simply destroying the morals of the people. He believed the Council ought to sustain morality and not destroy it. He was a soft-shell Ranter himself, and, perhaps, took a different view to others.

The General thought the Council required some lighting themselves before illuminating the city.

Councillor Bungleman could not see the extreme hurry of the measure. We had a good moon just now which cost nothing, why entail expense ?

Councillor Beefchops proposed, seconded by Goathead :

> "That the question of lighting be put off until the next meeting."

Carried by a majority of three.

Councillor Muttonhead called attention to the present state of the trees in Mud Lane. They had now been planted twelve months and were a very sickly sample of beauty. The Mayor had told him confidentially that the said trees were of the order "Cyclobranchiata," and would thrive better if the tops were planted and the roots aired.

Here the Mayor jumped up and indignantly denied saying anything of the kind about the trees—Muttonhead should be ashamed of himself.

The Council came to the conclusion that if trees would not grow with their roots soiled, they stood less chance if they reversed the order of things.

Muttonhead seized the opportunity to state that the next time the Mayor favoured him with scientific talk, he would take care to have witnesses,

Mayor, derisively, " order !" " order !"

The Mayor then read the following resolution :

> "That in the opinion of the Council it was incumbent on that body to appoint a committee for the purpose of passing such measures as would tend to the public health."

Seconded by Gaspipe.

The Mayor then proceeded to inform the Town Council that he had not been installed in office long, but during that time he had tried to be impartial in his office. He wished that was the chief trait in the character of the Council. He had been told by a friend of undoubted veracity that old "Ironsides," who lives at the extreme corner of the city verging towards Waaihoek, had assured him that if a Town Councillor, or a road party, a city engineer, or any of the plant belonging to the Council, were seen at that corner they would be looked on by the inhabitants as a curiosity; and yet they were not overlooked when rates had to be collected. The only servant of the Council they knew was Zaccheus the tax-gatherer. Things should not be so. It would be invidious to point to any single Councillor as being more guilty than his brethren, but it was notorious there more people than "Ironsides" ready to empty their cups of woe when an opportunity afforded. Shakespeare puts advice to a young man in the following way:

"To thine own self be true."

He (the Mayor) did not think Town Councillors ought to be guided by that line; but as regarded the health of the town, he was prepared to lay before the Council many of the causes that produced mortality amongst the citizens. He had observed that whenever the North-East or Nor'-West wind blew, the air was generally loaded with an impure gaseous substance called ozone, which brought in its train diphtheria, neuralgia, and rheum. To avoid the effects of these winds, the first thoughts of the Council should be directed towards mitigating the evils. They should, firstly, build an Ovipositor with a longitudinal inclination towards a Libethenite formation or Luteolin, and also collect lycodontes during every Novennial year, bearing in the direction of the Nubigenous with a corruscation of infinitesimal radiations, involving a complete phalanx of notoriousness. "*Rara avis in terris, nigroque simillima cygno*," and further consolidate the ramifications evolved from a distinct tracery of "*tempus edax rerum*," which causes, I may say, "*Vox faucibus haesit*."

At this stage the General found he was æsthetic in tastes and travelled to Bridger's hotel. The rest of the Council settled one by one into a deep, deep siesta, and the Mayor went in for tail-lashing on his darling subject. How long he would have stayed, and how long the Council would have slept, it is impossible to say ; but a boy rushed in and called out " Fire !" " Fire !" The Council was equal to the occasion, and walked in great dignity to the burning store. And here they enjoy themselves by looking on in an abject state of sheer helplessness. It was amazing to some Councillors to note their ex-Mayor frantically rushing about and spoiling a good tweed suit, worth £7 10s., in order to save half-a-dozen Kafir pots, worth 15s.

Wolsey's advice to Cromwell might have been quoted to the ex-Mayor :—

"Cromwell, I charge thee fling away ambition,"
For by that sin the angels fell."

BLIKOOR.

Our Sanitary Surroundings.

Bloemfontein, 12th Dec., 1881.

To the Editor of the *Friend :*

Sir,—The impurity of the town spruit has been the hue and cry of the inhabitants of this city for many years past.

The town spruit has been represented as the infested nest from whence nearly all the diseases the town folk suffer, emanate from. Only a few weeks ago we noticed in the local column of one of our newspapers that a certain medical gentleman here had, under his treatment, over fifty cases of diphtheria within two months ; these facts speak for themselves, and certainly demand the prompt interference of the Honourable Town Council of this city to see to our sanitary surroundings.

The spruit, with all its stagnant waters and other objectionable impurities, poisning the centre of our town, is bad enough, but is the Honourable Town Council aware that nothing less than a hide and skin curing establishment is added to the unpleasant and unhealthy odours of the spruit, and that, in the very heart of our town ? I, for one, begin to apprehend all manner of calamities, such as "putrid typhus," or some other dire epidemic, to follow the toleration of such sinks of impurity.

I believe it is the duty of our worthy Sanitary Inspector to report to the Honourable Town Council the existence of such nuisances as the above-named, which, if allowed, cannot fail to vitiate the general health of the town. The Sanitary Inspector being in default in this instance, allow me through the medium of your valuable columns to call the attention of our worthy Corporation to the existence of such a public nuisance.

I am, &c.,

An Inhabitant.

Such was the want of common sense—especially on the part of Ex—Ton—Mare that the town was in a constant state of insolvency and had to borrow at a high rate of interest from the bankers.

Paying the Piper.

"The building of a Town Hall in excess of our requirements is beginning to bear bitter fruit. The Corporation has already borrowed £2,000; and now a public meeting of householders is called for Wednesday next, May 9, at 8 o'clock, for the purpose of appealing to the householders ' for power to borrow a sum not exceeding £3,000, to meet engagements for the current year.' The placing of £3,701 10s. on the estimates to be ' derived from prospective sale of erven,' was

> ' To swallow gudgeons ere they're catched,
> And count their chickens ere they're hatch'd.'

And the piper must be paid somehow. Hence the Town Council is in a quandary.

> ' So comes a reck'ning when the banquet's o'er,
> The dreadful reck'ning, and men smile no more.'

We were always averse to the expenditure of so large a sum as £15,000 on a Town Hall, and looked upon it as the hobby of a few ambitious but irresponsible citizens who had become 'too big for their boots.' Such has been the prodigality of our 'guardians' that the town is now £5,500 in debt—a debt that will probably be augmented by £2,000 before the current year has expired. All our available resources are exhausted, and Bloemfontein will be like a lame dog limping over a style for the next ten years. Retrenchment, therefore is imperative; and we trust the householders in public meeting assembled will discountenance the reckless game of burning the candle at both ends, which has been going on of late so consumedly. The virtues of economy must be impressed upon the minds of the Town Councillors, and the folly of 'outrunning the constable' dilated upon. In these hard times frugality must be practised : it is the only safe card we can play. We are in debt, and it behoves the town to get out of the quagmire, and not sink deeper into it."

Now all this could have been prevented if the State and Council had but understood how to build and construct public Municipal waterworks, &c., by means of public National Paper-money. They could not plead ignorance, because I specially drew their attention to the subject when I read my paper on "How to Construct Free State Railways and other Public Works without the burden of Loans, Bonds, Mortgages or Interest"—since printed and to be had from all booksellers with my other works. Time after time suggestions were made for the storing up of water for the use of the citizens, and notably the scheme here appended.

Our Water Supply.

"We have always advocated a good water supply for this town. When we considered that the town was likely to 'outrun the constable' in building the new Town-hall, we said we should not so much mind the extravagant expenditure if the Municipality spent a pound upon securing a good water supply for every twenty shillings it expended upon the new building. But, we are sorry to say, our advice was not heeded. We have now an expensive structure—very useful no doubt, but not a neccessity—but very little money has been expended on securing a supply of water. Now, the Corporation are in the position of the man who gave his children a stone when they asked for bread. They have secured, by boring at the Park Springs and at Kafirfontein, an ample supply of water, but the expense of bringing it into town baffles them. An Engineer has been consulted. An elaborate plan has been drawn up. We have been made to long for the rich store of the precious element which we can have simply by paying for it, but, alas our spending power is exhausted ! Although we should be glad to witness the supply of water running through our streets as promised by the scheme of Mr. Schurmann—and should not object even to the Modder-river being brought into town—we really do not see how our finances are to stand it.

> ' Utopia is a pleasant place,
> But how shall I get there?'

It strikes us that a much more modest scheme, would have sufficed the inhabitants of this town for many years to come. Our Town Council has evidently lost its head in financial matters. Erven have in late times been sold at such ridiculously high prices ; the morning market dues have brought up such a pretty figure ; the rateable property, as we have previously pointed out, has by a sleight-of-hand trick been increase nearly double ; so our town-fathers think that there is money in galore. *Wij zwemmen in het geld !*

But they should remember that the times, instead of improving, are decidedly getting worse. That it is no use in going too fast. 'Go slow,' should be their motto. These are the times of retrenchment, rather than of increased expenditure. It seems to us a rather reckless spending of money to give any local man £200 for any scheme for supplying water. No body of men who cared for the pockets of their constituents, unless they had the funds of the City of London at their command, should have voted such a large sum of money merely for a scheme, before they had ascertained that there were means sufficient to carry out the plan when brought to maturity. If the Corporation had been in funds, then the competitive principle should have been brought into vogue. A reward of £100 in these hard times would have brought plenty of schemes to the fore. Mr. Schurmann in his Report says :

> According to measurements taken by me at different times during the last four months the undermentioned springs are able to give the following mean number of gallons per day :—1st, Park Springs every 24 hours about 50,000 gallons ; 2nd, Kaffirfontein every 24 hours 150,000 gallons; 3rd, Bloemfontein every 24 hours about 100,000 gallons. Together about 300,000 gallons per day, which quantity is quite sufficient for ten thousand inhabitants.

So that it appears there is no want of water in and around our town for our population, which is probably under 2,000. After stating that the amount of rainfall in the town of Bloemfontein during a certain number of years has averaged about twenty inches per annum, Mr. Schurmann proceeds to say :

> If the same quantity of rain water falls on the area of the above-mentioned kloof [between Tempe-road and the Spitskop], which may be reckoned on, and from this rain water 8 inches only are caught, this will give a quantity of not less than 76,554,240 gallons of water per year, and if all is stored up, an average of 209,710 gallons per day.
>
> At present a reservoir to store up 20,000,000 gallons of water will be sufficient for the town supply, if the Town Council is willing to adopt a combined water scheme, according to the plans and specifications.
>
> In accordance with the above-mentioned scheme, all parts of the town, which are lower than 50 feet above a certain 0,oo point shown on plans, will be supplied with spring water from the Park, by means of the 50,000 gallon tank ; all parts of the town which are on a higher level than 50 feet above the 0,oo point, will be supplied with water from the High Level Reservoir.

> The fire hydrants as shown on the plan, can be used under high pressure only; the above-mentioned reservoir will give the pressure required, and will save the cost of a fire-engine.
>
> The tap-posts as shown on plan are made for the public in general, as well as for those who can afford the expense of having the water from the main pipes laid into their houses.

The following is the plan proposed by Mr. Schurmann for paying for the outlay necessary for this large undertaking:—

> According to the valuation roll, the value of property in Bloemfontein is about £500,000, and if the Town Council adopts the scheme with the High Level Reservoir, which will cost about £35,000, the water rates must be 1¼d. in the £.
>
> £35,000 at 6 per cent. interest will give £2,100 interest per year. 1¼d. in the £ on £500,000 will give about £2,600 per year.
>
> From this can be repaid in the first year £500, and in the following years more, so that in a certain number of years the Waterworks will be the absolute and free property of the Municipality.

The scheme matured by Mr. Schurmann in accordance with an order of the Mayor and Town Council is no doubt as good as could be devised under the circumstances, but we maintain that there is no necessity for such a *grand* undertaking, and if there were, there are no funds at the disposal of the Corporation to pay for the carrying out of the same. What we want is a small practical scheme to cost at the outside about £5,000. We believe the ratepayers never dreamed that the Council ever intended to clap threepence in the £ in perpetuity on their erven. We say, threepence in the £; for the estimate of 1¼d. would never pay the interest. A penny rate on the present fictitious value of property brings up, according to the published Estimates, £1,720; therefore, a penny farthing rate would produce £2,150. There would be expenses attending the reservoir and pipes, as well as the salary of another water bailiff to be provided for, which might be set down at £500 or £600 a year. If this were added to the interest of £2,100 per annum (which our readers will observe is reckoned at the rate of 6 per cent, per annum only, whilst the cheapest money the Town Council can get is at 6½ per cent.), it would bring the yearly charge up to £2,700. Before the ratepayers agree to such a scheme a re-valuation of property is sure to take place, and that would probably bring down the receipts 25 per cent. We note that Mr. Schurmann in his report says that 1¼d. in the £ is equal to £6 per erf, which would be a very high rate for landlords to pay on small tenements. And how about the hundreds of vacant erven? Would their proprietors be called upon to pay their quota? Although their value is included in the rateable property, it surely would not be fair to tax the proprietors if no water was consumed.

In addition to the above, other schemes were proposed, but to please the Ex—Ton—Mare, a sum of about a thousand pounds was spent in digging a trench to drain a hollow, born of bog and always dissipated by drought. I am bold enough to state that it is not for want of water that prosperity does not follow the white man in South Africa. It is want of wisdom in not knowing how to gather up Nature's solid stone and other material and storing up the waters that run to the rivers and seas. Of course, the one thing needed in South Africa or elsewhere is money, or exchange mediums, to enable the people to carry out all undertakings necessary for their comfort and welfare; and this necessity, with its attendant train of discomforts, will always exist so long as we place our sole reliance upon bankers or gold money.

The ancients knew nothing about our modern system of money, and yet, by their labour, they constructed aqueducts and other public works as can be seen to this day, as I have fully explained in my *National Paper-Money and Its Use*. If, in the past, the ancients could construct such works without money, surely we, the scientific moderns, can do so; and, with our improved system of legal tender paper notes, even much better.

By adopting this course we should free ourselves and our children from being debt-slaves to the gold money-holders. It must and will be done when the light dawns upon our State and Town

Councillors, and then there will be a chance for all to have pure water in their houses and in the streets. It is quite saddening to think of the want, waste and deaths that result from the want of a supply of pure water. With a large dam at the top and bottom of the town, millions of gallons of the precious fluid could have been blocked back by simply pulling down and removing the big hills at the back of the town by gravitation. The one could have been placed in the way of the water, and finally banked up by stone work, that it would at all times—by means of gravitation—have supplied the whole of the town for drinking and all other purposes, and thus the whole district might have been converted into a beautiful garden. But no; though the hills were crying out, " Come and take us : " and the water asking to be stopped and used for the benefit of man and cattle whilst rushing away in sufficient volumes to supply the whole country, and for want of gold money the unemployed were standing still and living upon charity.

With a sufficient supply of water, and manure from the waste materials of the town, the lands of Bloemfontein could have grown all the food that was needed, and thousands of pounds would have been saved,—that were lost through cattle dying in the winter for want of food in consequence of the insufficient water supply. These facts being known, one can only feel contempt for men who sit on Town Councils—not only in Bloemfontein but all the world over. In the days to come these are the works that will remove all want and trade depression and give everlasting work to all our workers, and thus :—

> In our distress bid Legal tenders chase
> All fear of want from Labour's hardy race,
> Bid Aqueducts be form'd to bring the rills
> Of purest water from from the neighbouring Hills;
> Bid Lakes expand where youth may safely float;
> Bid deepen'd Streams the Health of Towns promote.
> Bid Harbours open, public Works and ways extend,
> Bid Temples worthier of Art and Science ascend;
> Bid the broad Arch the dangerous Flood contain,
> The Mole projected, break the roaring main.
> Back to her bounds the subject Sea command,
> And roll obedient Rivers through the Land.
> Lastly, let Government such Wages give

On Public Works, that all may toil and live:
Then, all who toil will find life pass along,
Happier sustained by Labour than by wrong;
Then, will our Virtuous Poor be better fed,
Nor workhouse test,—nor destitution—dread ;
And all around them rising in the scale
Of Comfort, show that humanity's Laws prevail.

Chapter XVI.

THE month of May was an important month in the history of the Free State. For twenty long years John Brand had served the Free State as the State figure-head; but certainly not as the *head* of the State. For many reasons he had been chosen: but I am prepared to vouch for the truth of the assertion that, in no sense, had these reasons been verified. I have already made frequent allusion to this man, and shall have to continue to do so; but, in the first place, let me say there is no desire or intention, on my part, to draw attention to him in his private capacity. I consider him to be, like thousands more, a good husband, a good father, and a good man; but goodness in private life is not all that is needed in a public official.

On the eve of his fifth election occurred one of the most convincing proofs imaginable that—after twenty years of official life—he was a complete failure in his public capacity, an opinion that is thoroughly borne out by the following article from the *Friend*, of May 8th:—

The Volksraad.

"Pursuant to notice, and in accordance with the Constitution, the honourable Volksraad assembled at ten o'clock on Monday last. There were about forty members present. It being the annual session, a Chairman for the year was elected. The choice fell on Mr. J. George Fraser, the member for Bloemfontein.

"Mr. Tobias De Villiers, who has acted in this capacity since the death of Mr. Gert Visser in 1879, said his health did not permit him to accept the high and honourable situation. Many members, notwithstanding the expressed wish of Mr. De Villiers, voted for him as Chairman, twenty-three voting for Mr. Fraser, and nineteen for Mr. De Villiers. We cannot but commend the Raad upon its choice, for Mr. Fraser's legal knowledge, tact, and business capabilities, pre-eminently qualify him for the responsible position. He is also thoroughly conversant with the new rules of order, and it is thought that public business will be much expedited by his election. Mr. De Villiers has done his work in his day and generation, but his friends have lately observed that the new rules of order were very trying to the old Chairman, whose health has been failing recently.

"Messrs. Louw and Kruger were appointed as a Commission to escort His Honour the President to the Council Chamber, and the Raad adjourned.

"At 2.15, the President arrived, the Band striking up the *Volkslied*.

"The Rev. C. S. Morgan offered up a fervent prayer to the Most High that He would pour down on the assembly the continual dew of His blessing.

"His Honour, who was in good voice, then delivered the opening address, a copy of which, and a translation of the same, our readers will find in other columns.

"The Raad has made some progress with the public business brought forward in the Speech by His Honour. We are sorry to observe, however, that the low state of the Treasury Chest is having its effect on the legislature, for it has not only refused to entertain the question of building a new Presidency, which can be done without for a time, but it refused to consider the subject of building a new Post Office, of which there is much need.

"The Report of the Treasurer-General on the past financial year and the Draft Estimates of revenue and expenditure for the year 1884-5 were laid on the table. The latter was referred to the Commission on the Estimates. The Treasurer-General estimates the revenue from all sources at £229,598 10s. 10¼d., and the expenditure at £269,327 15s. 2d., showing a debit balance of £39,729 4s. 3½d. This statement will no doubt frighten some of our *landsvaders*, who have been used to an annual surplus of nearly the like amount. It must not be forgotten, however, that £84,157 11s. is brought up as an item of expenditure. This large amount appears to have been obtained during the past financial year, as follows :—Promissory Note, National Bank, £7,000 ; Loan from said Bank to Treasurer-General, £40,000 ; overdrawn account in the said Bank, £26,057 11s. ; and borrowed from the Government Loan Funds, £11,100. Of this amount, £40,001 1s. 5d., which sum has been paid for reproductive works, will be repaid from the Debentures when floated. The Treasurer-General having brought this amount of £40,001 1s. 5d. up as revenue, it therefore follows, that the debit of balance of £39,729 odd is a serious deficiency for us.

"The great depression of trade has a very injurious influence on the revenue ; and the tightness of the money market and the low price of all kinds of farm produce at present ruling do not allow the usual sales of land to take place. It therefore appears that the Raad will have to ' cut its coat according to its cloth,' and retrench as much as possible. We trust, however, that all reproductive works will be allowed to be carried on as promised."

The Bad Times.

" Never since March, 1854, when the British garrison marched out of the Fort, has Bloemfontein presented such a wobegone appearance as it now does. Never since the epoch of the Abandonment, has the capital exhibited such a list of empty tenements. Never since the country was thrown overboard by its sovereign, have ' sovereigns ' been so scarce. Never since the establishment of the Free State, have ' establishments ' been so pitilessly reduced. Never since President Brand secured for us peace and plenty by the subjugation of the ' nation of thieves ' and the circulation of a forced paper currency, have trade and enterprise been at so low an ebb and " accommodation ' at such a high consideration. Never did the cheery motto of our blithe-hearted Chief Magistrate (' Alles zal regt komen ') sound so vapid and meaningless as it does in these ' hard times ' when an almost imperceptible rise of the commercial barometer would be hailed with inexpressible delight by the entire community."

"The speech of His Honour the State President and that of the Governor of the Cape Colony offer much scope for the discussion of questions that may justly be called burning questions. Both are characterised by what we may be allowed to call, in opposition to the progressive legislation of former years, a tendency to consolidate existing measures and provide for a period of difficulties and short comings. To exult in the position now occupied by this State and the Cape Colony would be sheer madness, yet it may be sound sense to acknowledge that nations as well as individuals derive incalculable benefit from being subject to laws as natural as they are necessary.

"One of those laws is, that unnatural growth is followed by disease or decay, that upon every period of inflation follows one of depression. But the lesson would be a vain one, if the latter state was not really acknowledged and truly made use of to return to life's real and best objects, which are so often overlooked in the race for what is called in this world success. Thus, both the Free State and the Cape Colony will be occupied with legislation that concerns the regulation of their finances upon a more sound basis, and touch the prosperity of the country by an attention to questions, that are too easily disregarded and overlooked as long as each country—out of a sense of independence and selfishness—is mindful only of what it deems its own profit.

"The contemplation of what is of mutual interest to both countries forces two or three questions to the foreground, which we intend to discuss on this occasion. Looking at the securing of peace as a main condition of prosperity, the question of Basutoland deserves to rank foremost in our consideration. Colonel Clarke's visit to Bloemfontein and his journey thence to confer with the Governor of Capetown, regarding the immediate measures calculated to ensure peace and good government shows the mutual interest both countries take in the future of Basutoland. We have been told that his intention is to raise a force of something like a thousand volunteers—here and in the Cape Colony—destined to protect our boundary and to enable him to govern Basutoland, if need be, by an application of force. We are again told that the Colonel has bluntly refused to lend a shadow of his authority to Jonathan, and that in consequence thereof the chief, loyal to the cause of his countrymen's enemies, is on the verge of ruin.

"The two statements, coming as they do from trustworthy sources, do not harmonize, and we feel at a loss to offer advice to our Government, except to postpone action until the policy of the Administrator has passed the limit of intentions, and has made itself apparent in measures. The danger of a sudden change of policy, to which we are now as subject as we always have been, is too apparent to allow of our leaving the strict confines of caution and prudence. The more so as the imminent change of Ministry in the Cape Colony threatens to influence the position of the Colony towards Basutoland. Though we may at once add that we should hail the change, promising as it does the constituting of a Ministry, which will lay greater stress upon our needs and what is due to us than the present Ministry has exhibited.

"A new Ministry in the Cape Colony means, if not a Dutch South African Ministry, certainly one in which that party—our party—will have a decided influence. It means consequently a reversed policy in the native question, and that is necessary. It means the retention of the Transkei, and a check upon 'the new departure,' by which colonists are placed in opposition to natives, and unmethodical philanthropy takes the place of a practical policy. It means the avoidance of complications in Stellaland, an eventuality in which we, as well as the whole of South Africa, are more deeply concerned than appears on the surface. It means that this country will have reason to expect justice from a sister State that has preyed upon us and abused our natural weakness.

"Thus we come to the second point, in which both countries are alike deeply interested. His Honour the State President and the Governor alike touch upon the question of a rebate on customs, the former in an appeal to the sense of justice of the colonial people, the latter in an acknowledgment that the colonial trade will be benefited by such a concession. It matters little whether feelings of honour or self-interest dictate the actions of the Cape Colony in this matter, as long as justice is done to us. This we fondly hope, for the sake of the Colony as well as our own. For the refusal to listen to the dictates of common justice will be fruitful of disappointment and distress, and we think it will not be out of place to quote here an extract from the *Natal Witness* bearing upon Railways, a question that is entirely dependent upon that of Rebate of Customs :—

> The railway question, however, as is well known, touches the financial question, and the financial question touches also the Customs question. These are also points that have to be kept in view in respect of any plan for the future. In discussing this on former occasions, we have spoken of it as the interest of Natal to assist in railway construction from her own border as far as Bethlehem, and as the interest of the Cape Colony to assist in railway construction from Colesberg to Bloemfontein. This is, no doubt, a convenient mode of stating the problem so long as we are arguing on the basis of the rival interests of the Cape Colony and Natal. There can, however, be little doubt that, viewing the question from the basis of the general interests of South Africa, a different and more comprehensive view will have to be taken. It will be necessary to follow the system adopted in Algeria by dividing railways into two classes, viz., "lines of general interest," and "lines of local interest," the former cared for by the South African communities in common, and the latter by the local Government by which they were constructed. The classification would not be difficult to arrive at. "Lines of general interest" would be clearly those which connected the different communities together, and brought their centres of population into communication with each other. "Lines of local interest" would be lines other than these. Hence the lines from Capetown to Kalk Bay, from Capetown to Malmesbury, from Capetown to Stellenbosch, from Port Elizabeth to Graaff-Reinet, from Port Elizabeth to Grahamstown, from Durban to Verulam, from Durban to Isipingo, and from Ladysmith to Newcastle would undoubtedly all be "lines of local interest." Probably the same classification would apply to the line from East

London to Aliwal North; possibly to the line from Capetown through Beaufort West. It would be at least impossible for South Africa at large to recognise as "lines of general interest" lines which have been notoriously constructed as competing lines to serve party purposes. The individuals who have profited by the construction of such lines should pay for them themselves, if they can. They cannot expect South Africa to pay for them. So, too, the line from Pretoria to Delagoa Bay could only be regarded as a "line of general interest" as far as the Portugese boundary. Within that boundary it is Portugal's concern. On the other hand, it is very plain that the lines constructed within the Free State would be all of them "lines of general interest," inasmuch as they would all be lines of intercommunication between the different South African communities. The importance of recognising this principle will be at once admitted, while the effect which it cannot but exercise on the future of the whole South African question will be very great. In all probability it be will found both desirable and necessary for united South Africa to undertake the responsibility for all money spent in the construction of "lines of general interest," and there can be no doubt that the Customs receipts at the various ports will rightly constitute the fund out of which liabilities of this kind are to be met.

The three questions of Native Management, Customs Dues, and Railways, seemingly unconnected and independent of each other, are thus brought under one focus. If an attempt is made to deal with them on a broad and liberal basis, the times that are and have been will soon be forgotten, in an era of true prosperity and progress. Alas, if to our present troubles should be added the result consequent upon a disregard of what concerns South Africa's best interests!

The above forms so serious an indictment that people may well wonder at the glowing eulogies that had been heaped upon the

President. The fact is, that but for the connection with England, the Free State would have become an uninhabited wilderness. The diamond fields were the one cause of an appearance of prosperity in the past; and, as I shall afterwards prove, not one single effort was made on the part of the officials to improve the condition of the people.

But for the golden shower of English sovereigns, the Dutch, as of old, would have been but mealy eaters, with now and then a piece of biltong as a relish, and the wearers of leather breeches. All this may be repudiated by the brainless lads born since the the abandonment, but it will certainly be endorsed by those who recollect the period of the English occupancy, and who long once more for the power, protection and wealth of the English nation; and now that money is so scarce the people are having their eyes opened to the truth. It may well appear that it was owing to some special merit that President Brand was elected for the fifth time; but it was nothing of the kind, as all who know the circumstances are fully aware.

The Dutch are proverbially slow, and history proves that it is only on such occasions as when they feel the pinch of hunger, or property or life is endangered, that they can be moved to energetic action. During the whole of the President's career the Dutch had made money out of the English and that to them was sufficient. During this period, the German and Hollander have rushed into the Free State, and having occupied the official positions they are determined to keep the man in power that helped them into such good quarters at the expense of the Dutchman. The inhabitants of the Free State are getting so poverty-stricken that they will not stand another term of five years for Brand or any other President with a horde of German and Hollander human asvogals, who look upon the Dutch people as so many carcases with which to gorge themselves for the remainder of their lives and their children after them. The Dutch have been and are good natured; but they cannot stand the beaks of these wretches at their very vitals without turning like the worm when trodden upon, and in their turning I feel that they will smite hip and thigh the settled and roving vagabonds all over the country eating them up so continuously.

The month of May was the official May Day. Having a holiday, I determined to see the sights provided for the Dutch people by the official Hollander class. Children are at all times pleased with firearms, and if not a *living* then a *rocking*-horse. Now you cannot move the youth of the Dutch inhabitants so readily as to mount him on a horse and give him a gun with an inexhaustible supply of powder to blaze away. Now this was the great enjoyment of the day. The show so far as the bunting was concerned was a sight not fit for niggers much less the gods. It was not of sufficient quality even to please the children, and must have disgusted the men.

Simple-minded women will laugh and giggle at a little, and for an opportunity to show up and be admired will risk any amount of disappointment. But the miserable, ludicrous figure that the aspiring officials cut was something so saddening that one wondered how they could expose themselves before the conquered natives in such a burlesque. It was a daylight, walking pantomime of the grotesque order.

To parade the streets, to conduct the President to the Dutch Church to swear an allegiance for another five years of good things in the shape of £3,000 a year and an honorarium of £2,500 to clear himself of debt after the many thousands he had had during the past years of his Presidency. It was quite annoying to me to see how happy he looked as he passed along thinking how nicely he had made the Free State a "Tom Tiddler's ground" for picking up English gold and silver at the expense of the Dutch. One wag facetiously intimated that he would swear and fulfil the office for a third of the sum.

What a vile thought of a Radical in a Republican State—but really this aping of older countries is truly disgusting. A big show may be possible in a European country, but the attempt to parody the swindling ceremonies of Europe is something outrageous. At a given time the burghers on their nags in some of the most wretched clothing and "show ups" that it has ever been my lot to witness were proud to salute their chief. The word of command was given by a half-blooded Sheriff Ruff, for the time being made Commandant because he had a splendid mount. Then the march commenced to the Dutch Church. We passed, on the way, the Town Hall, near which were placed some damaged salmon tins charged with fat for the evening illuminations.

The poverty of the town was such that the Town Council voted the magnificent sum of £10 to celebrate the occasion. Think of it ye gods; £10 for a National day of rejoicing. O glorious simplicity of a Republic.

Arrived at the Church, in the midst of guns firing, the officials at last entered the church of man—it had long ceased to be the Church of God—and then commenced a combination of blasphemy and eulogy that was simply a compound of insolence and audacity. Thanks to the conceit and narrow-mindedness of the Dutch, the minister was no longer allowed to speak in English in this structure—so that I, not having learned the *patois* of these simple Dutch farmers and their kitchen Dutch, was not able to follow all the orders of the Masters of the Ceremonies; reserving to myself the pleasure of its translation in the *Friend* afterwards. Having sat through the mimic torture of a spurious Republican swearing-in, I retired in the midst of guns firing to my tiffin, hoping to enjoy that better than all this childish mimicry.

The Swearing-in

of

HIS HONOUR J. H. BRAND

as

President.

On Friday last, the 9th May, the town presented quite a gala appearance—flags waved in the wind from every flagstaff, pennants and banners hung out from many a building, and the streets were thronged with people in holiday attire. Soon after sunrise horsemen galloped about the city—some with rifles with which they ever and anon fired off a *feu de joie*, and others bearing the Free State colours unfurled. About nine o'clock the armed and mounted burghers, who had arrived in town on the previous day, began to muster under their different field-cornets. These came from the four wards and the town, and were distinguished by different coloured puggarees. The town burghers, numbering about 60, under Mr. Nicolas Raaff, wore orange; the Boven-modder-river wore green; the Middle-modder-river, red; the

Kafir-river, blue ; and the Kaal-spruit, orange. Mr. Field-commandant Prinsloo, who was in command, wore an orange scarf. At ten o'clock the President in his carriage, accompanied by Messrs. Roux and Siebert, two of the oldest members of the Raad, especially selected to accompany His Honour, arrived on the Market-square under an escort of about 500 armed and mounted burghers, *en route* to the Council Chamber, where it was arranged the Volksraad would receive him, and the procession should be formed. As soon as His Honour arrived, the school-children sang the " *Volkslied.*" Six masters of ceremonies, appointed by the Raad, and twelve assistant masters of ceremonies, after some little time, formed the procession as follows :

  The Town Burghers under command of Mr. N. Raaff.
    The Artillery Band.
   Two M.C.'s (Dr. Krause and Mr. Salzmann).
The Chairman and secretary of the Volksraad and the Minister of the D. R. Church, Bloemfontein.
    The Members of the Volksraad.
   Judge Reitz and State-Attorney Vels.

Armed and Mounted Burghers.	HIS HONOUR THE PRESIDENT and Messrs. Souz and Siebert.	Armed and Mounted Burghers.

   Members of the Executive Council.
  Consuls of Holland, Germany, and Portugal.
    The Moderator of the Synod.
 Ministers of the various congregations and Members of the Synod.
 Heads of Departments and the Rector of Grey College.
    The Mayor and Town Council.
  Officials and school teachers of Grey College.
     School children.

Burghers on foot.
Armed and Mounted Burghers.

The head of the procession, which had come down Maitland-street, arrived on the Market-Square exactly at ten o'clock. It turned to the right, passed in front of the Club, went down the south side of the Square, traversing the east side by the Free State Hotel, and then by the *Friend* office to Upper Church-street. It was about 400 yards long, and reached from the Club corner to the Police-station. The public walked four deep and mounted burghers six deep. Whilst the procession was moving along minute guns were fired. The President alighted at the Dutch Church at about half-past ten o'clock. About 500 persons were assembled at the building, the inside of which was crowded, space only being left for the Members of the Volksraad, the Executive, and other privileged persons. The Chairman of the Volksraad received His Honour at the Church and led him to his appointed place, followed by the two delegates from the Raad, the organ playing a voluntary in the meantime ; after which the swearing-in ceremony was commenced by the Minister of Bloemfontein offering up prayer. An eloquent address was then delivered by the Chairman of the Raad, who requested the Volksraad's Secretary to read the oath. It having been demanded of the Psesident whether he was prepared to take the oath, His Honour replied in the affirmative, took the oath, and signed the same. The "*Volkslied*" was played on the organ, and a salute of 21 guns notified the enactment of this part of the proceedings. After an address from the Rev. C. S. Morgan, to which His Honour the President replied, the solemnities were closed with prayer, and the Raad adjourned to the Council Chamber. The Chairman and Secretary of the Raad and the Landdrost of Bloemfontein escorted His Honour to his carriage, and he was accompanied to Government House by the two delegates from the Raad, under escort of the whole of the mounted burghers. The Chairman and Members of the Volksraad returned in the same order in which they came to the Council Chamber. There was no real recession, as the President proceeded to the Presidency by one route, and the Members of the Raad took another to their destination ; while the other bodies returned home without any formation whatever. A great number of people who fully expected that there would be a recession similar to the procession, and who had been waiting for an hour-and-a-half—the time the ceremony occupied—were, in consequence, disappointed in missing a view of the expected pageantry.

Soon after His Honour had returned home, the Chairman and Members of the Raad repaired to the Presidency and presented the President with an address from that honourable body and the gift of money voted last annual session. At half-past one the W.M.s. of the two Masonic Lodges in this town presented an address from the members of the Craft, to which His Honour replied in cordial terms. Then Mr. Attorney Mathey, the Agent for the Chief Sepinare, handed in an address from that Chief congratulating His Honour upon his election for the fifth time as President, and expressing the wish that the cordial and friendly relations which had always existed between the Barolongs and the Free State would long continue. His Honour, who appeared much gratified with this thoughtful token of respect of the Chief Sepinare, said he trusted that the friendly relations which had hitherto existed between the two people would last, for the Barolongs had always been allies of the State, and in the early days had much befriended the original settlers in this country. This deputation was no sooner bowed out than the Mayor and Corporation waited upon His Honour and presented an address to the President, to which he gave a gracious reply. The Chairman and Committee of the Bloemfontein Club then presented an address to their Honorary Chairman, and were cordially received. The Moderator and Ministers of the Dutch Reformed Church also presented an address on behalf of the Synod, now in convocation.

The amusements and illuminations of the evening were positively marvellous. I may truly say that the English at their clubs and houses were as fawning as the Germans and Hollanders. The Jew—as ever, parsimonious in the land where he gathered up his wealth, even the bankrupt unbelieving Thomas and the German Old—Sons of the fountain of *dis*honour—again went into debt at somebody's expense to lighten their residence, but no longer their house. May they never know what it is to own another place is all the harm I wish them after all my special kindness. The town, like the unfortunate land, is full of sycophants who, believing that John Brand can help them in getting hold of English money, fawn and flatter without stint.

The Germans and Jews are low and grovelling when poor, and insolent and snobbish when well supplied with English money. The Dutchman may love his Africa with all his heart and would perhaps fight for his land, but the Germans and Jews, directly they find there is nothing to be gained from the Free State, will leave all to their wretched fate.

Chapter XVII.

ROM the time when the Colonial Government gave to the Free State the sum of £100,000, as compensation for the supposed loss of the diamond fields at Kimberley, the banking power there has been to all intents a monopoly. That money was made the means of taxing, under another form, the inhabitants, and the income derived from usury was devoted to the payment of the Free State officials.

In the early days of the Orange Free State, the then Government issued on the public credit, and the security of what were at that time known as the public lands, a sufficient number of paper notes called "Bluebacks"; but as time rolled on, these lands were stolen, or passed away to private holders; thus, the security, upon which the notes were issued, vanished, and as a matter of course the market value of the notes diminished. This was just the result any sane person would expect. Destroy all or part of the securities, whether moveable or unmoveable property, upon which the English or any other Government made an advance and the whole value would at once depreciate to the exact amount of loss by such destruction.

Although this was well known, the Government gold Bank, the one private bank of Africa, and other interested parties opposed the issue of paper-money; but I am bold enough to assert that in future the English Capitalists will not lend to the Dutch Free State; and they, like many others, will have to consider the expediency of making their own money for home use, and the products of the country—whether many or few—will have to be the purchasing medium for foreign goods.

Gold money has been the cause of the downfall of all ancient Empires, and as it was in the past so will it be in the future. Thus it becomes the duty of all statesmen to consider well the present money and exchange conditions if they desire to prevent the destruction of the governing classes.

The legal humbugs in Bloemfontein were so unreliable that it was impossible to secure an honest opinion from *one*. This is not to we wondered at when we consider how they constituted themselves black ornaments to their profession. The original history of the whole is so peculiar that posterity must not lose the advantage of watching how, under a Dutch Republic, such things could be possible.

First and foremost, the President—a Cape Town lawyer, a failure in Cape Town—a place-man from the beginning in Bloemfontein. The Attorney-General, so rank an impostor and swindler that no one desired his services; and, with £700 a year, always in debt, and being a lawyer no one "went for him" for fear of losing in any just cause of complaint they might have against him. The keenest and most successful lawyer was a most immoral and outrageous man; always in debt, and, as a retired German missionary and Kaffir killer and an ex-policeman, was very little respected. Another was so black a sheep, that even his black brethren did not care to know him; who, although at one time I paid him £100 for services not worth twenty pounds, never finished the work for which he received the sum above-mentioned, and at last sent me a most piteous letter begging the loan of two pounds, which was never repaid. Perhaps Mr. What-is-the-matter and the Future will accept this as a gift to buy a Bier for him when he ceases from troubling. The magistrates of the Free State were totally unqualified for their office, as the constant appeals against their decisions in the High Court (so called) bear witness.

The Hat—Ton of Bloemfontein was a most miserable man both in and out of office. With all the impudence of a Dutch Boer he offered an Englishman, who needed work and help, 10s. a month, to work in his garden; mark it well,—less pay than that given to a black man. This man for two months refused to issue a warrant for the apprehension of a man who outrageously robbed me of over £1000. It was suggested that a fellow-feeling would not allow him to be hard upon this vagabond. At last, under the influence of public pressure, he consented to see into it; but when I respectfully accosted him about the matter, he assured me that he was not sure if he had the power to do as I wished, but would look up the "authorities" on the subject.

Fancy, the Chief Magistrate not knowing his duties; no wonder it was said that he was an officious fool, making up in bluster, for lack of knowledge:—

This state of things becoming intolerable, I demanded justice from the State Attorney, who wrote for the warrant to be issued immediately, with results that will be seen later on.

In December at the introduction of a broker, I sold to a man who called himself a merchant, £142 worth of flour on a month's Promissory Note. This man was dishonourable enough to attempt to assign his estate, the very day after this transaction, and never paid the balance remaining. Finding I could get no satisfaction, I at last secured compulsory power of sequestration, and then the Law wreckers carried on their work of destruction. Think of the conditions that could allow such damnable conduct on the part of a trader!

"*Victim*" *on Commercial Trickery.*

"The worth of a State in the long run is the worth of the commercial individuals composing it."

Pietermaritzburg, Oct. 25th, 1883.

To the Editor of the *Friend*:

Sir,—Having noticed some very trenchant remarks in your local column of the 18th inst, relative to the unsatisfactory manner in which business is transacted in the Free State, I shall esteem it a great favour if you will allow me a space for these few lines apropos of the subject.

It has been a matter of great surprise to many for some years that in the face of such apparent rascality and business trickery that has, and is still taking place within the South African Colonies, that merchants are not more careful in the entrusting of their wares to the credit of petty shop-keepers throughout the country.

It is a generally admitted fact that the existing laws between the creditor and debtor will bear a deal of modifying, for the former's better security, but at the same time it is passing strange that a trader upon finding his business proving an unpayable one, is privileged with the consoling expedient that he has only to stow away to some distant part a third of his stock, and declare himself insolvent when he may shortly reappear upon the scene affluently circumstanced with his name *visibly* untarnished. Others with a fiendish longing to obtain gold at any cost, speculate in a fire insurance policy, and cruelly charge the domesticated animal of their household with having set the matches in a blaze, thereby causing them to become "burnt out of house and home." Lor' how pitiful a story to work upon the feelings of a compassionate community ! !

How easily the Fire Insurance Agent's warm sympathies are touched too, so much so that he actually will not waste time duly investigating the fire's cause, but out of pity for the homeless shopkeeper, "shells out" like a lamb without further delay.

It is indeed a cold country for an honest man where the great majority of men would sooner be calculating the money in your pocket than the virtue in your breast, but truly this is the general characteristic of a very large proportion of our shop-keepers.

We hear so much of illicit diamond buyers and their severe sentences, but is the crime of the I.D.B. an iota worse than the shop-keepers ?

Then why are our merchants not alive to the necessity of forming some means of detecting or preventing this accursed and doubly illicit system of roguery ?

And I may further ask why are the Fire Insurance Agents not more alert to the cunning speculators upon their policies ?

Hoping these home-thrusts will not fail to reach the many for whom they are intended, and that men of recognised probity and thorough straightforwardness will endeavour to impede the further increase of this gentlemanly clothed system of swindling by bringing the matter out more forcibly and thoroughly ventilating it through the medium of the Press,—

I remain, &c.,

A VICTIM.

It has often been said that lawyers have no conscience, and that very few of them can possibly enter heaven. If making a hell for other men is worthy of reward, then indeed these men deserve a future hell, as we have proof of from the time of Judge Jeffries. Some may say we complain too much. Good heavens! whatever we may say of the legal profession, can hardly be too strong when we have been victimised in Parliament, out of Parliament, and in every turn of life by these legal swindlers.

There may be a few honest men among lawyers, but in these days no honest man would care to belong to the legal profession. Even the simple-hearted Boer-farmer has felt his swindling practices so long that in very self-defence he has had to pass the most stringent measures to protect himself from being ruined in the Free State by the army of foreign-German lawyers.

Chapter XVIII.

N May it became necessary for me to settle with my so-called landlord, but who in reality was nothing better then a "house thief." The reader will as he follows the narrative be able to form some idea of what this German missionary, Freemason, inhuman legal and illegal shark and exploiter—who assured me that Equity was not understood in the Free State —was like.

During my tenancy of three years and a half he had received from me over £800 in rent, and more than £1,000 from the previous tenant, these two sums defraying the cost of the property for which he now demanded £2,500. During my occupancy I had erected on the premises at considerable expense an iron building which upon my leaving he refused to allow me to remove, claiming the same as his own property under what he called the Roman-Dutch law, and which even he admitted was in no sense of the word—Equity. What a land to live in although with a man at its head who had not only secured his legal right to absorb other people's chattels in Cape Town, but, it is said, sat his terms in one of the English Inns of Court, during the twenty years he was president of this Free State Alsatia no laws were passed upon which any man could look with pride, nor could the head of the State say with Solon "I left them a guide to regulate them." To resume :—I at last had to agree either to pay him (my landlord) the sum of £25 for permission to remove what by all moral right was my own property or to allow the same amount out of the original purchase-money from my successor ; and as he required the structure, and to save myself from further plunder, I allowed him that amount of money. To embitter me the more and ultimately cause me to leave the Free State with feelings of hatred against all such barefaced robberies, this man was a member of the Legislature, and a constant attendant at Church, where equity was preached but not practised. Truly the world needs the removal of these inhuman skunks—a Deluge or earthquake to swallow up the whole of them with all their wickedness and injustice.

Notwithstanding these facts, this swivel-eyed thief declared in the presence of others that he did not wish to deprive me of a single sixpence that I had worked so hard for, and then tried to gloss over his plunder and robbery of myself by flattering me, somewhat as follows :—" no man had ever stepped into the Free State who had worked harder, or did more to enlighten the public upon all matters pertaining to the improvement of their condition, &c., &c." Still, all this did not prevent him robbing me in as shameless a way as ever an Irish landlord robbed his tenants who improved their properties at their own expense and could get no compensation. The insolence and impudence of the demand I was compelled to submit to was almost unbearable, and if ever I felt hatred towards a squint-eyed man, it was at the moment when I recollected a former robbery on his part, wherein he gave me a further display of legal treachery by the monstrous charge of £55 for what was simply three days work on the part of his clerk! To slay such men would almost be a public blessing. No law worthy of the name, no justice, no equity. —Advocates pretended to sympathise with me in my heavy losses. Death is the only justice for such wretches!

This swindler admitted that I had always paid him honourably and yet he was low enough to rob me at the last moment. Personally, I might have passed even this over, but my case was by no means the only one. This defender of Kaffir cold-blooded murderers, illicit Jew diamond stealers, a supporter of the tyrant Sepinare, because he, like the missionaries in the territory, received grants of land plundered from the general domain of the tribe, a mean despicable detainer of the ill-gotten wealth of these murderers, and who, upon being compelled to disgorge the same, imposed upon his brother Masons by borrowing from them with all the effrontery of a practised beggar. Truly the Free State—

from the President downward—was but a home for all the murderers, thieves and vagabonds of South Africa. With fear at my heart that I should be skinned of my very all, I held my peace for the time, knowing that with such a monster of iniquity, and in their Courts of in-Justice I had no chance. Surely such vile acts must ultimately compel men to rise and with sudden power crush and stamp out such man-devils.

Perhaps it may be asked why I submitted to such extortions? In reply I would ask, after all the experiences I have related, would anyone think it possible to contend against such odds single-handed? The information vouchsafed to me and others was that although it was not *legal* to rob me in such a way, still—even if I gained a formal judgment in Court—he would find out some Roman-Dutch arrangement whereby to fleece me and turn me out of the Free State shorn of the results of all my many years of self-denial and hard work. I could enumerate other cases, but they only sicken me. The examples I have given are more than enough.

In order to prove that the record of these gross and seemingly incredible villainies is thoroughly well-founded I append, for the satisfaction and instruction of my readers, the following extracts from the *Friend* and the *Express* of the Free State :—

The Free State branch of the Africander Bond is reported to have passed a resolution : " Whereas lawyers are not among the necessaries of life, this meeting of Bondsmen hereby pledges itself to use every constitutional means to extirpate them, and calls upon all affiliated members of the Bond to do likewise. Our reason for this course is, that, in the Orange Free State, lawyers of every grade in the profession unite marked professional incapacity with a great power of bloodsucking, and this is being borne in upon the community in a manner no longer to be tolerated."

There is little doubt that there has been for some considerable time a feeling growing in the country so adverse, and we may almost say hostile, to the legal profession that if to-day a plebiscite were taken, the great majority would undoubtedly vote in favour of the abolition of a profession which, under ordinary circumstances, men are too apt to look upon as a necessary evil, but which, under our present circumstances, is most certainly regarded as something much worse. Whosoever doubts our statement has not read the papers, and has not taken cognizance of what goes on in the country. If he should not attach much weight to these utterances he may go to the sittings of the Volksraad, and listen attentively to what is said there, and, looking upon that Hon'ble body as as representative a one, as exists, he will without hesitation endorse the view expressed above. In itself, and without approaching the question as we do for the purpose not merely of discussing the same, but with a view to advising measures calculated to effect an improvement, the prevailing sentiment is of sufficient interest to a writer of contemporary history, to note the same and to investigate its origin and the causes of its development. If in doing so we should appear harsh, we may be permitted to state at once that we write less with a view to criticise than to improve. Dictated by such a sentiment, laudable as it must be even in the eyes of the legal profession itself, the statement will be accepted as correct, though very disagreeably correct, that the legal profession, as a whole, occupies so low a standard in this country that upon the raising thereof the very first move towards amelioration depends. It would be unjust and ungrateful if we omitted here to mention that our Bench of Judges is of as high a standing as that of any country, that we possess members of the Bar and Side-Bar who would be an ornament to the profession anywhere, and that the Judges, by their endeavours to raise the standard of efficiency, have already attained a marked improvement. That, finally, the additions to the profession in late years leave no doubt of a complete ultimate change. Thus, all that remains, and indeed it is the burning point of the question, is that the period of transition may not be too prolonged a one, and that it should be marked by the utmost severity towards those members, who, through want of proper qualification, are already enjoying so much forbearance, that they should not be permitted to encroach further thereon through want of professional usages, irregularity, and, finally, dishonesty. We are aware that we are treading on delicate ground, and that we are dealing with a militant profession. However, the truth must be told, and that openly. As things have gone, it has not been an unusual occurrence that men who have held powers of attorney have abused their power, to the detriment of their mandators. It has occurred that men entrusted with the settlement of estates have used money collected in those estates, for their own private ends, and could only be made to disgorge after an appeal to the court. It has, finally, frequently occurred, that men collected accounts, retained the moneys, and that their clients are either still awaiting settlement, or obtained such only after employing a second agent to collect the money from the collector. That this was wrong, who doubts ?—that it was a grave wrong at the hands of men who owned a position of trust who will gainsay ?—that it was a wrong that threw discredit upon the whole of an honourable profession the feeling of the entire country testifies to. Yet the last is a fortunate accident, in spite of its misfortune. For it suggests the only remedy extant. To think that oppressive laws and a ruinous tariff will effect an improvement, people may believe and hope. We share neither their hope nor their belief. In the very fact of oppression there is the danger of illicit dealing, and by the very act of oppression the man who never scrupled to act dishonestly, is challenged to extend his crooked and dishonest manipulations, whilst the honest and upright lawyer, who is indispensible to the community, is condemned to sufferance, exposed to poverty, and forced to seek a living elsewhere. The remedy lies with the profession, and from them the *only* improvement can be expected. If honest lawyers wish to protect themselves, they must do so by protecting the public. They must combine and remove the cancer from their body, and that without feeling or false compassion, and they must do so without loss of time. To show neglect would be tantamount to despising public opinion, and would only invite retribution and defeat. For, whatever mode of expression is indulged in with regard to this question, the feeling that the public must be protected is a general one. Who is to do it ?—we or the profession itself ? That is, we repeat, the question, and we should trust that, by a sincere effort—for but the slightest effort has hitherto been wanting—the legal profession will enlist on its side the sympathy at least of all moderate men, which they cannot be said even to possess now. How to do this, we need hardly say; the *modus operandi* is better known to themselves than to us, and the example of other countries shows clearly the road they have to follow. That they may do so, is in their own interest first, though it is in ours as well, and we therefore sincerely hope that they will do it soon, and, moreover, do it well.

At this period of time, according to the *Daily News* and the *Express* of the Free State, the whole town—from the highest official of the land to the lowest, whether the municipal paid Page, a sanitary scavenger or clerk of commissioners—stunk with rottenness. It was supposed that with the exception of about ten business houses, none could call themselves free men, and who expected by every mail notice to shut up and clear out. The credit of the State was nowhere. All were expecting the insolvency of one another. Immovable property could not be sold for money, and all trade was but a system of barter: the working and principles of which are thoroughly explained in my *How to Construct Free State Railways*—read before the Bloemfontein Literary Association, Chief-Justice Rietz in the chair, when a resolution was passed expressing entire approval of my views and proposals.

Mortgages did not buy, they simply absorbed; and the continual cry was that John Bull alone could save them in that hour of their extremity by a loan of his gold—and that as the Hollander and German could not help them, England should be requested to take charge of them once more and for ever.

Chapter XIX.

I MAY here mention a case in which an unfortunate wretch who through drunkenness allowed the Sheriff to get into my business in the country—a business I had bought right out—and in various other ways helped to deprive me of my means.

Now it happened that in the course of a conversation, I had spoken unkindly of his behaviour in repeatedly making outrageous demands upon me, and stated that I refused compliance with the same on the ground that during the last twelve months I had been victimised by a set of low scamps and practical thieves.

This conversation reached his ears, and for his own knavish purposes he asserted that I had used the offensive words mentioned—personally towards him; and at the instigation of an insolvent, lying builder, backed up (as he afterwards said) and assisted by a juvenile shark of the law, he demanded of me for loss of character the modest sum of five hundred pounds.

I was fortunate enough however to defeat this conspiracy; for it turned out that the very men he alleged had informed him that I used the words reflecting upon his character, denied that I had said anything of the kind, or that I had spoken otherwise than in a general sense.

I afterwards found out that this fellow had neglected his wife and subsequently been convicted of felony, so that he had to give up as a bad job the hope of fleecing me upon the pretext of loss of character. The affidavits of several persons saved me from having to eat a leek of such gigantic proportions as would be represented by the sum of £500, and a proportionate bill of costs to the young shark of a limb of the law or justice of the Free State.

I make bold to state that the hard times in Bloemfontein had turned half the inhabitants into sharpers; no one felt sure of his neighbour, and the attempt to rob and plunder universally was intensified among all. I was glad at last to wipe the dust of Bloemfontein off my feet.

I may mention that the two others stated to have heard me speak some truth of this human leper, afterwards denied that I had used such words in the personal sense; but finding that six vagabonds were prepared to swear that I must have said so, and knowing that if I got into the what is called the High Court of Justice my means would have been eaten up by the lawyers, I admitted that if I did so use the words I had no business to do so —the law not allowing me to speak the truth in self-defence. If this whitewashed the *quondam* felon, he was welcome to the statement; and I felt that if any other six in any other made up six cases had demanded of me to contradict anything that they were prepared to swear and maintain, and if my whitewashing the rascals, by so doing would save me from the money-stealing sharks of lawyers of Bloemfontein, I would have saved my cash from such swindlers and stated, that if Brutus was an honourable man so were all these unfortunates.

What a hell of torture a place may be made to the man who dares to speak against State, Church, Political and Social outrages.

The reformer who dares to open his lips may not in these days find himself in a stone dungeon, but he is even now hunted down by legal Inquisitions, and when unable to pay damages, thrown into a gaol not fit for a " Christian martyr "—one who should turn the other cheek when smitten on the one side, and give up his coat if possessed of two—much less a rational truth utterer. It was with perfect loathing against the shams, as I have yet to describe, that I left Bloemfontein whose very atmosphere at last was contaminating to me.

The Reformer.

All grim and soiled and browned with tan,
 I saw a Strong One, in his wrath,
Smiting the godless shrines of man
 Along his path.

The Church, beneath her trembling dome,
 Essayed in vain her ghostly charm;
Wealth shook within his gilded home
 With strange alarm.

Fraud, from his secret chamber, fled
 Before the sunlight bursting in;
Sloth drew her pillow o'er her head.
 To drown the din.

Grey-headed Use, who, deaf and blind,
 Groped for his old accustomed stone,
Leaned on his staff and wept to find
 His seat o'erthrown.

Yet louder rang the Strong One's stroke,
 Yet nearer flashed his axe's gleam;
Shuddering and sick of heart I woke,
 As from a dream.

If the rascality of the legal fraternity was intolerable, no less had the medical profession become a huge system of thieving. Quack doctors were continually running over the State, and to cover their malpractices, they sent their sons over to England to secure a diploma, under cover of which they hid their own misadventures.

Dr. Carouser could not fill the position of Town Doctor, but as a vendor of drugs he had amassed a fortune and made his son an M.D., and who, not finding his skill appreciated, was during the small-pox scare appointed medical officer for the examination of Kaffirs and others. Although he received three guineas per day, or over ninety pounds a month, he failed to fulfil his duties and finally got kicked out without notice through his want of skill and decency. But these charges were moderate compared with some of the ex-Lord *Mayoress* quacks of Bloemfontein who charged £17 for two days' professional "kill or cure" services to a struggling Winn of a baker.

The rascality at last, as previously mentioned, got so outrageous that the members of the Raad, in self-defence, passed an Act imposing severe penalties—and not before it was time—which brought down upon them the following letters which truthfully depict the state of rascality and openly practised quackery then existing in the Free State. I unhesitatingly say that all the medical men thought it their duty to make fortunes as speedily as possible, either by saving the living or arranging to make money out of the dead.

One missionary quack bought of a patient—who thought he was dying—his farm for a very small sum to be paid at his death to his family, and although the man would not die for some time after, this doctor secured a most valuable farm which he afterwards sold at a very enhanced price and thus defrauded the man's family.

Those who knew the doctors can quite understand the necessity for legislation, but to enable them to expose themselves I reprint the following letters that were written in the interest of the medical profession.

Medical Scandals.

We wish to draw the attention of our readers to the very great injustice which has been, and is being, done to the medical profession in this State. As we have no medical schools as yet, we are dependent on gentlemen who have had, at great cost of time, money, and brain, to make themselves proficient in other lands. Thanks to the general wealth of the country, men of good attainments have been induced to settle here, and the State is all the better for it in more ways than one. At the present time the members of the medical profession can compare very favourably with those of the Cape Colony or Natal for general proficiency in their profession, and for honours obtained in the medical schools and universities of Europe. This being the case, we should do well to keep them in our midst. We should not lay upon them burdens too grievous to be borne; nor should we allow the quack and the charlatan to sow tares while the husbandman sleeps. We do not approve of the principle of taxing medical men at all; but if we do force them to pay a licence, we should extend to them some protection. Of course, we know it will be said that some one must pay the taxes, and the doctor—as he knows how to make long bills—should be one. We quite see that the Raad is going strongly on the principle that every interest but the farming interest should be taxed. But even allowing that the Raad as a body is particularly careful not to tax themselves, it might be just in taxing others. It should place a tax on ignorance and presumption by making all unqualified people who dispense medicines, or give advice, for a monetary consideration, pay at lease five times as much as a duly qualified man who is registered; and it should allow qualified men to charge such fees as a Board of medical men would be satisfied with. We do not advocate that the fees of medical men should be raised. Far from it. We only suggest that gentlemen, who give their time, day and night, in wind and rain, who have spent much money and many years in endeavouring to acquire knowledge of diseases, and skill in treating them, should be paid as well as a journeyman bricklayer or joiner, who pays at present no licence; and that the public should be protected from quacks and charlatans who have an immunity from all taxes. We wish to draw the attention of our readers to the letter of Dr. Brock, which appears in another column. The writer has made out a good case for the doctors. He has shown the injustice of reducing the tariff of fees, and the absurdity of allowing quacks more privileges—except the very important one of contributing to the State exchequer—than legally qualified registered medical men. We know there is a weakness among a good many of our legislators that the farming population, which is often few and far between, should have even the doubtful advantage of being attended by a quack when no qualified man is to be got. This has, doubtless, much weight with many. There might be some such plan adopted with qualified medical men as the Government selects with bridges. To protect the tolls over a bridge, the law stops all drifts ten miles on either side of it. If the Government prevented a quack from practising five or six hours from a *licensed* medical men, there would be some protection for him. At present the licence carries nothing with it except the forced acceptance of a tariff which is now bad enough, and may be at any time made worse. If things do not soon mend, the qualified men will have to change places with the quacks—pay no licence, accept no district surgeoncies, and give no evidence or testimony before a court of law. When the Raad has duly licensed quacks doing all this, they will perceive, when it is too late, that you cannot measure a man's brains by a bucket, or his accomplishments by a footrule. A memorial to the Volksraad has been drawn up which will, doubtless, be generally signed by the medical profession. The following is an English translation of this document :—

> That the Raad has passed in its Extraordinary Session of 1884 a certain Tariff Ordinance, which was published in the *Government Gazette* of the 12th March, 1884, and which came into force directly after publication ; that in the said Tariff, amongst other things, a Scale of Fees is laid down for Medical men, and the said Scale of Fees not only applies to the Criminal work for Government, but is also in force as regards the relationship between doctor and patient; that in the same *Government Gazette* above mentioned, a certain Draft Ordinance is published, in which, amongst other regulations, it is enacted that all qualified Professional Men are prohibited from charging any fee above the amount as laid down in the said Tariff Ordinance under the penalty of being prevented from practising their profession in the Free State ; that your Memorialists feel greatly aggrieved at the said Ordinance, on account of their not being sufficiently protected by this State, in which no law exists against quackery by unqualified men ; that these Quacks not only injure the public at large, and are directly or indirectly the cause of a number of deaths, and of much chronic ill-health, but also interfere greatly with the proper performance of a medical man's duty to his patient ; that the public, by the false representations of these men, are induced to employ them to the damage of the health and pecuniary well-being of the community ; that the said Ordinance completely prohibits freedom of contract between doctor and patient, and that the Scale of Fees laid down in the Tariff Ordinance of 1884 is not sufficiently high,

especially with regard to extraordinary cases in Medicine, in Surgery, and in Midwifery, to Journeys, and Expert Evidence, to be an adequate remuneration for the trouble and expenses to which a medical man is subject in such cases; that your Memorialists consider that, if Quackery were totally abolished, the Tariff in the main, with the above exceptions, seems satisfactory; that if this Draft Ordinance becomes law, and Quackery be not abolished. the Ordinance will materially affect the public as regards the procuring of properly-qualified practitioners; that your Memorialists, considering their having to pay heavy licences, ought to be protected by the State against Quackery, against which there is no protection whatever at the present moment; for which said reasons your Memorialists humbly petition the Volksraad that the said Draft Ordinance be not extended to the Medical Profession. and further that the Volksraad should introduce a measure to totally abolish and prohibit the practice of Quackery, or the giving of advice or medicine for money or value by non-qualified men.

Medical Tariff Ordinance.

Mayfields, dist. Rouxville, 7 April, 1884.

To the Editor of the *Friend* :

Sir,—I, in common with I have no doubt the whole body of qualified medical practitioners in the Free State, have read with satisfaction Dr. W. J. Brock's letter in the *Friend* of the 3rd inst., as well as the apposite remarks it has called forth from yourself, respecting the unfair restrictions imposed upon them in the recent tariff ordinance passed by the Volksraad. It is further satisfactory to note that action is being taken to bring our grievance in a formal manner before the Raad, and that our effort to obtain fairplay is so heartily supported by yourself.

I fully concur in the observations of your Rouxville correspondent both as regards the injurious nature of the enactment referred to in its dealings with qualified men, and as to the urgent necessity for legislation directed against the crying evil of quackery. That the scale of fees set down in its ordinance by the Volksraad is too low, I have not any hesitation in saying. The restriction on fees for operations concerns the public perhaps more than the profession, for in such a scattered population the amount of surgical practice is small and counts for little in our income. To the public, however, it is a serious matter, for where considerable risks are involved in any operation a surgeon is asked to perform; in justice to himself he will probably refuse to undertake it. But it is otherwise with the restriction on the charges for travelling, since such a restriction must sweep away no small part of a medical man's income. The sum of ten shillings per hour is inadequate, and it would be safe to prophesy that the proposed penalty for exceeding that charge in one or two instances, would lead to a general exodus of the best men in the State.

For what attraction does the Free State offer for the carrying on of medical practice? It has no natural beauty to recommend it as a desirable residence. Such a thing as society, except perhaps in your own favoured city, can scarcely be said to exist. It is with the greatest difficulty and at a great expense that the ordinary comforts of life can be obtained. From the sparseness of the population, and consequently the paucity of patients, the professional interest of practice is reduced to a minimum; while for the same reason and because his visits to them can only be made at intervals of weeks or months, the study of special diseases is rendered either impossible or very unsatisfactory.

The only really accurate means of studying disease, viz., by examinations (*post mortem*) is denied to the physician of this country by the prejudice and ignorance of the people. Last, but not least, we are precluded by distance from intercourse with our professional brethren, and that interchange of ideas so stimulating to a faithful and intelligent discharge of our individual duties. What attraction then can the Free State offer to induce good medical men to settle within its boundaries, in spite of this species of social and professional ostracism to which they are condemned? There is but one plain answer to the question: They must be well paid.

Medical men are not more worldly than their neighbours, but

it is foolishness to think that good men—who are, of course, the men to succeed wherever they go—will, out of choice, select for practice a field where, with actually less remuneration, the drawbacks are so great and so numerous as they are in the Orange Free State. Seeing what a large proportion of his earnings is derived from journeys, I cannot but think that the new restriction upon the doctor's rate of charging for them must have practically the effect of preventing any man from practising in the State, who can make his way elsewhere, say in the Colony or any other division of South Africa.

As to the unblushing quackery so freely carried on among the farmers, every qualified man in the State can corroborate the statements of your correspondent. I could cite only too many sad instances of its miserable effects in this same neighbourhood. The indiscriminate use of the most potent drugs in the pharmacopeia by these unscrupulous persons, whose only extenuating plea could be their ignorance, is frightful to contemplate. It is not too much to assert that quackery is often synonymous with culpable homicide; and who can be sure that it does not sometimes cover murder as well?

It is sincerely to be hoped, Mr. Editor, that in the interests, not only of medical men, but of the public at large, the Volksraad will see fit to remove these irksome restrictions upon the freedom of action of an honourable and hard-working class, and that instead of indirectly setting a premium upon dishonesty and charlatanism, our legislators will recognise the pressing necessity for some stringent measure for the suppression of quacks and the proper protection of those, who, under so many discouragements, place their dearly acquired knowledge at the service of the community.

I am, &c.,

Geo. S. Brock

M.B., Edinburgh C.M., late Assistant Professor of Pathology in the University of Edinburgh.

How to put Down Quackery.

Orange Free State, 12th April, 1884.

To the Editor of the *Friend* :

Sir,—Permit me a short space to ask Mr. E. H. Croghan, who seems to take to heart the extensive system of "Quackery" being sanctioned by the Orange Free State Government, how he would deal with another "form" of "Quackery" of a worse kind, to my ideas of thinking, than that exposed by his letter in your issue of the 10th instant, but which seems to have escaped his notice? I am morally convinced that if the form of quackery, to which I refer below, is stopped by the O.F.S. Government, the real object of the memorialists will be speedily attained and the respectability of the medical profession in the Free State will be raised on a par with the sister States.

Mr. Editor, I ask you, is it dignified, is it respectable for medical men to advertise their diplomas, their testimonials, their past defunct appointments in the same manner as a merchant advertises his soap, candles, tobacco and snuff? Is it respectable for a medical man to seize every opportunity of parading in print what he is, what he has been, and almost what he will be? "Only come and try me," &c. This advertising by some Free State doctors has assumed such extraordinary development of late that one expects to see some famous nostrum or other added to the list, such as inventor of the famous "wind pill," or the inventor of the medicine that cures cancer, &c.

Fortunately—I say fortunately advisedly—very few inhabitants understand the real meaning of half the alphabet being placed after a medical man's name. Take for example what I mean—a medical man signs L. & L.M., F.P S.G. & L.A.H.I. after his name. Probably, if the O.F.S. inhabitants did understand what this flourish of letters meant, those who use them would scarcely venture to tax your compositor's fingers again. However, this is simply an example of advertising I refer to, and it would be interesting to hear how Mr. E. H. Croghan would like the Free State Government to deal with this kind of "Quackery."

There are reasons why a limited amount of modest advertising should be looked upon in a favourable light in a country not having much local communication; but it would be very useful to hear Mr. Croghan's ideas upon this system of quackery in the O.F.S., when I will trouble you with some further examples of the system I refer to.

I am, Sir, yours, &c.,
M.D.

District Surgeoncies.

Rouxville, 5th April, 1884.

To the Editor of the *Friend:*

Sir,—May I be permitted through the medium of your paper to call upon all my medical brethren in this State, who hold what is euphoniously called the office of District Surgeon, to join me in an attempt to get these so-called District Surgeoncies put on a proper footing. There is now an Ordinance existing (which may be found in the law-book) which says that District Surgeons may be appointed in every district.

Now what is the present plan? One quite undeserving the notice of an honourable profession. Tenders are called for the supply of drugs to the sick prisoners, and the lowest offer gets it. Now, in the Colony and also in Natal (in both of which I have held office) District Surgeons are appointed by the Government at a fixed salary with stated duties, and with extra fees for certain services, such as journeys, post-mortems, &c., and they hold office during good behaviour.

Let everyone of us, in his respective district, see the member of Volksraad for his town and get him to bring forward this Ordinance. A District Surgeon properly appointed is a Government official. He can be referred to by the authorities for information on all matters respecting the public health, and holding some position can speak with authority. He would have certain specified duties, and would know what he had to do, and being a Government official and appointed by the Government would be responsible to them. Though we have no real existence, we are practically.

recognised by being ex-officio members of the gaol committee as District Surgeons. And in connection with this point the District Surgeon should be a V.R.

How often is the D.S. perhaps sent out to see some serious case of assault and finds his patient dying, and there is no one to take the deposition! Of course, all of us cannot write Dutch (I do only in a way), but we all know enough to take the deposition and can write " Afrikanse."

Now, Sir, through you I will ask all my brothers holding appointments to stir in this matter. It is a disgrace to us this tendering business, and leaving out ourselves it would be a gain to the public at large and a saving to the exchequer if permanent appointments were made. Let each of us get his member to present a petition to the Raad, praying them to put the Ordinance in force, or to take steps for putting us in the same position as our brothers in the Colony and Natal.

I really believe this is the only State in South Africa which gives the right to medically attend the sick prisoners to the man who tenders the lowest, even if he be the veriest ignoramus going. The principle is thoroughly bad. If a man has done Government work for some time and faithfully, he has certainly gained some considerable knowledge of public medicine which enables him to save the public purse; and it is only a just reward to allow a man to retain an appointment, the duties of which he has always faithfully fulfilled.

I shall be glad to hear from any of my brethren on this matter.

Yours truly,

CHAS. WM. BROWNE.

P.S.—The Ordinance above referred to is entitled: "Ordonnantie No. 19, 1877 (Ordonnantie over Geneeskundigen No. 2.). Volksraad's besluit dd. 24 Feb , 1866 :—De Raad besluit dat er Districts Doctoren kunnen worden aangesteld door ZHEd. den Staats-president, tegen een salaris, niet te bovengaande £50 sterling per jaar."

Having finally closed up my business, and during my close attention, and family society and national banishment, having expressed myself somewhat strongly, upon all things, I was urged by many to give a parting lecture. At a great sacrifice of time and attention, I at last prepared to do so, and such was the strong feeling on the part of all who knew my peculiar manner, that, as they expressed it, a farewell treat was expected.

My novel style of advertisements had given them an idea that I should treat the subject of the lecture in an unusual but in all points most edifying way, and when I announced the topic the universal cry of the men of light and learning was one of satisfaction; and it was felt that it would be the lecture of the season.

In due course I waited upon the Town Clerk, hired the Hall and gave him the subject—"The Rise of the European Dutch Republic, and the Downfall of the South African Dutch Republics.' Now this title fairly took away the breath of the Town Clerk, and I had to explain that, although I used such strong expressions as "the downfall, &c.," I did not advocate violence or dynamite, and so well was this known that the Town Committee passed a resolution to let me the Hall; but the Ex-Groom of a Baumann, and the successful house and rent exploiter, that was supposed to be an old woman in most other things, showed himself in his proper colours. Now this Hard—God, who with all his Chapel attendance was certainly God—less, got so alarmed, and so great was the fear of Boon in his organ—called his heart—that he immediately summoned a full meeting of the Town Council to decide whether I, the Boon of Bloemfontein, should have the opportunity—in the presence of the Town Raad and the Government in general—to express myself on the old public affairs of Holland, and the momentous questions affecting the South African Dutch Republics. I regret to state, that the fear of the Council was such that they decided to refuse to the Boon of the Free State, the right of free speech in what is called the Free State, to the disgust of all right minded men in the town. Others were surprised that a bankrupt town should have refused good English sovereigns, but alas when conceit and prejudice hold sway, there is no controlling ignorance, even when found in a Mayor like their God—Hard or their Ex-Groom of a Stock who with all his German impudence believed in free speech, but not in my speech of freedom.

It was well known that my lecture would have been the event of the season, and being on the eve of my departure, a not to be forgotten one ; and the subserviency of the Council was an outrage upon the freedom of the subject. May they never have greater crimes to answer for. The same week, this same Council could let the Hall to a black gang of lunatics, headed by one not Pay-up, who on loafing around the hotels, at last was run in to answer for his " op schrijven " propensities.

Another leader of this black gang of imbeciles, was the Son of an old minister among the Settlers ; one who could mouth out on a platform, with blackened face all the *double entendres* and look the general fool and smut he was, cheat and swindle the Boer during all the week, and then with his ugly face, make grimaces at the girls, while singing at the Lord-be-praised church on a Sunday.

Such was the awful fear of these little men called a Council, that they justified their action in refusing me the Hall by stating that I should "go for" the humbugs in such a way that the Germans would " go for" the English. Bah !

I here tender my thanks to the Hobbs and Co. of the town, who would have protected me from the violence of such German scum. It is something so disgusting to think that Englishmen and Scotchmen should be so villified and set upon by the descendants of the Prussian thieves, that I felt the time had come to denounce and show them up in their right colours. They, under a pretence of helping the Dutch, are always " egging them on " to insult the English—using the Dutch and Africanders as monkeys to snatch the chestnuts out of the fire, for the Germans to consume, and the ignorance of the Dutch and Africander is such that they play their part to the piping of the German band, that howls out at every convenient spot that they can stand upon. In the Dutch colonies they are doing their best to undermine English rights, and influence to secure the lands for a Greater Germany, as they are in Europe to secure Holland as their naval outpost to commence a system of buccaneering all round the world, thinking that they may be as successful as they have been with Austria, and poor enslaved Poland. O these lovers of Fatherland ; how they do love to steal and rob in the lands of other fathers. In other lands they may succeed for a time by sheer Brute-force and bullet-heads, and gross-animalism ; but the time will come when they will be found out, and known in their true colours and be swept back once more to eat sour-cabbage and black-meal. In English colonies they enjoy liberties that they never struggled for, and with all the insolence of men suddenly made rich, not by honest labour but by swindling and cheating at every opportunity, they fancy with all their course natures, they are the Peculiar People of Jehovah, to join company with the Jews, to plunder the nations of the earth.

Let them take warning; they are now found out, and being found out, there is no chance for them to possess English colonies or Dutch-Holland. The English may appear to nap and the French to be quiescent, but the time will come when all old wrongs will be righted.

In further illustration of my views anent the Prussians, I quote the following by Edwin Heron:—

> This is the crew I fly from. Shall I see
> Hybrids, like these take, precedence of me?
> Shall these adventurers strive, and take our place,
> These men of guttural names and dubious race?
> Who some years since, before they made a noise,
> Come here with Hambro sherry, hemp and toys.
> Is it no matter that such stocks as ours
> Have been the source of all this country's powers;
> Have laid the broad foundations of the State,
> Built up the Colonies, made England great?
> That now, like vultures scenting out a prey,
> These supple tradesmen hustle us away.
> Give them their way, in every English place
> The rarest sight will be an English face;
> Give them their way, and then the ocean o'er
> Self banished, he will seek another shore.
> Where for some time, until there's cream to skim,
> These keen-eyed cormorants will not follow him.

The Saint Edmond of the Council answered me that the refusal of the Hall, was the saving of my life. Now, as I had no desire to end my existence in a German brawl. I suppose I must be thankful; and if such was the case, I trust that it may be a source of thankfulness to England and the world in general.

What to do with such a man as I was, was often asked, for they knew, I would leave no wrong unchallenged and if they shut me off the platform perhaps in the future, they would regret having done so when they came to read my writings, and, again ask: What shall we do with such a man?

In confirmation of my statement concerning the action of the Town Council, I herewith print the programme of the Entertainment I proposed to give, together with the reply of the Town Clerk to my application for the use of the Hall:

THE
ENTERTAINMENT

The Long Expected Come at Last.

By very special request

MARTIN JAMES BOON

Will Lecture in the Town Hall

On Tuesday, June the 3rd. Doors open at ½-past 7, Lecture to commence at 8.

On the following Subjects :—

"**The Rise of the European Dutch Republic**,"

And the

"**Downfall of the African Dutch Republics**,"

With Special Reference to the Free State.

And a few personal remarks to ease his conscience before he leaves these parts he hopes for ever.

At the close of Lecture opposition fearlessly solicited.

Reserve Front Seats, 1s. Body of the Hall and Gallery, 6d.

The above Charges to cover Expenses.

Any surplus after all expenses will be handed to the Hospital for Incurables, or for pocket money for the future occupiers of the New Lunatic Asylum.

          Town Office,
            27 May, 1884.

M. J. Boon, Esq.,
  Bloemfontein.

Dear Sir,

  I have the honour to furnish you with the following copy of the Council's Resolution, of this day, relative to the letting of the Town Hall to you on Tuesday next, 2nd prox.

  "Resolved that the use of the Hall, for the purposes required by Mr. Boon, cannot be granted."

    I am, dear sir,
      Yours faithfully,
        GEO. EDMOND,
          Town Clerk.

On Sunday, June the 1st, I, for the last [time, wandered over the town, and finally on to the hill, and like unto one of old, looked and mourned, and felt I too, would have gathered the people under my wing, as a hen gathers her young, but eaten up with all the vices of the Age they would not.

Drinking and smoking, had so eaten up, and into the nature of the inhabitants of this Bloemfontein, and the Free State in general, that they have become, like the Kaffirs, mere animals. The eating up process had converted the whole, from the President downwards, into one state of cannibalism, worse than the old inhabitants. To sell was impossible, and therefore absorption became the rule. It might be truly said that not one was a freeman in the town, and this explains the fact that not even one had the courage to express himself without fear. Freedom,

Dignity and Independance—were no longer the boast of any man in the Free State.

It was with a saddening of heart that my old customers bid me adieu, many feeling that now their Boon was going, there would be no longer light and sunshine in Bloemfontein ; truly if darkness covered the earth eighteen centuries ago, a total eclipse was now looked forward for when at last, I prepared myself for my final departure.

Having completed my arrangements, in every particular, on the Monday, I once more made ready to engage the passenger cart to take me away, and although I heard the "away, away with him, he knows too much to leave us alone." I felt that I could forgive even them ; and when I witnessed the moistened eye and faltering tongue I turned away with a full conviction (though the little nobodies say to the contrary) that many felt that it had been a good thing that I had spent three years is exile in Bloemfontein and I felt that after all my struggles and disappointments, that perhaps it was a good thing even for me that I had spent time and gathered experience to be related, ever after, while in Bloemfontein, of the Free State.

VALEDICTORY.

HE happy day of my departure from the Orange Free State arrived at last, and I hastily ran round and shook hands with all my friends in token of " good bye." Without waiting for that day of judgment and of doom which sooner or later will certainly overtake the Free State, with hatred at my heart strangely intermingled with feelings of delight at the prospect of leaving for ever Bloemfontein—the city of legal and illegal exploiters,—I once more mounted the Post-cart for my last ride in and out of the Orange Free State.

With the farewell cheers and heart-felt good wishes of my friends, broken by ill-suppressed emotion at the thought of losing their Boon perhaps for ever, still ringing in my ears I drove on, inwardly resolving to carry out the behests of those friends who urged and even implored me to strike and spare not, and thus prove myself an ever living Boon—not for the Free State only, but to all States and for all time.

In sadness too deep for utterance, and which even the efforts of my fellow passengers failed to shake off, I passed over the barren common. But with me as with all others, the bitterest grief must have its limits ; so that when we had passed through the desolate country that met my view on all sides and at last arrived at the first out-span, I had once more recovered my composure and flow of spirits. All can understand the pain one felt parting from the many associates one had met and made in a City like Bloemfontein ; the breaking up of ties where one had made some successes though they were more than counterbalanced by cruel, heavy losses. All this transitory grief and every trace of gloom vanished however as I realised the fact that I was on the way to meet loved ones in the Colony and relatives in England—that dear old spot the land of one's birth. My self communing was interrupted by my arrival and alighting at the hotel of the Simon Pure on the banks of the Modder River. Upon my attention being drawn to the dry bed of the river all my indignation was once more aroused as I remembered the possibility of damning up all rivers and thus storing their water for man's future use and gain. But alas, there were no statesmen capable of grasping the subject and appreciating the vital importance of providing irrigation works. This and other kindred subjects might be enlarged upon, but I have drawn special attention to them in my *Immortal History of South Africa* and other works. I shall, if I am spared, in my last but by no means least history of the Transvaal, Stellaland, Kimberley, Griqualand West, and the western portions of the Colony adduce further evidence of the true position and conditions, of these parts in the one hope that as I write only to reform, others will follow in my footsteps and also use their pens so that they too may leave the land of their adoption better than they found it.

Paradoxical through it appears I beg to subscribe myself yours with intense indignation but universal love,

M. J. B.

PRINTED BY
LONGMAN & DAVIES,
3, JERUSALEM PASSAGE,
LONDON, E.C.

MARTIN BOON'S & BRONTERRE O'BRIEN'S BOOKS FOR THE PEOPLE.

JOTTINGS BY THE WAY;

OR,

BOON'S MADNESS ON THE ROAD.

Being a Philosophical View of Life, Past, Present, and to Come, in the Orange Free State, Natal, and the Cape Colony.

PRICE, TWO SHILLINGS.

HOW TO CONSTRUCT FREE STATE RAILWAYS.

BY

MARTIN JAMES BOON.

Read before the Bloemfontein Literary Association, 1883, Judge Reitz in the Chair.

'Tis to create, and creating live
A being more intense, that we endow
With form our fancy, gaining as we give
The life we image.

PRICE, SIXPENCE.

Advertisements

How to Nationalize England's Commons and Waste Lands.

Dedicated to the Prime Minister, Reformers' Union and to the British People

By MARTIN JAMES BOON,

Author of "Home Colonisation," "Protest against Emigration," "Remedies for the Present Time," &c.

PRICE, SIXPENCE.

National Paper Money and Its Use

BY

MARTIN JAMES BOON.

The Remedy for the Present and All Time.

PRICE, ONE SHILLING.

HOW TO COLONIZE SOUTH AFRICA,

AND

BY WHOM?

BY

MARTIN JAMES BOON.

PRICE, TWO SHILLINGS.

The One True Remedy for "Outcast London," all other Cities and the World all over,

HOW TO CONSTRUCT RAILWAYS,

Ship Canals, Waterworks, Electric Light and Gas Works, Harbours, Docks, Tramways and other National and Municipal Works of Utility Without Loans, Bonds, Mortgages, or the Burden of Interest.

By MARTIN JAMES BOON.

PRICE, SIXPENCE.

THE

RISE, PROGRESS AND PHASES

OF

HUMAN SLAVERY.

How it Came into the World, and How it Shall be made to Go Out.

BY THE

NATIONAL REFORMER, BRONTERRE O'BRIEN, B.A.

PRICE, THREE SHILLINGS & SIXPENCE.

Works by William Maccall.

	s.	d.		s.	d.
National Mission (16 Lectures)	10	6	The Individuality of the Individual	0	6
The Elements of Individualism	7	6	Sacramental Services (sewed)	0	6
The Agents of Civilization. A Series of Lectures	1	6	The Lessons of the Pestilence	0	6
The Education of Taste	1	0	Creed of Man	0	4
The Doctrine of Individuality	0	6	The Unchristian Nature of Commercial Restrictions	0	3

TRUBNER & Co., Paternoster Row.

Outlines of Individualism	0	6	The Career and Character of C. J. Napier	0	2
Solomon's Song of Songs	0	2			
The Land and the People	0	2			

E. TRUELOVE, 256, High Holborn.

Via Crucis, 2s. 6d; The Newest Materialism, 1s; Russian Rhymes, 6d.

GEORGE STANDRING, 8 and 9, Finsbury Street, E.C.

Just issued, Crown 8vo., 96pp., Cloth Gold Lettered, with Vignette Title Page.

PRICE, 2s. POST FREE.

MOODS AND MEMORIES

BEING MISCELLANEOUS POEMS, BY

WILLIAM MACCALL.

LONDON: W. STEWART & Co, 41, Farringdon Street, E.C.   EDINBURGH: J. MENZIES & Co.

Advertisements. v.

MALTHUSIAN QUACKERY.
THE TRILOGY OF SKUNKISM.

HISTORY ALLEGORICAL & CATEGORICAL

OF THE

TWO PRIMORDIAL SKUNKITES

BRASSY CHEEK

AND

BREEZY BOUNCER

By the Famous German Traveller,

HERR VON SCHLAGSCHARKE.

1.—The Dunhill Dancers.
2.—The Deification of Bestiality.
3.—The Creed of the Cesspool.

PRICE ONE PENNY.

Can be had of all ANTI-Malthusian Booksellers; also at 108, Farringdon Road, W.C., where all Boon's Books, and the Land, Labour, and Currency Literature, can be procured.

THE IMMORTAL HISTORY
OF
SOUTH AFRICA.

(COMPLETE IN TWO VOLUMES.

THE ONLY TRUTHFUL, POLITICAL, COLONIAL, LOCAL, DOMESTIC, AGRICULTURAL, THEOLOGICAL, NATIONAL, LEGAL, FINANCIAL AND INTELLIGENT HISTORY OF MEN, WOMEN, MANNERS AND FACTS OF THE CAPE COLONY, NATAL, THE ORANGE FREE STATE, TRANSVAAL, AND SOUTH AFRICA.

By MARTIN JAMES BOON,

AUTHOR OF

How to Colonise South Africa, and by whom ; Jottings by the Way in South Africa; Home Colonisation; How to Construct and Nationalise Railways; National Paper Money, to enable all Nations to Construct Public Works without Bonds, Mortgages, or Interest, &c., &c., &c.

Vol. I.

LONDON:
WILLIAM REEVES, 185, FLEET STREET ;
MARTIN JAMES BOON, 170, FARRINGDON ROAD.

SOUTH AFRICA:
HAY BROS., WHOLESALE AGENTS, KING WILLIAM'S TOWN.

1885.

CONTENTS

OF VOLUME I.

CHAPTER I.—Boon Starts on his Travels from Bloemfontein—The Capital of the Orange Free State Republic, South Africa—Describes the Town and exposes its deplorable sanitary condition.   1—13

CHAPTER II.—Objections to youthful marriages — Definition of a "gentleman"—Health and happiness synonymous — The distinctions between pleasure and happiness—Education of the feelings as well as of the intellect erects a temple of virtue in every heart — Knowledge the groundwork of virtue, and virtue the foundation of happiness   -   -   -   -   -   14—25

CHAPTER III.—The climatic conditions of Bloemfontein misrepresented by doctors to entice visitors and secure patients—Cremation—The Jews, the vilest race on earth: their money-making dodges exposed—The Bible and the New Testament — Jesus Christ as God and Man — Christianity an instrument for degrading the masses and for enriching the priests, pastors and ministers of all sects—The pharmacopœia of the Church — Rationalism — Quackery: Medical and Theological—Huxley's Lay Sermons—The Eucalypticus — Luther and Shakespeare — Human Amelioration, Man's noblest work —Rainfall and drought: their effects on agriculture — Water Storage and Irrigation—Sheep Farming: defects and remedies   -   -   -   -   26—58

CONTENTS.

CHAPTER IV.—Dutchmen's homes — Dutch Farmers and Jewish Traders—Anti-English feeling of the old Boers—The English language prohibited by the Boers in their Schools—The fighting powers of the Boers — The Colonial Government an organised conspiracy of cheats—Military bunglers—An Officer burnt in effigy— Dutch greed and mendacity— Sisters of Mercy — The Diamond Fields — The Chiefs Sepinare and Samuel— Dangers of the Road to travellers—Burning grass — Forests and the drought—The Grahamstown Scandal—Agricultural and industrial conditions—The power of the pen—Boers and Basutos—The Treaty of Aliwal North, *verbatim et literatim* 59—78

CHAPTER V.—Lord Derby and the Colonial Government on the Basuto Question, official despatches, &c., &c.   -   -   -   -   -   -   79—99

CHAPTER VI.—Trouble in store for the Colony—The Basutos our auxiliaries and faithful allies—Cetewayo, John Dunn, and the Zulus—The Indenture system pure and simple slavery—The British Lion and the Transvaal — Execution of Mampoer: shocking scene upon the scaffold—The G.O.M. and President Kruger — The National Pitso — Starving, shooting, and mutilating the Chief Morosi: horrible disclosures — Basutoland, the natural granary of South Africa   -   100—112

CHAPTER VII.—From Aliwal North to St. James Town —A genuine woman and good mother—Government frauds—Districts and Reserves exclusively for Natives—Missionaries the fomenters of rebellion—Sprigg; a placeman in a stateman's position; a land-hungerer, and selfish mercenary failure — Sprigg's brother-in-law a disgrace to human mind—General Gordon in Basutoland: his masterly plans, and sweeping abolition of sinecures and reduction of salaries, including his own, resulting in his dismissal from the post of Colonial Commandant   -   -   -   -   113—127

CHAPTER VIII.—The Coal Fields of South Africa—
King Alcohol capsizes *Cobb's* Coach, with some
serious, and many ludicrous results—The late
Prince Imperial and the Zulu Campaign—Human
Man-Eaters—Hereditary transmission of disease
128–136

CHAPTER IX.—The Journey continued to Dordrecht
—A midnight bugler—Cattle-Lifting, the Dutch
and the Kaffir methods, and how to prevent the
same—Boon falls in with "Satan" *en route*—
Dordrecht described — Wealth of the Dutch
Farmers—The Dutch Church : courting and proposing therein—The Malpractices of the Jews in
the Colony—Gross official corruption—The great
mineral wealth of the district—Preference of the
Dutch girls for English settlers   -   137—155

CHAPTER X.—Exeter Hall a curse to South Africa—
More about the Missionaries. Cetewayo and the
Zulus—The blood-sacrifice : terrible vengeance—
Monogamy and Polygamy—Isandula—Cetewayo
defended   156—175

CHAPTER XI.—A narrow escape—A contrast between
modern missionaries and the monks of old—The
Koranas or Bushmen —The Missing Link—Dr.
Brimstone's sermon — Over the Stormberg and
Bongola Mountains to Queenstown — Colonial
poverty and immorality–Gold-worship—Business,
the God in Queenstown—A protest against the
Emigrationists—A Market built for nothing
176—202

CHAPTER XII.—The Africander Bond—The future language of South Africa—Triumphs of the English
language—English self-esteem   -   203—225

CHAPTER XIII.—Land and money lords — Colonial
farming–Disastrous effects of the drought amongst
stock and sheep—The indolence and apathy of the
farmers contributing to their calamities — The
subjection of agriculture   -   -   -   226—251

CHAPTER XIV.—The Waterford experimental farm—Agriculture—Water-wealth—Colonial statistics—The different Nationalities in the Colony—The "Native" Question—The "pass" system—A Trek threatened—Tree planting: what it will do for the Country—The locust tree shown to be drought-resisting - - - - - 252—282

CHAPTER XV.—"The Fruits of Philosophy" and the High Priest and Priestess of *The Modern Precautionary School*—Modern Malthusianism exposed—Theatricals in South Africa and the Morality of Modern Stage Plays criticised—The Pastor of Wheatlands and the Black Cabbage Seed—Education and the State—The Schoolmaster and the Conqueror - - - - 283—309

CHAPTER XVI.—On to King William's Town—Land Lords are bad, but House and Money Lords are worse—The Christian Idea of Eternal Torture and the Dante Purgatory—Science the Helpmate of Man in Subduing the Earth—Production, Commerce, and Finance—Producing Pilgrims and the Load on their Backs—Bankruptcies and Suicide—The War-Sprigg Party and the Scanlen Dodgers—The Cape German Colony—Beaconsfield, Bismarck, and Salisbury The German Emperor and *Ig*-nobles of Germany—The German Connection a Curse to Englishmen—Filthy Lucre-loving Parsons and German-Wastelings—The Unregarded Toil of the Poor—A One-foot-in-the-grave Old Man—A Never-satisfied, Asthmatical, Young-old Man, and his Exhausted Wife and Young Family of Consumptive, Asthmatical, Small, Puny, Wizen Weaklings—The Union of Young Diseased Persons and the Evil Consequences Thereof—Bishops and Parsons Condemned for Marrying them—Blue Stockings—Boon in the Jaws of a Tiger—Sucking Poison—Boon's Remedy for Outcast London—A Second Daniel come to Judgment—The Jews as Diamond Salters—The Truth, the Whole Truth, and Nothing But the Truth - - - - - - - 310—344

Reviews.

—:0:—

IMMORTAL SOUTH AFRICA.

By Martin James Boon.

"We have just had the pleasure of perusing the first volume of one of the most remarkable, instructive, and entertaining books ever presented to the public—*Immortal South Africa*—by Martin James Boon. Past, recent, and current events, all combine to enhance the interest and anxiety that we doubt not exist in the public mind with regard to all that pertains to the African Continent; and assuredly no Englishman, worthy of the name, can look with indifference upon the kaleidoscopic-like events now passing before his mental view in that veritable *terra incognita*. Egypt, the Soudan, the Transvaal, Basutoland, Zululand, Bechuanaland, &c., &c., are names now "Familiar as Household Words" in every English-speaking home, and naturally so; for where is the one to be found of the Anglo-Saxon race, from lisping infancy to the threshold of the grave, who has not read or heard, and on reading or hearing, of our African triumphs or disasters, felt the warm glow of patriotism and pride suffuse the brow, or sought refuge in tears from the agony of unavailing grief, and mentally resolved that the transient stain upon the national escutcheon must be removed? Under such influences and conditions as these, we feel not only that no apology is needed for inviting and commending to public attention *Immortal South Africa*; but that it makes its appearance at a singularly opportune and felicitous moment; and we confidently hope that it will obtain what it undoubtedly merits—the liberal patronage of the reading world. Although, as indicated by its title, the work is mainly devoted to South Africa, including the Orange River, Free State and Transvaal Republics, nothing has been left untouched where "British

Interests" are concerned—and where are they not? Few men have had better opportunities than Mr. Boon of acquiring the materials necessary to complete the Herculean task he has so successfully accomplished; and certainly no contemporary writer has brought to bear upon the subject greater natural ability and honesty of purpose, or more dauntless courage in maintaining the right and denouncing the wrong. As a resident in the country during a period of eleven years, Mr. Boon writes with all the authority of personal experience, and a sincerity as apparent as it is exceptional in the penultimate decade of the nineteenth century. "Fear, favour, or affection" on the one hand; "malice, hatred, or ill-will" on the other; appear to be *unknown quantities* to Martin James Boon. His descriptions of the natural features of the country are realistically beautiful. His defence of the poor Aborigines, plundered, cajoled, goaded, banished, and at times wantonly murdered, is a marvel of eloquent pleading, that appears unanswerable on the part of the oppressors. His denunciation of the Jews and their malpractices; of all shams, humbugs, and impostures, whether Governmental, official, or individual, are couched in language of crushing impetuosity, convincing and overwhelming. With unerring precision, and resistless force, he strikes at every abuse; tearing away with the mighty power of righteous indignation, the mask that has too long concealed them, and ruthlessly exposes them in all their nude hideousness, to the scorn and contempt of the world. Mr. Boon is far too much of an Englishman to have left untouched the German element—a by no means unimportant factor in the great South African problem; more especially now that Bismarck has shown the cloven hoof of acquisition in his Colonial Policy at Angra Pequena and New Guinea, &c.; combined with his ill-disguised hostility to us in Egypt —and with a master-hand, he has cleared away all the obscurity in which that portion of the question was enshrouded; and by virtue of his rare powers of perception and description, presented it to us in a form as intelligible, as the subject is interesting and important. Nothing worthy of notice appears to have been overlooked. Politics and agriculture in all their bearings; social, sanitary and domestic topics, the "Race" question, and a thousand and one other matters are dealt with in an able and comprehensive manner, revealing to the reader the *minutiæ* of the conditions of daily life in South Africa, as distinctly as though he looked upon the subject through the medium of some powerful mental microscope. Throughout the entire work

—for we will take the public into our confidence, and say at once, that we have enjoyed the pleasure of a peep into the second volume, which is in an advanced stage of the arrangements necessary to enable it to follow Vol. I. into the "Hearts and Homes," doubtless waiting to welcome its arrival, where we opine it will prove to be of "metal more attractive" even than its predecessor—the readers interest is never allowed to flag. The diversified contents of the book, and their mode of treatment by the Author render *Immortal South Africa* a mental *pabulum* upon which the appetite never palls. All English-speaking folk who value the principles and attributes of right and justice, truth and purity, will greet Mr. Boon's book with a hearty welcome; whilst to the agriculturist, the settler in South Africa, or the intending emigrant, it is of supreme importance that "one and all" should be possessed of it, as they undoubtedly will be, if they have any genuine regard for their own interests. Although Mr. Boon makes no pretensions to literary style or polish, he is a writer possessing singular power and originality of ideas, fascinating by reason of their very freshness, accompanied by a rich vein of humour and keen sense of the ridiculous, whereby he at times completely deprives us of all control over our risible faculties. On the other hand we are now and again moved to the tenderest of human emotions by his simple, pure and unaffected pathos. Neither can we pass over without notice his trenchant criticisms of evil-doers in high places, his scathing sarcasms when dealing with organised or individual hypocrisies, or his truly terrible power of invective when delivering an onslaught upon social, political or ecclesiastical malefactors. With his perfect freedom from all conventualism, Mr. Boon is a literary gem of the first water, a veritable rough diamond; and it requires no great stretch of imagination to picture his pen as the magician's wand, whose vigorous strokes shall bring about the moral redemption of South Africa, and hand down to posterity the name of Martin James Boon, as the Nineteenth Century literary Bayard. *Sans peur et sans reproche."*

MONEY AND ITS USE.

In these days, when "hard times" is the universal, and unhappily but too well founded cry, certainly, any proposition, that appears feasible, for the amelioration of matters must be somewhat more than welcome. Whatever the cause, it is a fact, which cannot be gainsaid, for all of us are only too painfully aware of it, that our country in common with others, is in a state of commercial prostration, the like of which has rarely, if ever, been experienced; and thousands upon thousands of our "horny-handed sons of toil" are in a state of semi-starvation through want of employment. Of such gigantic proportions is the evil, that private effort, however well intended, is utterly helpless even to mitigate it to any appreciable extent, and our wilfully blind or mentally paralysed Government seems to be either unwilling or hopelessly incapable of grasping the difficulty, and dealing with it in an effectual and statesmanlike manner. Innumerable plans and suggestions—all of a more or less impracticable character—have been promulgated by the Press, and mouthed from the platform or in the Senate, but nothing—absolutely nothing has as yet been *done*. The latest scheme for improving our condition and exorcising from our midst, or stalling off that rapidly approaching dread gaunt goblin Famine aye, famine; surrounded by plenty, wealth, luxury and sumptuousness, appears to be the construction of subways in different parts of the Metropolis, thereby providing employment for a considerable number of our idle hands. Employment! Yes; just the thing English working men want, and "don't they wish they may get it?" Whilst our Municipal or Local Government pettifoggers are discussing the matter, and turning about in all directions to find the ways and means—the indispensable, the *sine qua non*, absolutely and indisputably of our very existence on this sublunary planet, it is simply but a repetition of the "old, old story" that *while the grass grows, the steed starves*. What then is to be done? Why simply this:—Let every statesman, every politician, every political economist, every philanthropist, the clergy and ministers of all denominations, in fact, every man who wishes himself and his country well, procure at once the little *brochure*, entitled "Money and Its Use," by MARTIN JAMES BOON, author of "The Immortal History of South Africa," "History of the Orange Free State," &c., &c., &c. Having purchased it, let them read and ponder carefully its contents. Having done so, we are persuaded that all then remaining to be done, will be for every one in his respective sphere and capacity to do all that lies within him to carry, or cause to be carried immediately into practice the great and indisputable truths, and plans sketched out by the author. Let what was done in Jersey be repeated to the extent necessary in England, and then we shall have achieved our emancipation for the greatest and grossest thraldom that ever disgraced, outraged, and held in bondage the world of manhood—that of the gold exploiters and monopolists. Then shall we have effected, noiselessly and peacefully, the greatest social revolution of this or any other age, and we make bold to prophesy that the name of Martin James Boon will be hailed with universal assent and acclamation as the talisman whereby this wondrous transformation was brought about.

THE RISE, PROGRESS, AND PHASES OF HUMAN SLAVERY: How IT CAME INTO THE WORLD, AND HOW IT SHALL BE MADE TO GO OUT. By JAMES BRONTERRE O'BRIEN, B.A. London: William Reeves, 185, Fleet Street, E.C.; G. Standing, 8 & 9, Finsbury Street; Martin James Boon, 170, Farringdon Road, W.C.

THIS little Work, by an eloquent denunciator of the manifold evils of Profitmongering and Landlordism, whose entire life was devoted to the advocacy of Social Rights, is now given to the world for the first time in complete form.

The Author, in his lifetime, was frustrated in his design of finishing his History, through the ceaseless machinations of working-class exploiters and landlords. This has been at length accomplished by the aid of his various writings preserved inprint. The object steadily kept in view has been to give the *ipsissima verba* of the Author, so that no foreign pen may garble or mislead.

In order to provide room for so much additional matter as was essential to the elucidation of the great reforms needed in the subjects of Land Nationalisation, Credit, Currency, and Exchange, it has been found expedient to omit from this edition some disquisitions on subjects of ephemeral and passing interest, not closely connected with the scope of the Work. Ample compensation has, however, been given in the additions which have had to be made for the elucidation and enforcement of the saving truths therein contained.

> A man who lived for truth, and truth alone,
> Brave as the bravest—generous as brave;
> A man whose heart was rent by every moan
> That burst from every trodden, tortured slave;
> A man prepared to fight, prepared to die.
> To lighten, banish, human slavery.
> The mighty scorned him, villified, oppressed;
> The bitter cup of poverty and pain
> Forced him to drink. He was misfortune's guest

Thro' weary, weary years: his anguished brain
Shed tears of pity—wrath—for mankind's woe;
For his own sorrows tears could never flow.
He loved the people with a brother's love:
He hated tyrants with a tyrant's hate.
He turned from kings below, to God above—
The King of kings who smites the wicked great.
The shame, the scourge, the terror of their race,
Those demons in earth's holy dwelling place.
Thou noble soul! Around thee gathered those
Who, poor and trampled patriots were like thee.
Thou art not dead! Thy martyred spirit glows
In us, a band devoted of the free:
We best can celebrate thy natal day,
By virtues, valours, such as marked thy way.
WILLIAM MACCALL.

We have been privileged with a sight of the proof-sheets of O'Brien's "Rise, Progress, and Phases of Human Slavery,' and are sure that the thousands of Socialists throughout the world will hail with delight its appearance, for the first time in a complete form. It seems to us as the rising from the dead, after a long sleep, of the mighty great who electrified his audiences with his eloquence. With what convincing arguments does the writer show the horrors of slavery, tracing its progress from brutal chattel-slavery down to its more refined and diabolic form of wage-slavery. He does not, however, leave us here; but in fixing the evil, he also, at the same time, gives the full and sufficient remedy. It is like the voice of the Deity, speaking from the dead to living. Let the people heed the voice, and their redemption draweth nigh.

HISTORY OF THE ORANGE FREE STATE.

UNDER the above title, another aspirant for public favour will shortly make its appearance in the book market. The work will be complete in one handsomely bound volume, and is from the able pen of MARTIN JAMES BOON, author of "The Immortal History of South Africa," a work we had occasion to notice with unqualified eulogy, some short time back— "Money and Its Use," and other works on social and political economy. "Immortal South Africa," with all its encyclopædic comprehensiveness, from the immense variety of subjects it dealt with, could hardly do more than touch the fringe, as it were, of that many-coloured geographical entity, the Orange Free State. Those who have been fortunate enough, or had the good sense, to read Mr. Boon's more general work, cannot but have felt eager, when perusing the valuable and interesting generalities, anent the Free State, therein contained, for more detailed information from the same authoritative source; and in the work under notice they will find it in abundance, variety and beauty. Mr. Boon has handled his subject, as only one in possession of absolutely personal knowledge and great natural gifts, could. In this book we positively feel as though we were onlookers or participators in the stirring events described. Public affairs generally—State, Local and Municipal—are treated with a copiousness that leaves nothing to be desired, and with a boldness of assertion, welcome and refreshing in these degenerate days of pandering to "authority," and cloaking its manifold transgressions and iniquities. Semitic and Teutonic rascality, appears to be rampant in the Free State, and the victims thereof seem, for the most part, to be Englishmen. So mean, contemptible, and dastardly; so utterly abhorrent to all the instincts of right and justice; in short, so fiendish, one might say, are the practices of these degenerate Cousins-German, and nefarious descendants of Abraham, that the Orange Republic must indeed be a sort of terrestial pandemonium. If Mr. Boon is correct—and he certainly fortifies his assertions, both by direct and collateral evidence—the malpractices referred to are openly encouraged, or secretly connived at, by the Free State officials of all grades. Whilst the experiences narrated, are engrossingly interesting, throwing a flood of light upon that mysterious, but ever existent inner circle of social and political life in the Free State; the warnings given should not only be read, but engraven upon the memory of every Englishman contemplating a residence in that unfortunate and really little-known Republic. Whether as a supplementary, or companion work to "The Immortal History of South Africa," or from its own inherent merits and attractions, "The Orange Free State" should find a welcome and a home in every public and private library.

"HOW TO NATIONALIZE OUR COMMONS, WASTE LANDS AND RAILWAYS."

Such is the title of a little work of very unpretending appearance, but whose contents are of paramount interest and importance to all classes, and especially to that unfortunate stalking-horse of political parties—the working man. Whilst the author, who has evidently studied the question carefully and earnestly, expresses his views with all the energy of an enthusiast who has unlimited confidence in the soundness of his conclusions; he is remarkably felicitous in his mode of illustration, which is characterised by such force and perspicuity, that not even the humblest capacity can fail to grasp his meaning. The author contends that the appropriation, with the public money, of our Commons and Waste lands is the only way to work out the great Land Question; and he urges that if this were done, and the whole brought into a proper state of cultivation, there would be no necessity for our agricultural labourers to emigrate, and that our own lands would yield sufficient sustenance for a population of "one hundred and twenty millions." The historical and legal bearings of the Commons Question are ably and copiously dealt with; and the statistics upon which the author bases his deductions, are collated from the most authoritative sources, including the report of the Enclosure Commissioners, from which he estimates the annual loss of revenue to the United Kingdom, through the present condition of our commons and waste lands, at the enormous sum of forty millions. Formidable as this amount appears, the author has something still more astounding in store. He says that if these lands were to be allotted to farm labourers for cultivation, they would in a few years yield, in the form of rent, an annual income to the State of "from sixty to eighty millions!" Such are a few only of the numerous items of interest contained in this truly valuable pamphlet, which not only points out existing evils, but—what is of infinitely greater importance—it shows the way out of them, in "short, sharp and decisive" fashion; and greater, better, and more wonderous still—"without a farthing's loss or cost to any one." Of the "Railway Question," the exigencies of space only permit us to say—without intending a joke—that it is dealt with exactly on the same lines. In conclusion, we cannot give better advice concerning this marvellous little work, than that contained in the words, "Go and buy it." The price places this little treasure within the reach of all, and it is written by that staunch, true friend of the working man, MARTIN JAMES BOON, author of the "Immortal History of South Africa," "History of the Orange Free State," "Money and Its Use," &c., &c., &c.

"JOTTING'S BY THE WAY, OR BOON'S MADNESS ON THE ROAD."—By MARTIN JAMES BOON.

LONDON: GEORGE STANDRING, 8 & 9, Finsbury Street.

" This is a very remarkable book by a very remarkable man. Mr. Boon is an ethusiast of the most indomitable type. He is irrepressible in his hopefulness. He presents us, in this volume, with a philosophical view of life—past, present and to come—in the Orange Free State, Natal, and Cape Colony. He has lived long and travelled much, and seen a great deal in these parts; and he believes that his thoughts, speculations, fancies, and facts will be of service to Englishmen—hence this work. Mr. Boon is a most pronounced Republican, and an ardent advocate of the nationalization of the land. He is a reformer, and is never happy, but as he is either destroying what he believes to be evil, or is uplifting and supporting what he believes to be good and true. His volume is interesting, instructive, and suggestive, and ought to be read by all reformers and those who take any interest in foreign policy. Mr. William Maccall, well known to advanced thinkers in this religion, introduces this book of colonial genius. We must not say, for the author is English born—but his ideas seem to have been strengthened, if not developed, by his colonial life and experience. In 1869 Mr. Maccall, at the Hall of Science, London, delivered four lectures on Pauperism. Among his hearers were the author of this book. The lecturer and his boon companions recognised a kinship of spirit, and this kinship has been strengthened by time. He is a merchant at Bloemfontein, Orange Free State. His "favourite ideas" do not let business muzzle his soul. *Maworm*, in the play of the Hypocrite, boasted that "he extorted [exhorted] all who came to the shop," and Martin Boon, who is a true man and no hypocrite, finds that his ideas being freely communicated and fearlessly maintained, do not hinder his progress in business. As Mr. Maccall's name is a sufficient voucher for the book we have only to add that it abounds with racy writing, which will amuse the cursory reader, and with thoughts that will interest the graver student of this mad world."—*Western Times.*

GEORGE STANDRING, 8 & 9, Finsbury Street, London, publishes "Jottings by the Way," and "How to Construct Free State Railways," by Martin James Boon. They are two thoughtful, earnest, and vigorous works. They are fresh, striking, drastic; brimful of all sorts of information and suggestions, and ought to be read by all reformers.—The PROPAGANDIST (Vail & Co., 170, Farringdon-road), is a twopenny monthly of the most advanced type, edited by Martin James Boon. It is a fearless, outspoken, daring periodical, advocating views of the most uncompromising kind. Martin Boon is far ahead of his age and country.—*Oldham Chronicle.*

"A SCHEME OF IMPERIAL COLONIZATION:
How to Coloninize South Africa, and by Whom."
By Martin J. Boon.

Many readers must recall with pleasure and esteem the name of Martin James Boon, who, twelve years ago, played a conspicuous part as a social and political reformer, and who was the first popular champion of what has recently attracted so much attention—land nationalisation. The more disinterested and devoted we are in the service of truth, the more we have to suffer; and brave, benevolent Boon was not an exception. His worldly affairs having fallen into confusion, he went, early in 1874, as a settler to South Africa. If in England he had been a hero, in Caffraria he was destined to be a martyr. For a considerable time he has resided as a merchant at Bloemfontein, Orange Free State. His tribulations have not diminished his enthusiasm, and he continues to write and speak with the valiant zeal which he displayed in England. His pamphlet, "How to Colonise South Africa," contains many ingenious suggestions.

At the risk of being called a Jingo, I think that England should have a great foreign policy and a great colonial policy, and that England should be for the modern world what Rome was for the ancient world. I was amused the other day, when reading a lecture by Mr. Conway, to find Benjamin Disraeli treated as an earnest man, with something of the old Hebrew prophetic fire. It seemed to me the height of comicality that the most detestable impostor of modern days should be regarded as a serious and honest personage. It is enough to make me hate Benjamin Disraeli that, by his contemptible trickeries, he brought a vigorous foreign and colonial policy into disrepute. To that policy we must return if England is to maintain or to extend its place among the nations. Whenever that policy is revived South Africa is sure to be sought as an admirable field for colonizing experiments. Boon's main idea includes the rapid extension of a peasant proprietary in connection with an immense issue of redeemable paper money. As all money is simply representative, I see no reason for deeming Boon's plan unworkable. But I cannot discuss the plan here, and must content myself with trying to excite the interest of the reader in Boon's pamphlet. My own currency has always been extremely limited; and I might be too much influenced by prejudices if I were to enter on the debate of currency questions. That these questions have been profoundly studied and are thoroughly understood by Boon, I am convinced; and his sincerity and generosity are beyond the reach of doubt. William Maccall.

HOW TO CONSTRUCT FREE TRADE RAILWAYS, &c.

"The manifold advantages of a thorough system of railway communication are so well known and appreciated in those countries fortunate enough to possess this universally recognised desideratum, that any recapitulation thereof is totally unnecessary. The chief ground for surprise in connection with the matter is, that any Nation or State, claiming to be considered civilised, should be without, or inadequately provided with railways; and as we cannot for a moment imagine any people to be so blind to the interests of themselves and their country as not to be possessed of an earnest desire to have them, we are forced to the conclusion that the want of *means*, rather than the want of wit, is the real stumbling block in the way. We are led to these observations by the perusal of a pamphlet bearing the title at the head of this notice, written by that well known militant Apostle of Progress, Martin James Boon, author of the *Immortal History of South Africa, National Paper Money and Its Use, History of the Orange Free State*, &c., &c. The author having for a considerable time been an observant resident in the Free State is pre-eminently entitled to speak upon the question, which he treats from the point of view that the railways should be constructed by and become the property of the State, the cost thereof being provided for by the issue of State paper-money in the form of Notes, marked to denote the purpose for which they were issued, and made legal tender for all purposes within the confines of the Free State. The security upon which the notes were issued would be the railway plant and works themselves. Upon the completion of the line five per cent. of the receipts after paying all expenses to be called in, and notes representing that amount cancelled annually, until the whole would be passed out of circulation and the property left as a source of income, either to carry out other works or to relieve the burdens of the taxpayers, and all effected, entirely free of cost. Such is a brief outline of the author's general idea, and it is worked out in detail with admirable reasoning, illustrated by convincing examples. Every member of that somewhat cosmopolitan community, The Orange Free State, should invest sixpence, and study the question for himself."

www.ingramcontent.com/pod-product-compliance
Lightning Source LLC
Chambersburg PA
CBHW032104230426
43672CB00009B/1633